THE PRIMARY CURRICULUM

This book is concerned with the relationships and tensions in education between children's needs and societies' demands, tensions which primary teachers everywhere face on a daily basis.

The existence in many countries of national curricula might be expected to ease part of the stress felt by teachers by prescribing what should be taught and, possibly, how it should be taught, thus removing from them the individual responsibility of ensuring a broad and balanced curriculum for each child. If, however, the content and methods suggested by a national curriculum seem to the teacher to be inappropriate or irrelevant to children's needs, the teacher may be faced with a conflict likely to increase the levels of stress he or she suffers. The younger the children, the more their immediate needs and interests will appear to compete with remote long-term societal needs likely to be emphasised in a national curriculum.

This book seeks to present a range of international pespectives on the interplay between childhood, curriculum and classroom practice. The first part of the book offers a framework for thinking about primary curricula, while the second part presents a range of international views on the primary curriculum from South Africa, Australia, New Zealand, south-east Asia, Europe and the USA.

Janet Moyles is Senior Lecturer, and **Linda Hargreaves** Lecturer in the School of Education, University of Leicester, UK.

D0219315

THE PRIMARY CURRICULUM

Learning from international perspectives

Edited by
Janet Moyles and Linda Hargreaves

London and New York

First published 1998
by Routledge
11 New Fetter Lane, London EC4P 4EE

Simultaneously published in the USA and Canada
by Routledge
29 West 35th Street, New York, NY 10001

Typeset in Garamond by J&L Composition Ltd, Filey, North Yorkshire

Printed and bound in Great Britain by
Biddles Ltd, Guildford and King's Lynn

British Library Cataloguing in Publication Data
A catalogue record for this book is available from the British Library

Library of Congress Cataloguing in Publication Data
The Primary Curriculum: learning from international
perspectives/edited by Janet Moyles and Linda Hargreaves.
p. cm.
Includes bibliographical references.
1. Education, Elementary – Curricula – Cross-cultural studies.
2. Curriculum planning–Cross-cultural studies. 3. Curriculum
change – Cross-cultural studies. I. Moyles, Janet R.
II. Hargreaves, Linda.
LB1570.P678 1998 97–17424
372019–dc21
CIP

ISBN 0–415–15832–X

CONTENTS

ILLUSTRATIONS

Figures

Plates

TABLES

NOTES ON CONTRIBUTORS

Bob Adamson is an Assistant Professor in the Department of Curriculum Studies at the University of Hong Kong. He has taught and published in the fields of English language teaching and teacher education in the People's Republic of China and Hong Kong since 1983. A consultant to the State Education Commission in the PRC, he has worked on textbook and teacher education projects related to the national English curriculum in Chinese secondary schools.

Geva Blenkin is a Senior Lecturer in Early Childhood Education at Goldsmiths' College, University of London. She was previously head-teacher of an infant school in East London. She is also currently Director of the Early Childhood Education Research Project, 'Principles into Practice'. Her major research interest is the interface between developmental psychology and the early years curriculum. She has published widely in this field, and her best known works are the trilogy of books she has co-edited with Vic Kelly.

Dr Martin Cortazzi is Senior Lecturer at the University of Leicester and specialises in primary education, linguistics and language teaching. His publications include two books, *Primary Teaching: How It Is* and *Narrative Analysis* and articles on literacy, vocabulary learning, cross-cultural communication and learning English in China. He has recently given teacher training courses in Spain, Turkey, Lebanon, China and Taiwan.

Glen De Voogd is an Assistant Professor at the University of Houston in Texas with an appointment in the Department of Curriculum and Instruction. A former bilingual classroom teacher in the primary grades, technology staff developer and founder of a programme to teach children of migrant workers, his research explores innovative and multi-cultural approaches of education with particular focus on beginning literacy instruction and the uses of technology in literacy instruction. His publications focus on the shifting roles of teachers and students that contribute to a more inquisitive and democratic society.

Maurice Galton is Professor and Dean of the Faculty of Education and Continuing Studies at the University of Leicester. He has directed numerous research projects concerned with the observation of teaching and learning in the primary classroom (ORACLE 1975–1983). His current work involves curriculum provision in small primary schools. He has numerous publications to his credit, the latest being *Crisis in the Primary Classroom*.

Dr Linda Hargreaves is a Lecturer in Education at the University of Leicester, having been a primary school teacher and psychology tutor. She teaches research methods on the taught doctoral course in the U.K. and abroad. She has contributed to observation research studies including the ORACLE project, Science Teaching Action Research (STAR) project and studies of curriculum provision in small schools. Her current research concerns 'Education Superhighways' and primary–secondary transfer.

Vic Kelly is Emeritus Professor of Curriculum Studies at Goldsmiths' College, University of London. He was formerly Dean of the Faculty of Education there. His research interests have focused on conceptual issues in curriculum discourse, and in the present climate, this has increasingly entailed a conceptual critique of political policies and practices in education. His more recent publications have, therefore, been centred on the significance of current political interventions in school curricula and in the organisation of education. The most notable of these are *The National Curriculum: A Critical Review* and *Education and Democracy: Principles and Practices*.

Dr Paul Morris is a Reader in the Department of Curriculum Studies at the University of Hong Kong, where he has worked since 1976. From 1986 to 1992 he was the Dean of the Faculty of Education, and from 1988 to 1993 he was a member of the Education Commission in Hong Kong. He has published extensively on issues related to the school curriculum and educational policy in East Asia, and his most recent books include *The Hong Kong School Curriculum: Development, Issues and Policies* and *Education and Development in East Asia* (with Anthony Sweeting).

Janet Moyles is Senior Lecturer in Education at the School of Education, University of Leicester, having previously been headteacher of a primary school. Her main research interests are in the areas of children's play, assessment of learning and issues related to classroom and curriculum management and staff development. She frequently lectures and undertakes research in different countries – in 1994 she spent ten weeks as an invited Research Fellow at the de Lissa Institute, University of South Australia, and last year visited Sweden, China and Norway to support play and curriculum development. She has published widely on children's learning and classroom management and her books on play have been translated into several different languages.

Dr Anthony Pell was for eight years Science Education Consultant to the Gazankulu Government of South Africa. Born in Northampton, he was educated at the universities of Birmingham, Lancaster and Leicester. His main interests are curriculum development, educational research, physics education and science and society studies. After many years working in schools and a further education college, he is at present a Research Associate at the University of Leicester and an educational consultant.

Les Regan is Head of the School of Education at Southern Cross University in Australia where he lectures in education studies, assessment and reporting, skills of teaching and research methods, having previously lectured at the Universities of Macquarie, Western Sydney and Monash. In the second half of 1996 he was a Visiting Fellow in the School of Education at the University of Leicester. He is co-editor of the *Journal of Teaching Practice* and has served as a member of the National Executive of the Australian Teacher Education Association. He has published papers on the professional socialisation of student–teachers and on the impact of teacher education programmes on student–teachers' developing perspectives about teaching and learning.

Professor Colin Richards was a primary teacher before becoming a lecturer. He was the first editor of *Education 3–13* and has authored and edited books and articles on primary education. In 1983 he joined HM Inspectorate and later became Staff Inspector (Primary Education). From 1992 to 1996 he was OFSTED's specialist adviser for primary education. He now works as an educational consultant, as Honorary Professor of Education at the University of Warwick and as Visiting Professor of Education at the Universities of Newcastle and Leicester.

Paul Ryan is a Lecturer in Education in the Education Management Development Unit at the University of Leicester. He was formerly a deputy headteacher in a large inner-city primary school and he has also taught in a number of primary schools in inner London. His current research activities are concerned with primary school teachers' perceptions of the national curriculum in the UK, defining quality in the primary school and the implementation of the national curriculum in English primary schools. He has contributed chapters to a number of books and written articles in his specialist field.

Hidenori Sugimine is Professor of Education in the Graduate School of Human Culture and Principal of Nara Women's University High School. He teaches courses on curriculum development and the philosophy of education. His research and writing have focused on comparative history/statistics of school education and modern curriculum development. He has published widely in Japan on issues related to international perspectives on pedagogy and curriculum.

Dr Mel Vlaeminke taught for ten years in a large, urban comprehensive school, before moving to the University of Leicester to teach and research. She coordinated the professional studies course for some years and is currently responsible for the PGCE history course. Her research interests lie in the history of education, equal opportunities, especially gender related, the pastoral curriculum and, more recently, the moral and spiritual dimensions of schooling. Publications include *Developing Key Professional Competences* and *Developing Key Subject Competences* (both Pearson), *Young People's Attitudes to the Voluntary Sector* (NCVO 1996) and *Breaking the Mould* (DTI 1997).

Kazumi Yamamoto is Professor of Early Childhood Education at Heian Jogakuin (St Agnes') College, was Head of the Department of Early Childhood Education from 1990 to 1995, and is also Director of the College Library. She has visited the UK several times to study nursery and primary education. Her fields of specialist study are the philosophy of education, curriculum, children's play and methods of education, all as related to childhood and early childhood. She has published books and papers in Japan on early childhood education.

ACKNOWLEDGEMENTS

In a book with so many contributors it is always a delight when people adhere to set deadlines and manage to do so with patience, humour and enthusiasm: for this reason, we owe a debt to all those from around the world as well as in the UK who have ensured that this book has been produced within a relatively tight schedule. Particularly, we acknowledge Glenn DeVoogd.

We are also indebted to the publishers who have enabled us to develop this book, despite the undoubted difficulties of its focus, and encouraged its progress along with its sister volume, *Teaching as a Learning Relationship*.

Other people have been involved in the general preparation and we would especially like to acknowledge Deborah Phillpott and Andrew Farrow for their contribution to the final manuscript.

Part I

PRIMARY CURRICULA:
ORIGINS AND INFLUENCES

INTRODUCTION

Janet Moyles and Linda Hargreaves

This book is concerned with the relationships and tensions in education between children's needs and societies' demands, tensions which teachers of children between the ages of 3 and 12 years everywhere in the world face on a daily basis. The existence in many countries of national curricula might be expected to ease teachers' stress by prescribing what should be taught and, possibly, how it should be taught, and thus removing from them the individual responsibility of ensuring a broad and balanced curriculum for each child. If, however, the content and methods suggested by a national curriculum seem to the teacher to be inappropriate or irrelevant to children's needs, the teacher may be faced with a conflict. The younger the children, the more their immediate needs and interests will appear to compete with more remote long-term societal needs likely to be emphasised in a national curriculum. Teachers, therefore, may find themselves in practice trying to satisfy the demands of three fundamental sources of pressure, namely:

1   their society's perspective on children and childhood;
2   the dictates of their education system and any national curriculum;
3   the conventions of classroom practice, and teachers' beliefs and values.

This book presents a range of national and international perspectives on the interplay between these three strands, in short, *childhood, curriculum* and *classroom practice*. The book begins with an inward-looking but critical Euro-, indeed, Anglo-centric perspective which identifies contemporary problems in primary education systems. It leads, however, to the need to look for lessons and solutions beyond those Anglo/European shores, to take in a wide range of world perspectives. The structure of the book, then, is that Part I offers a basic framework for thinking about the primary curriculum and the factors – historical, ideological, political, economic and religious – which influence the development of primary curricula whatever their national or cultural contexts. Maurice Galton's chapter then provides a bridge from the Anglo-and-Eurocentrism of Part I to wider global concerns and the shifting locus of educational and economic attention from West to East, particularly south-east Asia. Part II subsequently presents a range of international perspectives on the primary curriculum, with examples from Africa, Australia, the Far East and the USA authored by educationalists living and working in these contexts. These writers have framed their contributions around the three main strands, which are elaborated below. Readers are encouraged either to trace a national perspective within a single chapter, or to examine a particular educational theme through several international contexts. The focus may be either on exploring differences in primary curricula or on accounting for the universal nature of primary curriculum for indeed both similarities and differences are identified by the various writers.

The three strands: childhood, curriculum and classroom practice

Childhood, curriculum and classroom practice, provide the basic issues on which the chapters are focused. Each of these strands inspires a series of questions which the contributions implicitly address.

Childhood and society

Each culture defines childhood in its own way and from such definitions determines what educational provision and, therefore, curriculum is appropriate. Our first question must be to identify how *childhood is perceived in different countries*. It might be recognised as a state in its own right, qualitatively different from the states of adulthood, parenthood or old age, for example. Alternatively, childhood may be seen merely as a period of quantitative deficiency, in which size, strength, stamina and sense gradually increase until the physical characteristics of adulthood are achieved. This question is intimately bound up with the status of formal schooling in a society, since the end of schooling may define the upper age limit of childhood, as traditional or ceremonial rites of passage have been eroded or displaced by national examinations, graduation and job-seeking. Further questions on how socialisation is achieved within each society lead inevitably to exploring how children take on the behavioural norms and social and moral values of the society.

Universal primary schooling is now a feature of most societies. Its roots lie in the late eighteenth and nineteenth centuries when European national states constructed mass schooling systems that eventually came to encompass all children and have effects on all classes of society. Learning became irreversibly equated with formal, systematic schooling and schooling itself became a fundamental feature of the state. Mass schooling almost every-

4

where is clearly intended to be the dominant means of the intergenerational transmission of culture. Clearly, where formal schooling is established, children spend considerable periods of every day away from their families and exempt from a remunerated work situation. Thus the school in itself becomes a socialising agent, as Vlaeminke points out in Chapter 1, established originally in England to 'wipe out the evil inherent in children' according to the Victorian church, and to produce an 'orderly, civil, obedient population' able to carry out commands, as Colin Richards observes in Chapter 4.

Today, as complex societies in themselves, to what extent do schools issue mixed messages? Blenkin and Kelly (Chapter 2) ask how schools can foster the development of pro-social, democratic and cooperative values in a competitive education system. On the other hand, where school is an irrelevance set against the demands of daily survival, far from being an extended process in a protected environment, socialisation is a direct confrontation with life's demands (see Chapter 6). It is within similar active real-life roles that psychologists such as Bruner, Lave and Rogoff (e.g. Rogoff, 1990) site the power of situated social learning and where joint socialisation *by children* and adults takes place. Such learning reveals limitations in school-based learning. Paul Ryan (in Chapter 3), in essence, points to the difficult role for teachers as the *interface* for the children between the often harsh reality of the outside world and the remoteness of school activities. In addition, evidence exists within many societies that the period we call 'adolescence', which sits in the uncomfortable phase between the periods of childhood and adulthood, is a time when having completed their formal schooling, many teenagers become bored, disillusioned and disaffected with school, and may try to establish their identity by undermining adult values and norms (as in Japan and the USA, Chapters 7 and 8, for example).

Families

One reason for this may be the changing nature of what constitutes a family in contemporary societies. Over the last two decades in the UK, for example, children increasingly are being brought up by single parents or within 'reconstituted' families. As marriage has declined and divorce has increased (over one-third of marriages now end in divorce in the UK), this has arguably put great strain on children with a related impact on educational achievement and success (Crockett and Tripp 1994).

In addition, a disturbing trend in many postmodern societies is the increasing number of children deemed to be living in poverty and the increasing income differentials across families (Graham 1994). It has been found in the UK that 'the lower your social class, the more likely you are to die in infancy and the shorter is your life expectancy' (Sparks 1995). In 1991 it was estimated that 3.9 million children were growing up in households below the unofficial poverty line (DSS 1993). This is reflected in other societies around the world to greater and lesser extents.

If schools reflect societal roles, norms and values, what models do they portray for children? In particular, how are gender roles linked to perceptions of childhood? A majority of primary school children must submit unwittingly to a hierarchical model in which the minority group, men, occupy the most powerful positions, with women as assistants and intermediaries, and the majority, i.e. the children, having little or no voice. Does this model encapsulate any notion of equal rights or opportunities? Even where school councils exist, in the UK decision-making is mediated by staff.

Perhaps it is only in countries where children's rights are more widely recognised, as in some Scandinavian countries, that children can internalise an equitable model of society based on school. Any societal construction of childhood has implications regarding the roles, rights and responsibilities of parents. But parents confronted with compulsory universal schooling for their children might wonder wherein these rights exist for them.

Education systems and national curricula

Here the concern is with who determines educational policy and to whom the education system is accountable. Is education policy decided centrally without any consultation with practitioners or consumers, or at another extreme decided locally with genuine community involvement? The emphasis on active community involvement in curriculum planning and implementation is enshrined in the national curricula of, for example, Norway and Finland.

In the UK, the Education Reform Act of 1989 appeared to give parents a voice as 'consumers' of education. In reality, however, the imposition of a centrally determined national curriculum drowned out any parental voice. Colin Richards (Chapter 4) details the career of the national curriculum, and, despite its supposed experimental status, the impossibility for teachers to respond when overloaded with content, and under threat of impending inspection. Richards traces the major phases of the primary curriculum in England, defining the nature, rationale and purpose of five eras from 1862 to the present day, concluding with a look to the future. His analysis which breaks down the curriculum into seven features including the nature and extent of the legal prescription, the rationale and contents of the curriculum, its assessment and monitoring, its susceptibility to change and the extent of its implementation, can usefully be applied to the curricula described in Part II. What he shows in the English context, is a series of oscillations from a narrowly prescribed curriculum emphasising core skills, to concern to provide a broad and balanced curriculum which promotes the 'spiritual, moral, cultural, mental and physical *development* of pupils', both positions overwhelmed by the nature of school assessment and evaluation. So, Blenkin and Kelly, in Chapter 2, discuss the conflict between this so-called a broadly based curriculum designed to promote pupils' development, and the restrictive influence of assessment and testing which have high stakes for schools.

From the international perspective, it is interesting to note that Benavot and Kamens (1989), in a study of curriculum emphases in 130 countries, found that primary curricula not only contained the same subjects but gave them the same relative importance with an overriding major emphasis on generating literacy in one or more languages. Of equal note is the fact that the main categories and outline of primary curricula have become surprisingly non-controversial in most countries, controversy stemming mainly from the analysis of detailed content or in implementation (see Chapter 10).

The inevitable question at this point is *how teachers are trained initially and how training is developed* to implement various curricula content and models. Can we find the real purpose of the curriculum and levels of prescriptiveness in the teacher training process? Is there, for example, a national curriculum or prescribed list of competencies which all teachers must acquire (as in the draft outlines proposed for teacher training in England – TTA 1997) or are teachers encouraged to reflect on their pupils' needs, their practice and the improvement of their teaching? (See Chapter 6; for example, Pell's description of teacher training in South Africa and the post-apartheid developments.)

Classroom practice: teachers' beliefs and values

This strand is concerned with how classroom practices are influenced by the management of the school, how the curriculum is perceived by education professionals and how it is implemented. It refers to 'what people do in classrooms', how teachers organise and manage the children, what they decide to teach and in what ways, the resources they use to support their teaching and, finally, the style of interaction which they use when face to face with the children. Chapters 3 and 10 highlight the significance of these practical decisions in the context of the increasingly variable and uncertain contexts of children's lives, while other chapters in Part II illustrate these points in detail through cameos and examples (see Chapters 8 and 11 for examples). This brings us neatly back to the dilemmas faced by teachers in conceptualising and implementing what is required of them when they are dealing with the 'official' curriculum as represented in official state or local documents, the 'enacted' curriculum which is detailed in their own planning documents, the 'delivered' curriculum which often carries an outside assessment and the 'received' curriculum, being that which their pupils understand, whether intentional or not (see Meyer *et al.* 1992).

To conclude this introduction, we outline the chapters in Part I, the outline for Part II being given in a separate introduction.

In Chapter 1, Mel Vlaeminke classifies the significant historical and philosophical influences on the curriculum into five general categories: religious, social, economic, ideological and political. She delineates the general nature of each main class of influence and then goes on to relate it, with specific examples, to the development of the English primary curriculum. In each category, the English system stands out as counter-exemplary. In relation to economic influences, for example, the nineteenth-century British economy succeeded in spite of the established education system rather than owing anything to schools and universities. Thus the 'piecemeal, evolutionary and essentially counter-developmental nature of elementary education in England' is contrasted with a more coherent and ostensibly strategic use of educational provision elsewhere to promote national identity, economic progress and understanding of political issues. Vlaeminke concludes that while religious, social, economic, ideological and political influences can be identified, the forces on education are typically more complex combinations of these, which each reader will recognise or seek in his or her experience of their own national education system.

In Chapter 2, Blenkin and Kelly examine the concept of a developmental curriculum against an increasingly antithetical political and ideological context in the UK. Their aim is to elucidate the conceptual background to a developmental curriculum and to justify its advocacy in primary schools. Beginning with Greek philosophical notions of education for personal development, they trace the demise of such liberal ideals to the emergence of education for all and utilitarian demands for an educated workforce. Their arguments are underpinned by the distinction between education, as defined by R.S. Peters in the 1960s and forms of instruction, training or indoctrination, in which activities exist solely for the sake of the exercise and its content, and have no intrinsic value for the learner. They present both social and moral arguments for a curriculum which focuses on individual development. Their moral argument returns to the fundamental issue of whether children are to be seen as means to economic ends or as ends in themselves. Ultimately, a curriculum founded on democratic moral principles, they argue, is in a strong position to promote the development of all pupils' own individually reasoned recognition of the importance of such principles. They then introduce a recent, cost-based analysis which if adopted would end state-provided education for all, and see in this the undermining of democratic principles and hence the efforts of those who seek to implement developmental curricula. Finally, they appeal to the moral reasons to recognise the entitlement of every child to a type of education which supports enhanced and enriched forms of participation in an economically, socially and culturally healthy society. Without a developmental curriculum, they regard democracy itself as under threat.

Paul Ryan, in Chapter 3, offers a sociological perspective on the primary curriculum and emphasises the relevance of the social context of the primary school to curriculum construction and implementation. He focuses on the challenge for teachers' of finding a balance between the legal requirement to teach to a national curriculum and the imperative of providing a curriculum relevant to the social context of the school. Teachers themselves must somehow mediate teaching to meet the societal demands of a market economy, supposedly embodied in a centrally controlled curriculum, with the immediate social context of the school itself. Ryan goes on to discuss teachers' accountability: if, as the present system would suggest, teachers are accountable to the government, they may be abdicating their responsibility to children by implementing a national curriculum which contravenes their own values. He argues that national curriculum implementation can inhibit effective teaching by limiting opportunities for creative, sensitive and socially relevant teaching; in other words, facets of quality in teaching. Ultimately, it is left with teachers themselves to clarify, and continually review, their own values in striving to ensure a curriculum that is inclusive, contextually relevant and will ensure equality of access and opportunity.

Colin Richards, in Chapter 4, provides a very clear account of changes (and potential changes) in the elementary/primary curriculum over a century-and-a-half from 1862. He identifies four main eras in the history of the English primary curriculum based chiefly on legal prescriptions, and then analyses each era in terms of its rationale (where one exists), its contents, assessment, monitoring/inspection, susceptibility to changes and extent of actual implementation. His account begins with the rigid standards of the Revised Code of 1862 set up to reduce expenditure on education and to make elementary education serve the needs of society rather than merely of the church. It moves on to the 'codified curriculum' of 1897 in which central government provided an overview of the curriculum, but local authorities were expected to adapt contents and teaching to local requirements. There was an emphasis after the end of 'payment by results' on teachers' thinking for themselves about the most appropriate teaching methods, and, unusually, a rationale for the elementary curriculum which included strengthening character, developing intelligence and helping children for the 'work of life'. The next sixty-two years are labelled those of the 'unregulated curriculum' which began with the 1926 Code's statement that it was not possible to lay down any rules as to the number of subjects in any school. This lack of prescription failed to result in a broad curriculum, however, as schools were subject increasingly to the tyrant of the secondary selection system. When the Plowden Report and comprehensive schools were introduced in 1967, still primary schools did not make use of their freedom, and retained a narrow curriculum. There was what Richards calls, 'a lottery curriculum' which depended on what primary school a child happened to attend. Finally, 1989 saw the introduction of the national curriculum which consists of nine subjects for primary schools (excluding a modern foreign language), and was accompanied by attainment targets, a new system of school inspection, and national assessment arrangements. After describing the results of the Dearing review which reduced the burden of the curriculum on teachers and children, Richards concludes with a set of options for the schools of the future. Based on past evidence he predicts that most will opt for the most limited option, but he invites a reconsideration of the traditional primary curriculum for the twenty-first century in which schools offering an enriched legal entitlement curriculum 'could have a significance out of proportion with their numbers'.

Finally in Part I, Maurice Galton's Chapter 5 serves as a zoom lens, which brings the everyday consequences of curricular decision-making into focus, and at the same time brings distant fields closer to us. The chapter marks the transition between the two parts of the book, linking the Anglo-European educational concerns in Part I to a wider set of perspectives. The chapter opens with examples of the ways in which curriculum decisions impinge on children's experience and classroom practice, and then moves on to show how the concept of curriculum has moved from Tyler's objectives model to Stenhouse's continually evaluated and evolving process model. Galton exemplifies these by contrasting the imposition of the National Curriculum in England and Wales with the school-based development of the Dutch national curriculum. Ultimately, he suggests, Vandenberghe's 'backward mapping' approach which provides for two-way transmission of decisions and concerns between policy-makers and practitioners may be the more effective. After a consideration of child-centred and traditional ideologies of the curriculum, and the paradoxical difficulty of separating these two in practice, he introduces global issues and the metamorphic impact which information and communications technology is having on the world's economic systems. In particular, he notes the shifting locus of economic and educational control from the West to the East, and especially the Pacific rim countries such as Singapore. He challenges curriculum developers to advance their thinking in the face of rapid technological advance and global restructuring. Thus Galton's chapter transports the reader to the wider contemporary cultures represented in Part II, preparing for the future and the communications revolution.

We would encourage readers, at this point, to begin by considering the typical antecedents of primary curricula explained in Chapter 1 before tackling the specific examples of Part II.

References

Benavot, A. and Kamens, D. (1989) *The Curricular Content of Primary Education in Developing Countries*. Washington, DC: World Bank PPR Working Paper No. 237.

Crockett, M. and Tripp, J. (1994) *Social Policy Research Findings No. 45*. Joseph Rowntree Foundation, February.

Department of Social Services (DSS) (1993) *Households Below Average Income: A Statistical Analysis 1979–1990*. London: HMSO.

Docking, J. (1990) *Primary Schools and Parents: Rights, Responsibilities and Relationships*. London: Hodder & Stoughton.

Graham, H. (1994) 'Changing financial circumstances of households with children'. *Children and Society* 8(2), 998–113.

Hoyle, M. (1989) *The Politics of Childhood*. London: Harvester Wheatsheaf.

Humphries, S., Mack, J. and Perks, R. (1988) *A Century Of Childhood*. London: Sidgwick & Jackson.

Meyer, J., Kamens, D. and Benavot, A. (1992) *School Knowledge for the Masses: World Models and National Primary Curricular Categories in the Twentieth Century*. London: Falmer.

Munn, P. (1993) *Parents and Schools: Customers, Managers or Partners*. London: Routledge.

Newell, P. (1991) *The U.N. Convention and Children's Rights in the U.K.* London: National Children's Bureau.

Pollock, L. (1984) *Forgotten Children*. Cambridge: Cambridge University Press.

Rogoff, B. (1990) *Apprenticeship in Learning: Cognitive Development in Social Context*. New York: Oxford University Press.

Sparks, I. (1995) 'The shape of childhood in 2001'. *Children and Society* 9(3), 5–16.

Sylva, K. (1994) 'The impact of early learning on children's later development'. In Sir Christopher Ball, *Start Right: The Importance of Early Learning*. Report for the Royal Society of Arts, London.

Teacher Training Agency (TTA) (1997) *Consultation on the Training Curriculum and Standards for New Teachers*. London: TTA.

1

HISTORICAL AND PHILOSOPHICAL INFLUENCES ON THE PRIMARY CURRICULUM

Mel Vlaeminke

Introduction

This chapter aims to identify the many and diverse strands which have shaped primary education in the United Kingdom, in a way which encourages readers familiar with the education systems of other countries to see similarities and comparisons. It can be argued that the British system is a poor candidate for the central role in this discussion. Whilst all national education systems have distinctive features which are particularly related to their historical and cultural origins, the British experience contrasts more sharply with international patterns than most. Significant trends and influences which can be identified in many other nations are notable by their absence or neglect in the UK. Whereas other countries, sometimes during periods of great stress, have confronted the big issues – like what education is for and how much national effort should be invested in it – the UK has favoured an evolutionary, piecemeal approach which has been characteristic of its endeavours in other fields too.

There are advantages to such an approach. Change can be accomplished relatively smoothly, building on proven experience of good practice rather than by imposition. For much of the twentieth century, educational decision-making has been a shared responsibility between central and local authorities, enabling the latter to be genuinely responsive to local needs and often creative in their solutions. For example, the training of teachers, special needs provision and school meals and medicals were all local initiatives which were subsequently absorbed into national legislation. Teachers themselves, who have enjoyed considerable professional autonomy compared with those in many other countries, have often played a significant role in developing policy based on practice. The British 'system' has therefore permitted a degree of variety and experimentation which, certain aberrations notwithstanding, can be seen in a very positive light.

The main drawback, on the other hand, is that because until the 1980s legislation permitted rather than initiated, followed rather than directed, it concerned itself with structural organisation and repeatedly avoided stating an educational rationale. This has tended to leave primary education at the mercy of forces which have very little to do with the education of young children. The competing claims of nationalism, regionalism, social class and religious denominationalism have never been fully resolved, and there is a long history of compromise, evasion and partial solutions. If a national system of education is a set of coherently interrelated institutions provided mainly by the state for the education of its children, the UK has never had one.

Indeed, it is difficult even to agree accurate terminology. English traditions have profoundly influenced the other parts of the United Kingdom, but Wales, Scotland and Northern Ireland have been very different in the past and still retain distinctive features in their educational provision. The Isle of Man and the Channel Islands are different again, and the Republic of Ireland has had long, if often acrimonious, associations with England for much of its history. The terms 'Britain' and 'British' tend to be loosely used in educational history; this chapter will attempt to be accurate in its use of descriptors, for the sake of readers understandably perplexed by these nuances of geo-political distinction. It is an important consideration because, as will be seen in the course of this chapter, issues to do with nationhood and the development of state formation are crucial determinants in the shaping of most educational systems.

It could probably be agreed worldwide that young children have the right to be given the opportunity and encouragement to acquire the essential basic skills of literacy, oracy and numeracy, along with an introduction to wider areas of knowledge and the skills associated with accessing and understanding those areas. To provide that entitlement through formalised schooling affords, in addition, important opportunities for the socialisation of young children, so that they learn to behave towards their peers and towards adults in a way deemed appropriate by the older generation. It would also be commonly held that a necessary function of primary or elementary education is, in some sense, to prepare members of the young generation for what lies ahead in their lives. The interesting debates arise out of such questions as: What are they being prepared for? How should it be done? Who will provide and pay for it? There are no universal answers. Perceptions of what each new generation is being prepared for are invariably coloured by social, economic, political, religious and ideological contexts. Whilst the innate enthusiasm of human beings for knowledge and ideas should not be underestimated, it remains true that the amount, content and style of education sought by, and offered to, a nation's population are closely related to prevailing concerns which have little to do with 'education for its own sake'. Let us now examine some of those concerns which recur in a number of countries, relating them particularly to the experience of the UK. They have been grouped under five broad headings – religious, ideological, social, economic and political – though links between the categories need constantly to be borne in mind.

Religious influences

The UK is not unusual in demonstrating a long-established association between religion and education. Religions typically generate quite early in their existence a written record and an organisational structure, which then require people (nearly always men) educated in the literature and the form of the religion to continue conducting and promoting it. In Western Europe, the hierarchical and centralised structure of Christianity in the form of Roman Catholicism incorporated 'schooling' into its network of churches and cathedrals, so that by the time of the Reformation in the sixteenth century, it can be said that 'educational provision within the British Isles had probably reached the highest level of uniformity that it has reached at any time in written history' (Bell and Grant 1977: 54). Then the sixteenth-century Tudor monarchs turned schools into Protestant institutions, as well as encouraging the addition of many more, some of them enjoying the titular distinction of 'royal' or 'grammar' or both, but many others comprising inadequately endowed and supported parochial elementary schools. Their efforts influenced Scotland and extended to Ireland, where the proselytising function of these English-speaking Protestant establishments was paramount. Only in Scotland, where the Parliament made local lay authorities – rural landlords and town councils – responsible for maintaining elementary schools, was there anything like a system of education at this time; the Scots, it was said, were the best educated people in Europe (Bell and Grant 1977: 57).

By the beginning of the nineteenth century, some of these grammar schools had disappeared for want of patronage, others had struggled on as elementary or trade schools, and a few, thanks to fortuitous endowments, were poised to become the prestigious elitist public schools of the upper and aspiring middle classes. The vast majority of the population – the working class – whose expectations did not include full-time schooling, was untouched by any of them. Basic literacy and numeracy were acquired, if at all, either from private teachers, often local and informal, or from one of the many church-related Sunday schools, or from limited attendance at the increasing number of small fee-paying schools run by the churches and other charitable organisations. Philanthropic voluntary effort by religious groups was the foundation of England's present primary school system. Its limitations – randomly located, underfunded, often poorly taught, narrow in scope and unconnected to any other educational institutions – were considerable, but its attractions to successive nineteenth- and twentieth-century governments ensured that reforms were grafted on to the denominational primary school system, rather than it ever being overhauled as part of a national evaluation of needs and suppliers. With buildings, however inadequate, and endowments, however small, to support the teachers' salaries, the cheapness of subsidising the existing 'schools' was irresistible. Hence a number of the significant developments in elementary education were designed to keep the denominational schools in business as cheaply as possible,[1] with the result that the education offered was based on mass instruction and characterised by authoritarian teaching styles and much drilling and rote learning, and rarely incorporating anything beyond the 'four Rs' – reading, writing, arithmetic and religion. It was a fortunate coincidence that this limited and uninspiring approach conformed with religious assumptions that children are innately bad, anarchic and amoral, and therefore in need of firm control and discipline.

The reasons why England was willing to settle for such a lowly version of elementary schooling – while all its neighbours were elevating their educational aspirations – will be discussed in later sections of this chapter, but here the enduring religious strand in English primary schooling is explained. The Tudor legacy was crucially important in determining that the dominant religious orthodoxy was created by the monarch and has remained, as 'the Church of England', the established church ever since. As such, as well as being the most popular church, it has been closely identified with the ruling elite and with the social and administrative fabric of English life. The Church of England has always, in consequence, been a safe and supportive locus for the education of the nation's children. Church and state are virtually one and the same, with the former posing no challenge to the latter, nor identifying itself with any organisation or authority outside the nation. Contrasts with countries where the dominant religion is international – Roman Catholicism or Islam, for example – are obvious.

State support for church schools was rather more contentious in Wales, Scotland and Ireland, where the majority of the population was not Anglican, and is in marked contrast, for example, to France, where nineteenth-century republicanism was strongly anticlerical. There the church fitted into the national system rather than the other way round, until in 1904 French state education became wholly secular, as it has remained since. It is a good example of the pattern which Green (1990: 29) describes as typical of national education systems: 'Whilst religion played a major part in the proliferation of early schools . . . in most countries the creation of public education systems involved, precisely, a break with the traditional clerical domination of schooling'. At exactly the same time as

16

France was banishing the church from state education, England was cementing 'the dual system' which gave church voluntary schools equal status and funding with fully maintained schools. For much of the twentieth century, religious instruction was the only part of the curriculum prescribed by law, and its recently revitalised role in schools – along with the compulsory daily act of collective worship – has reminded us that it is still an enduring issue in English education.

Ideological influences

Religion is not the only source of ideas about what children should learn and why. At times philosophers' thinking about the nature of existence, which may of course be influenced by religion as by many other factors, develops an explicitly educational focus. The multiplicity of factors makes it impossible to offer generalised conclusions which fit all countries, but one particular strand of thinking is highly significant in the shaping of primary education. In Western Europe, it grew out of the Enlightenment, rationalist philosophy associated with Rousseau, Voltaire, Locke and Mill among others, and was developed further into a human and political rights programme by radicals like Tom Paine and William Lovett.

Simply put, it stated the principle of universal educability. People are formed by their environment, nurture is more important than nature, and so everyone could and should be educated as a basic human right and as a tool of emancipation. This potentially revolutionary doctrine was, in Marxist terms, the inevitable expression of the challenge to the aristocracy by the bourgeoisie (acting on behalf of the proletariat), and its echoes can be found in many parts of the world as educational provision has been extended to larger parts of the population. In Western Europe, it is in fact difficult to prove a close chronological relationship between the prevalence of radical, egalitarian thinking and the development of elementary school systems. For reasons which will be explored below, the state generally took control of educational provision, with an overriding concern for the promulgation of an ideology more concerned with social control, conformity and political acquiescence than with human enrichment and liberation.

But as a strand of thinking in primary education, it remains highly significant in its twentieth-century guise of progressivism. This was a multi-stranded movement which gathered strength around the time of the First World War, no doubt partly, at least, in reaction to the stultifying atmosphere in the typical English primary school. Significantly, its first prominent advocate was the then Board of Education's recently retired Chief Inspector, Edmond Holmes, who complained that 'blind, passive, literal, unintelligent obedience is the basis on which the whole system of Western education has been reared' (Holmes 1911: 50). It drew in international perspectives in the shape of Americans Homer Lane and John Dewey and Italian Maria Montessori, and by the 1920s was attracting support from almost all the leading educational reformers of the time. By no means did they all agree with each other, but there was a core of shared beliefs about the education of young children which included an emphasis on the natural goodness and individuality of the child, and the need for an atmosphere of freedom and creativity in which pupils could be self-directing, spontaneous and free of the fear of harsh punishment. The curriculum moved away from the segmentation of 'subjects' into cross-curricular projects, maybe conducted in open-plan areas and at least partially driven by pupil interest, with the teachers somewhat relinquishing their customary instructional role.

The 'success' of progressive ideologies in changing practice and pedagogy in British primary schools is difficult to assess. Selleck (1972: 156) claimed that by 1939 the progressives 'had captured the allegiance of the opinion-makers . . . they had become the intellectual orthodoxy', though it was not until after the Second World War that 'actual primary-school classroom practices were greatly modified'. All the major reports and publications of the twentieth century have endorsed significant elements of the progressive programme; hence 'the curriculum is to be thought of in terms of activity and experience rather than of knowledge to be acquired and facts to be stored' (Board of Education 1931: 93); and "finding out" has proved to be better for children than "being told" . . . . The gloomy forebodings of the decline of knowledge which would follow progressive methods have been discredited' (CACE 1967: 463).

The main deterrent to putting progressive ideas into practice would seem to lie in the fact that primary schools have nearly always been required to fulfil functions imposed by other parts of the education system, which have tended to militate against progressive approaches. These competing demands relate to another, very different, strand of ideological thinking which also blossomed in the 1930s, the belief in psychometry or intelligence testing. England's secondary schools and universities traditionally concerned themselves more with the family background than the ability of candidates; it was only when secondary schools started admitting scholarship pupils from elementary schools that any form of meritocratic selection became necessary. From very shaky beginnings, the business of testing intelligence grew into the 'science' of psychometry. Supported by research 'findings' and deductions which are now known to have been seriously flawed, the theory that children have a fixed, inherited amount of intelligence and therefore require different amounts and types of education attracted top-level support. Advocated by the Hadow Report of 1926 and enshrined in law in 1944, it created a differentiated secondary school system, which gave primary schools the unwelcome task of sorting the children out. It was unwelcome because, unlike many nations where different types of secondary and higher education institutions flourish and interlink, in England 'parity of esteem' between grammar, secondary modern and technical secondary schools was never remotely a reality. Grammar schools – predominantly middle-class institutions – were hugely advantaged and successful, creating a model of excellence, almost a mystique, which seems impossible to erase from English consciousness. Primary schools became driven by the need to chase grammar school places, often incorporating a lot of testing, repetitious practice, didactic teaching methods and streaming from a very young age – all very much at odds with progressive approaches.

The release from this pressure, with the widespread (though not complete) abolition of the eleven plus examination in the 1970s, liberated the primary school curriculum for the first time in its history. The liberation was short lived. By the 1980s, anxieties about the UK's performance in relation to other countries, especially in the economic field, had – with little hard evidence – focused on education. Typically, English nostalgia looked back to the days when streamed classes of children were 'taught' by the teacher, tightly controlled, tested a lot and made to compete for the carrot of better prospects in the future. Evidence from some of the world's most successful nations can be interpreted as confirming the efficacy of such methods. Ideologies which saw the curriculum more in terms of the child's learning than the teacher's teaching, and important research studies into primary education, such as the ORACLE project[2], seemed largely to have been forgotten or ignored. Hence, the introduction of a national curriculum with regular testing, criticism of mixed ability groups, calls for more whole-class teaching and more competition, and the proposed reintroduction of selective secondary school places, are all part of the response of the 1990s in the United Kingdom. Once again, it seems, primary education is destined to be shaped by an ideological polarisation which exists more in the rhetoric of outside observers than in the reality of primary classrooms.

Social influences

Social influences on primary education are another very wide-ranging and variegated set of considerations. They grow out of a whole range of causal factors, including ideological, political and economic ones, and they are expressed in a variety of outcomes. The emphasis here will be on relations between the different groups in a society, which shape the education given by some groups to others. All societies have some groups more advantaged and powerful than others, though the reasons for such inequalities are multifarious. There is, however, a fundamental difference between societies which so constitute their educational systems as to protect the advantaged and perpetuate inequality, and those which offer similar opportunities to everyone. It is in this part of the discussion that England comes into its own.

The distinguishing features of the English elite have exercised – even entertained – commentators from many different countries and from many different disciplines. The English elite can be characterised as conservative, nostalgic, rural, anti-intellectual, anti-industrial, snobbish, gentrified, tolerant and humane. It is undoubtedly very effective at self-preservation, and education is perhaps the single most important vehicle. The transformation of endowments intended for the education of the poor into that unique set of socialising institutions, the public schools, has been well documented;[3] what is of concern here is the impact that it has had on other educational priorities. Above all, it defined differential educational provision along social class lines. Secondary education (and the preparatory classes and schools leading to it) was for the upper and middle classes, and was entirely separate from elementary education. The labouring poor, both rural and urban, were not deemed to need much education; indeed it might even make them dissatisfied and rebellious. Hence England's very late development of a primary education system, and the grudging, penny-pinching way in which this has occurred.

The first decade of the twentieth century, which has often been acclaimed as the birth of the UK's national system of education, can be seen as a defining moment in the shaping of primary education. The last years of the nineteenth century were notable for an upsurge of educational achievement and aspiration from ordinary people, using the publicly funded board schools along with pupil-teacher centres, technical colleges and the new provincial university colleges, and encouraged by assertive urban authorities imbued with civic pride. The denominational elementary schools and the endowed secondary schools were struggling to compete, and turned for help to the Conservative, high church establishment elite, who were in government until 1906 and dominated the House of Lords at all times. Amongst other changes, the crucial 'reform' of defining secondary education as a fee-paying, socialising activity devoted to literary education and extending over several years, made it firmly a middle-class preserve; it put paid to pupil-teacher centres, countered the rise of technical and vocational education and reduced the scope of elementary schooling.

The effects on the last of these have been described as 'devastating' (Gordon 1980: 202); elementary schools were 'put into a strait-jacket' (Eaglesham 1963: 5) with the introduction of 'a new and artificial rigidity' (Maclure 1970: 50). Henceforth, the vast majority of English children spent their whole school career, normally until the age of 14, in elementary schools, where they were to follow a somewhat limited curriculum and be inculcated with habits of industry, self-control, truthfulness and loyalty.[4] There was a concentration of effort on children of 10 to 11 years of age as the scholarship examination approached, even though many chose not to take it and there were nothing like enough secondary school places for thousands who did succeed. Preparation for the examination, itself a rudimentary selection mechanism, was alleged to cramp the curriculum, encourage streaming, cramming and mechanical testing, and give children a lifelong distaste for learning.[5] It also left the 11- to 14-year-olds with no overt educational goal, and oral history has revealed that many of them recall their last years at school as memorably tedious and unpleasant. In time, the whole of elementary education became permeated by the demands of secondary education, and as Simon (1974: 232) has suggested, it was essentially a process of 'selection by elimination', masquerading as the more acceptable and positive-sounding 'selection by ability'.

The specification of elementary schooling in this way was a quite remarkably retrogressive strategy, profoundly anti-meritocratic, and consequently untypical of twentieth-century educational developments in the vast majority of nations. It set the pattern for at least the first half of the century, for heroic efforts by some local authorities to enlarge post-elementary opportunities for their poorer children – by increasing the number of free grammar school places or by creating central schools – did little to challenge the basic division between elementary schooling for the many and secondary schooling for the few. It constrained elementary schools, but not in a way which gave them any autonomy; in their selective function, they were made the servants of the higher parts of the system, a role which has continued even after the introduction of 'secondary education for all' following the Second World War. It was a strikingly successful manoeuvre by socially advantaged groups to protect their hold over the nation's educational riches, one which it is difficult to match with the experiences of any other country.

Economic influences

A vast body of work, emanating from many different academic disciplines, has engaged with the problem of trying to explain the UK's persistent economic decline, which has been characterised as an 'unbroken chain of abysmal failures' (Pollard 1982: 185). The debate is hampered by the absence of measurable indices tying education to economic performance, but it seems highly unlikely that the two are not mutually related. Certainly governments round the world, looking to effect economic progress, typically invest in education and training as key contributors. Hence, a number of European governments have quite a long tradition of direct state sponsorship of economic developments – such as the introduction and protection of new industries, transport networks, trading arrangements – so that the idea of the bureaucrat-entrepreneur was not new. In the nineteenth century some of them specifically programmed their educational institutions to compete with British economic supremacy;

21

Germany, it has been said (Reisner 1939: 181), 'was a land of schools before it was a land of factories'. In many developing countries in the world, education and training are high on the agenda for reform, ranging from mass literacy campaigns to careful nurturing of appropriate technical, scientific and medical skills.

In contrast, Britain's Industrial Revolution had succeeded in the absence of any formal encouragement or controls, and it had become a key part of the Victorian gospel not to intervene. Industrialists and entrepreneurs were largely placed outside the mainstream of political and cultural life, a process reinforced by the religious nonconformity of many of them. They had learned their skills and achieved their success by trial and error, giving rise to the time-honoured 'rule of thumb' and an enduring attachment to the apprenticeship model of 'learning on the job'. England's industrial transformation owed nothing either to the universities or to the schools of the governing class, whose members treasured the distance – geographical as well as intellectual and emotional – they were able to maintain from the world of factories, mills, mines, cities, sanitation, poverty and disease.

Such an economic model placed few expectations on the nation's education system. What it was required to supply was a labour force not particularly skilled or knowledgeable about anything, but sufficiently disciplined to operate in large-scale units of production and sufficiently docile to tolerate the hardships of urban life. Indeed, it can be argued that the harsh, repetitious mass instruction favoured in Victorian elementary schools was an invaluable practice for the world of work. The criterion of economic utility – which permeates educational provision in many countries – was in England unusually limited in scope, and inextricably bound up with the maintenance of social order.[6] Emile Durkheim asserted that education has the twin functions of providing the skills needed by industrial economies and of acting as the main vehicle of social cohesion through the transmission of a common culture and morality. But where there are marked social divisions and inequalities, the culture and values transmitted through education are, as Marxist interpretations argue, those of the capitalist dominant class for whom a subservient and underskilled workforce is desirable.

Such a view brings in issues to do with meritocracy. Whether from notions of egalitarianism or of efficiency, or a mixture of the two, many nations have at some time in their development realised that maximising the talent of their populations is a useful tactic. Prussia, for example, rebuilding itself after defeat by Napoleon, enacted compulsory elementary education in 1810, with universal enrolment largely achieved twenty years later. Other German states, Scandinavia, more settled parts of the USA and France had national systems of elementary and technical education in place by the 1830s. Ireland's elementary education system dates from the same decade, when even the Channel Islands and the Isle of Man benefited from full-scale educational reorganisation. Scotland's system was considerably older, dating from seventeenth-century legislation to provide, support and inspect a national network of parish schools. In all of them, a subsidised and regulated elementary school system was accompanied by at least the beginnings of a trained teaching force and by appropriate secondary, technical and university institutions; in other words, provision for the education of young children was perceived not only as desirable in itself, but also as part of a bigger investment in their potential as adults.

In England, it was almost the end of the nineteenth century before changes in the occupational structure opened up new possibilities for both sexes – in teaching, nursing, clerical work and retailing – at about the same time as pressure to upgrade the nation's industrial and technical skills by learning from continental rivals gave technical and vocational education a new respectability. As the previous section showed, the national system conceived after the 1902 Act did much to turn back the clock. The one significant concession to meritocratic ideals, the intro-duction of the free place system in 1907, established the principle that only a small proportion of specially talented elementary school pupils would be permitted to aspire, after due socialisation, to academic and professional success. It is interesting that when, after the 1944 Education Act, the eleven plus examination became the sole bridge between primary education and the tripartite secondary system, there was considerable resistance to what was seen as excessive emphasis on intellectual achieve-ment, to the detriment of character-forming and sporting rituals. Work-ing-class and trade union opinion, on the other hand, was initially rather keen on eleven plus selection because it allowed talented youngsters to demonstrate their potential by objective academic examination. And par-ents in Wales, Ireland and much of Scotland 'seemed to be more inter-ested in solid training that would lead to job success . . . rather than the mere social badging of the old school tie' (Bell and Grant 1977: 70–1). In many countries the adoption of meritocratic principles in education, for the purpose of maximising the nation's pool of talent, is exactly that; in France and Singapore, for example, promotion or advancement is decided solely on the basis of the highest marks. The United Kingdom, in contrast, has become practised at manipulating the notion of meritocracy as a social instrument, and with the continuing existence of a prestigious fee-paying education sector, it is difficult to see how it will ever be otherwise.

Political influences

In many countries an association between the growth of democracy and the development of educational provision can be demonstrated. Even in England there is quite a close chronological match between legislation which progressively extended the franchise and legislation which enlarged educational provision. In some developing countries, the difficulty of conducting election campaigns with a largely illiterate population has been one of the main spurs to national investment in education. Radical and revolutionary movements, recognising the truism that knowledge means power, have often included a strong commitment to self-education. The revered Paolo Freire, recognising the revolutionary potential of education, advocated lifelong community-based education in opposition to the institutionalisation of state provision. In the UK, study groups, libraries and lecture courses were significant features of the programmes of Chartists, the Co-operative Movement, the Mechanics' Institutes, early socialism and trade unionism – the Workers' Educational Association continues to be active in adult education. It can be argued that the subversive threat posed by such initiatives is one of the prompts to government intervention in the provision of education.

This is because education is one of the key features in the formation of the modern state. As nations develop a clear identity which requires the loyalty of their subjects, education has to become a state concern, emanating from the top downwards and demonstrating certain uniform features which contribute to national identity. It has functions in supplying trained and loyal personnel for the maintenance of the state – bureaucrats, tax collectors, military, sometimes industrialists and entrepreneurs. It also has a vital role to play in transmitting a cohesive national culture as defined by the ruling class, along with implicit social and political training. Education is uniquely placed to undertake a whole range of tasks deemed desirable for an aspiring national identity, with the added advantage that it has access to young minds. It can promote a common language; preserve vernacular literature, music and art; assimilate immigrants; spread preferred or new methods of calculation; formalise a new calendar or holiday pattern; develop particular vocational skills; select historical truths; encourage patriotic enthusiasm; promote certain religious doctrines; inculcate moral codes; and shape personal and national expectations.

This process of national consolidation can be traced in all European countries in the eighteenth and nineteenth centuries, with a close correlation between periods of intense state formation and spells of dynamic educational change. Both often followed profound social and political upheaval – Napoleon leading France out of its revolutionary turmoil, the Prussian aristocracy recovering from the humiliation of defeat by Napoleon, the early republic of the USA following the struggle for independence. England, having achieved national unification earlier than most, was the least interested in education as a tool of nationalism. Its sense of national identity was securely rooted in ancient institutions, including the monarchy, as well as demonstrably evident in industrial and imperial superiority. It never had to be forward looking, to struggle for solutions, to learn from others. Even so, it is significant that most of the major educational statutes immediately followed a war – 1870, 1902, 1918, 1944, even 1988. England's sense of security has been such that it has felt able to leave Wales, Scotland and Northern Ireland varying degrees of control over their education systems, which has meant to them the opportunity to preserve their own cherished elements of national identity, such as the Welsh language or segregated denominational school-ing in Northern Ireland.

This regional dimension brings us to a conclusion which rather defies the categorisation of the preceding pages. In seeking for determining influences on the form and philosophy of primary education, it is possible to identify strands which history indicates were significant. Certain facts and precepts can confidently be labelled religious or economic or political, though often it is a combination of factors which shape the thinking that gives rise to policy and practice. In some respects, political considerations dominate all others, as the strengthening of state power subordinates all aspects of the nation's life in the pursuit of independent and self-reliant nationhood. Yet there is a dimension to national identity which seems to lie in the realms of indefinable but none the less resilient cultural traditions which influence priorities and expectations. It is worth quoting from two of the UK's most distinguished historians to try to convey this dimension. Hobsbawm has written of the development of mining in Wales:

> It brought about something like the birth of a self-conscious Welsh nation out of a traditional Welsh-speaking peasantry. Its most obvious symptom was the mass conversion of the Welsh to unofficial religions . . . strikingly national in spirit, and a self-conscious interest in Welsh culture and antiquities. After 1800 [it] brought three extremely important consequences: a marked development of education, of Welsh literature, and . . . a native social and political leadership. It also brought an alternative set of ambitions to the economic. Thenceforth the characteristic hope of the young Welshman would not be to become rich, but to become educated and eloquent.
>
> (Hobsbawm 1968: 296)

And of late eighteenth-century Scotland, Trevelyan wrote:

> The Universities flourished as they did not in England, being the real cornerstone of a real edifice of national education. Learning

was fostered among the people by the Church itself, which was in much closer touch with all classes and their needs than in South Britain of that day. Every peasant with a clever son aspired, not without reasonable hope, to see him pass through the village school and the University into the sacred profession, which thus continued to be recruited from the people and to represent the best side of the national idealism.

(Trevelyan 1922: 48–49)

Individual readers of this book will, hopefully, be able to recognise the cultural and idealistic qualities, as well as the economic, political and social factors, which make each country's education system, and the primary schooling within it, unique.

Notes

1 Notably, the invention of the monitorial system in 1809, by which one teacher could 'teach' large numbers by 'training' slightly older pupils or monitors; the introduction of 'payment by results' in 1862, which paid grants to schools according to a limited annual examination of individual pupils and successfully reduced national spending on elementary education; and even the introduction in the 1870 Education Act of board schools, which were intended to 'fill the gaps' in the voluntary provision by giving basic instruction to the poorest and most ignorant children, and only later developed into more educationally ambitious institutions.
2 The Observational Research and Classroom Research Project based at Leicester University's School of Education was a large-scale observational study of the classroom practice of primary teachers and its effects on pupils' learning (see Gatton et al. 1980).
3 In, for example, T. Bamford (1967) Rise of the Public Schools. London: Nelson; I. Weinberg (1967) The English Public Schools – The Sociology of Elite Education. New York: Atherton Press; R. Wilkinson (1964) The Prefects: British Leadership and the Public School Tradition. Oxford: Oxford University Press.
4 According to Board of Education (1904) which remained in force until 1926.
5 Allegations made by the more progressive members of the 1920 Committee on Scholarships and Free Places, who emphatically dissented from the majority report in favour of testing all but subnormal 11–year-olds.
6 For instance, the major nineteenth-century enquiry into elementary education, the Newcastle Commission, recommended both that 'it is far better that it [the child] should go to work at the earliest stage at which it can bear the physical exertion than that it should remain at school' and that the pupil should 'know what are the duties required of him towards his Maker and his fellow-man'. Royal Commission to Enquire into the State of Popular Education in England (1861). London: HMSO.

References

Bell, R. and Grant, N. (1977) *Patterns of Education in the British Isles*. London: Allen & Unwin.

Board of Education (1904) *Regulations for Elementary Schools*. London: HMSO.

Board of Education (1926) *Report of the Consultative Committee on the Education of the Adolescent* (The Hadow Report). London: HMSO.

Board of Education (1931) *Report of the Consultative Committee on the Primary School* (The Hadow Report). London: HMSO.

Central Advisory Council for Education (CACE) (1967) *Children and their Primary Schools* (The Plowden Report). London: HMSO.

Dearden, R.F. (1968) *The Philosophy of Primary Education*. London: Routledge & Kegan Paul.

Eaglesham, E.J.R. (1963) 'The centenary of Robert Morant'. *British Journal of Educational Studies* 12(1), 5–18.

Galton, M., Simon, B. and Croll, P. (1980) *Inside the Primary Classroom*. London: Routledge & Kegan Paul.

Gordon, P. (1980) *Selection for Secondary Education*. London: Woburn Press.

Green, A. (1990) *Education and State Formation*. Basingstoke: Macmillan.

Hobsbawm, E.J. (1968) *Industry and Empire*. Harmondsworth: Penguin.

Holmes, E. (1911) *What Is and What Might Be*. London: Constable.

Maclure, S. (1970) *One Hundred Years of London Education 1870–1970*. London: Allen Lane.

Pollard, S. (1982) *The Wasting of the British Economy*. London: Croom Helm.

Reisner, E.H. (1939) *Nationalism and Education Since 1789*. New York: Macmillan.

Selleck, R.J.W. (1972) *English Primary Education and the Progressives, 1914–1939*. London: Routledge & Kegan Paul.

Simon, B. (1965) *Education and the Labour Movement 1870–1920*. London: Lawrence & Wishart.

Simon, B. (1974) *The Politics of Educational Reform 1920–1940*. London: Lawrence & Wishart.

Trevelyan, G.M. (1968) *British History in the Nineteenth Century and After (1782–1919)*. Harmondsworth: Penguin.

2

THE CONCEPT OF A DEVELOPMENTAL CURRICULUM

Geva Blenkin and Vic Kelly

The view that the focus of the school curriculum should be on human development is one of several ideologies in the age-old education debate. It is important that it be seen as such, and not as the intellectual aberration that its opponents would have us believe it to be. Similarly, the alternative views of education and curriculum proposed by those opponents must be recognised – and analysed – as ideological.

Ideology is a term which came into prominence within Marxist philosophy, where it was used to refer to those 'false doctrines' which deviated from or disagreed with the 'eternal truths' of Marxism. It is used in much the same way today by those politicians and their lackeys who offer their ideologies in the form of 'eternal truths' and would have us view all alternatives as in some way intellectually flawed and inadequate.

In the postmodern age, however, we must recognise that all knowledge is socially constructed, so that every value system is an ideology. And we must, as a consequence, further acknowledge that, despite the absolutes we have been offered by philosophers from the time of Plato and continue to be offered by those who, for their political purposes, would discourage debate, the school curriculum has always been a battleground of competing ideologies.

The view that the curriculum should be developmental must be acknowledged, then, as one of these competing ideologies. This chapter will seek to elucidate what this particular ideology is claiming, and why so many people continue to advocate it, by offering an analysis of the concept of a developmental curriculum and identifying its key elements.

In the current political context in most countries, where genuine debate on many social issues is discouraged, conceptual exploration is not very fashionable. The present-day emphasis is that of Thomas Gradgrind – an emphasis on facts and more facts. But, without careful conceptual exploration, educational policies and practices lack any secure intellectual base.

They thus become confused and consequently inadequate, since practice without theory is blind and practice without a conceptually secure theory is dangerous. Worse, conceptual analysis involves making explicit the values which underpin one's policies and practices, so that it is a lack of conceptual clarity that makes possible all the many deceptions that are practised on us – most notably again by politicians and their lackeys.

Hence it is particularly important to analyse policies and practices to identify their underlying ideologies, where, as in most current practice worldwide, these are not articulated by their proponents. And, conversely, when one is advocating a particular approach to educational practice, it is obligatory to elucidate its conceptual base, its underpinning values, and to offer some kind of justification for these. It is the dual purpose of this chapter, therefore, to attempt such an elucidation of the concept of a developmental curriculum and to offer justificatory arguments in support of its advocacy.

The concept of education as human development

It should perhaps first be noted that there is no logical or conceptual reason why the notion of education as development should be specifically related to the early years of schooling. Historically, in most education systems worldwide, this kind of approach to education has been most in evidence in early years provision, but the connection is contingent only. And, further, some people have been arguing for a long time that education, in its fullest sense, must be so conceived at whatever age it is being offered or experienced.

Education as development: a long-established tradition

In fact, if we look at the massive theorising which has gone on in the Western world concerning education, since the time of Plato, we will quickly see that it has always been understood in developmental terms. A major, perhaps *the* major, purpose of educational provision has always been seen as personal development. In Plato's system, for example, although education in its fullest sense was reserved for a chosen elite, that chosen elite was to receive a form of education which would promote personal qualities – moral as well as intellectual. Again, it is worth noting that he recognised this as also providing a route to social and political stability – another lesson which has recently been lost. For Aristotle, too, the central goal of education was 'the good life', a concept which should be seen as having connotations not only of moral upbringing but also in terms of that enrichment of the quality of life which such provision offers. For, as he said, 'a state exists for the sake of a good life, and not for the sake of life only' (*Politics* III. 9).

29

This view, then, has permeated educational theorising up to very recent times. There is no major educational theorist, no 'great educator', who has not begun from a concept of education as personal development. And, since the time of Rousseau, such theorists have also recognised the corollary of this position, that such development can only be promoted by the offering of genuine forms of personal experience – a view which was given perhaps its most telling statement in the work of John Dewey.

It is also worthy of note that, at least until recent times, this notion of what it means to be educated was a major part of the meaning given to the term 'education' in common parlance. We have reserved the description 'educated' not for those who can demonstrate wide-ranging factual knowledge but for those whose upbringing has had a recognisable impact on the development of their character, their life-styles and their general behaviour. And the expectations parents have had of their children's schooling have always transcended the acquisition of knowledge and even success in examinations, and have embraced some sense that they would become better people for their school experience, would enjoy an enhanced and enriched life-style, would in some sense 'grow up proper'.

In practice, before the advent of state-provided education for all, while there was always a concern to ensure that those who were fortunate enough to receive an education were assisted by it to 'get on in the world', there was always a parallel desire to support their development as persons, their moral and social as well as their cultural development. It is this combination of theory and practice which has given rise to the notion of a 'liberal education'. The rejection of this as an important goal for educational provision in current policies and practices thus represents a massive rejection of tradition rather than the 'return to traditional values' which it has been 'sold' as.

The concept of education

It is now more than thirty years since Richard Peters offered us his analysis of the concept of education (Peters 1965; 1966). Some views, however, while they may go out of fashion, do not lose their cogency simply because of the passage of time; and there are certain aspects of Peters' analysis which continue to have importance for those who are planning and practising education.

His concern was to identify those aspects of schooling which might be said to differentiate *education* from other forms of teaching, such as, for example, *instruction*, *training*, *conditioning* and even *indoctrination*. There are three such criteria which need to be stressed in the present context – not only of this chapter but also of current practice.

First, Peters argued that the use of the term 'education' to denote an act of teaching must imply that the purpose of that act is not extrinsic to the activity itself. Education, in the true sense, entails activities which are *intrinsically* worthwhile. Thus acts of teaching which are aimed at providing the pupil with useful knowledge, skills and understandings, or at supporting the economy of a nation, while not to be scorned, are nevertheless acts of *training* or *instruction* rather than of education in the full sense.

Secondly, and following from this, the value or worthwhileness of these educational activities must reside in the activities themselves rather than in what they might lead to. And, in a postmodern context, where certainty about knowledge can no longer be assumed, the value of an educational activity must be gauged in relation to its impact on the recipient – the subject of the educational process rather than its content. In short, the concept of education, the use of the term 'education', implies that the activity being referred to or denoted has as its main purpose supporting the growth, development and enrichment of the individual recipient.

Thirdly, if such development is to be effectively promoted, the recipient must be a willing participant in the activity. Education in the full and genuine sense is not something which is *done to* pupils; it is an activity in which the learner as well as the teacher must be fully involved and engaged.

Education as non-development

The importance of this analysis, and perhaps especially of the last point, becomes apparent if we attempt to imagine a concept of a form of education which is not concerned with the development of the recipient. For one very useful way in which we can get to grips with the essence of concepts is to attempt to conceive of their opposites.

To offer a form of schooling which rejects the idea of individual development is to reject education as we have seen it defined, and to replace it with forms of instruction, training, even indoctrination, which deliberately ignore considerations of the *intrinsic* value of our provision for the individual and of the willing participation of the recipient in the activity. It is of course a practice which is not uncommon, and which we might argue is becoming increasingly common worldwide, but, whatever else it might be, it is not education. It consists of what A.N. Whitehead many years ago (1932: 1–2, 2–3) called 'inert ideas', 'that is to say, ideas that are merely received into the mind without being utilised, or tested, or thrown into fresh combinations' – a process which he describes as 'the passive reception of disconnected ideas, not illumined with any spark of vitality'.

Some further quotations from those essays by Whitehead will illustrate the point we are making here and illuminate the thinking behind it. They also offer an amusing perspective on some 'educational' practices prevalent in Whitehead's day and recently resurrected. 'Knowledge does not keep any better than fish' (Whitehead 1932: v). 'A merely well informed man [or woman] is the most useless bore on God's earth (: 1). 'Education with inert ideas is not only useless; it is, above all things, harmful – Corruptio optimi, pessima' (: 2). 'There is only one subject-matter for education, and that is Life in all its manifestations' (: 10).

It was this view of schooling, as to be defined in terms of its content or its utility, rather than in terms if its impact on the development of the individual, which was explicitly rejected in relation to primary education by the Hadow Report (Board of Education 1931: para 75) in the United Kingdom. That report refers specifically to Whitehead's thinking, telling us that 'we must recognise the uselessness and the danger of seeking to inculcate what Professor Whitehead calls inert ideas – that is, ideas which at the time when they are imparted have no bearing upon a child's natural activities of body or mind and do nothing to illuminate or guide his [or her] experience'. And that is the main basis for the report's famous definition of the developmental curriculum as 'to be thought of in terms of activity and experience rather than of knowledge to be acquired and facts to be stored'.

In view of the foregoing, it might be felt that the idea that education should be planned as a form of individual development is almost self-evident. Certainly, it is a very compelling ideology. It must be asked, then: Why has it in very recent times been receiving a 'bad press' and why have educational policies and practices world-wide increasingly shifted to other ideologies and other forms? A major part of the answer to that question is to be found in the advent of universal education.

Universal education

The view of education as personal development held an almost unquestioned sway during the times and/or in the context of elitist forms of educational provision. It made good sense in Plato's highly selective programme; it seemed self-evidently right for the free citizens of the society in which Aristotle lived; in Roman times and in more recent times, it was seen as the right kind of preparation for those whose parents could afford to have them educated and for whom education was a preparation for a major role in the governance of society. In short, while it was not to be made available to all, its attractions – moral, social, cultural and intellectual – went largely unchallenged. With the advent of universal education, however, it became problematic and controversial. And it has never been generally accepted that this form of education should be made available to everyone. It has been recognised as a privilege, even a luxury, which, for a variety of reasons which will become clear, should be jealously guarded.

Universal education brought with it the conflict between liberal and vocational ideologies in education. From the beginning, the most influential agents in its generation and development were those who looked to universal schooling for a trained workforce and a 'gentling of the masses', for economic utility and law and order. Those who have advocated forms of schooling for all which would offer more than this, those who have sought to promote education in the full sense rather than forms of training, conditioning, even indoctrination, have always been a minority.

The conflict was well expressed in the United Kingdom in a government report presented by the Crowther Committee in 1959 (CACE 1959). For that report identified 'two purposes that education serves'. First, there is 'the right of every boy and girl to be educated', a right which 'exists regardless of whether, in each individual case, there will be any return', so that 'from this point of view, education is one of the social services of the welfare state' (CACE 1959: 54). On the other hand, there is also the need of the community to provide an adequate supply of brains and skill to sustain its economic productivity. From this point of view, education is a national investment.

What is perhaps more important, however, in the context both of this debate and of current policies and practices, is that the report suggested that this is a false dichotomy, that it does not make sense to ask whether education should be designed to support the national economy or to promote individual development. For it saw these as inextricably interwoven, and regarded an emphasis on either one at the expense of the other as misplaced, misguided and ultimately self-defeating. As the report says:

> the two purposes could not be disentangled even if it were desirable to do so . . . there are many persons the justification for whose education must be sought almost entirely in what it does for them as individuals. But it is hard to tell which is which at the start, and not always easy later on. There are indeed parts of everybody's education which have no economic value, and there is nobody whose education is entirely without it.
>
> (CACE 1959: 55)

Subsequent governments, not only in the UK but also in most other so-called 'advanced' nations, have lost sight of this last point, have resurrected the dichotomy and have resolved it in favour of the notion of education as a national investment. It is for this reason that the idea of education as individual development has become lost. Its implications for the health – economic as well as social – of society have been overlooked, and it has come to be seen again as a luxury which no government feels it can afford to provide for the non-productive members of the school communities.

Hence curricula are now almost universally utilitarian, planned in terms of what is seen as economically useful knowledge-content, aimed at precisely pre-specified attainment targets and subject to regular assessment of progress, with that progress being judged in terms of the individual's advance through a pre-set programme of knowledge rather than in terms of personal development.

We must now complete this discussion of the view of education as development by exploring the main components of a curriculum designed to promote such personal development.

A *developmental curriculum*

To a large extent, the main elements of the form of curriculum appropriate for the promotion of individual development will have emerged from what has been said so far. Certainly, there are negative points to be gleaned from that discussion.

For example, individual development is not likely to be promoted by an off-the-peg curriculum which consists of prespecified syllabuses which *all* pupils are expected to follow. It is the imposition of this form of curriculum on all state-maintained schools in the UK which has led to the loss of the developmental dimension of education, with particularly unsatisfactory consequences for education in the early years. It has also made its contribution to an acceleration of the progress towards alienation and its consequent law and order problems. Educational development, like diet, like health, like all aspects of the human organism, is an individual matter, and thus requires a bespoke or tailor-made curriculum.

Secondly, this in turn necessitates that decisions about the content of each individual's education must be taken at the personal level. This does not obviate the need for an agreed national curriculum, but it does require that such a national curriculum should dictate not a rigid body of subject-content to be imposed on all regardless of suitability but broad guidelines, areas of experience which are seen as constituting a proper form of educational entitlement for all (DES 1977). Furthermore, those areas must be conceived as embracing all dimensions of development, all forms or modes of representation (Eisner 1982). This also, of course, requires a teaching force which has itself been educated to make such professional judgements and decisions, not a body of technicians trained to carry out the dictates of central government and/or political quangos.

Thirdly, a developmental curriculum entails that the learning be *active* learning, the learner must be directly engaged with the learning activities offered. Such learning must, therefore, be founded on the provision for every pupil of genuine experiences. Development, as we have seen, is not promoted by the plastering of 'inert ideas' on to passive minds. As every major theorist from the time of Rousseau has appreciated, development can only come through first-hand and genuine experience. A developmental curriculum must seek to provide such experiences; schools must be resourced to support such provision; and teachers must be capable of planning for the personal development of each of their pupils. Without this, schools become teaching shops, and education reverts to training, instruction or, again, even indoctrination.

Nor need such experiences be entirely idiosyncratic, as some of the more simplistic criticisms of this view assume. Perhaps the most important lesson which research into development in the early years has taught us is that learning is a social activity. And this constitutes a strong argument not only for the importance of recognising individual development as having a crucial social dimension to it, but also for an acceptance of the notion that a genuine form of education must be centrally focused on supporting development on all fronts – social, moral and emotional as well as intellectual.

This final point has taken us back to a consideration of what might be seen as a factor specific to education in the early years, although we lose sight of it at our peril in the later years of schooling. It also draws our attention to a further dimension of a developmental curriculum for the early years, namely that it must have a 'caring' dimension to it. The notion that early schooling – and, indeed, what is sometimes called 'preschooling' – involves an element of care as well as education has long been established in the traditions of early education throughout the world. We must note this here as another central element of a developmental curriculum. For, without the emotional support which this implies, development of the kind we are seeking to promote is unlikely to occur.

We began this chapter by noting that the view we have been seeking to analyse and articulate represents a particular ideology and one which not everyone subscribes to. Indeed, we have referred throughout to the fact that it has become distinctly unfashionable in many countries in recent years. Like all ideologies, therefore, it needs to be not only asserted or even analysed; it must also be justified. And it is to a justification of the adoption of such an approach to education in the early years that we now turn.

The justification of a developmental curriculum for the early years

Much of the justification for the adoption of this form of developmental curriculum is implicit in our attempt at analyzing its major components. We need now, however, to try to make this explicit.

Broadly speaking, there are two major justificatory arguments for the implementation of a developmental curriculum at all levels of educational provision, but again perhaps particularly in the early years. Firstly, there is a social/pragmatic argument. And, secondly, there is a powerful moral argument – powerful, that is, to those who are open to moral discussion and understand the concept of acting according to principle. We must now briefly consider each of these. In both cases, we will again see that a major part of the justification they offer is the negative argument deriving from the unsatisfactory aspects of other approaches or ideologies.

The social/pragmatic argument

As we have seen, the notion of education as development has always been predicated on the view that the development we are concerned with is all-embracing, that it goes far beyond mere intellectual or cognitive or even cultural development and includes, in particular, the emotional, social and moral aspects of human development. The concern has always been to support the young in their growth towards personal maturity; and the affective dimension of such growth is central to this.

The appropriateness of this perception has been clearly demonstrated by recent advances in developmental psychology, particularly as the centrality of the social context to human learning and development has become plain. 'A quiet revolution has taken place in developmental psychology in the last decade. It is not only that we have begun to think again of the child as a *social being* but because we have come once more to appreciate that through such social life, the child acquires a framework for interpreting experience, and learns how to negotiate meaning in a manner congruent with the requirements of the culture' (Bruner and Haste 1987: 1).

There are a number of important points to be unearthed from this very brief quotation, not least the notion of the centrality of negotiation to educational development. What concerns us here, however, is the claim that, through appropriate forms of social interaction, the child will develop not only intellectually and cognitively but also socially and morally, that this is the route to a smooth and successful entrée, as a fully participant member, into the culture of society. In fact, it points us to a new concept of cultural development, defined in terms of initiation not to the 'high culture' of a society but to its whole social, cultural and communal milieu. Children need the experience of acceptance into the social collective of the school if they are to develop into adults who can recognise the importance to their own individual lives of that social collective we call society. In short, social and moral development require a curriculum within which the pupils are of central rather than peripheral concern. Law and order issues within society are likely to be most effectively tackled through the implementation of such a curriculum.

And here we come to the negative aspect of this justification. For the alternative to the kind of social integration we are describing is those forms of social alienation which are increasingly a feature of all societies.

Perhaps the most disturbing feature of recent changes in educational policies and practices is the emergence of alienation among children in the early years (Barrett 1989).

Social integration cannot be achieved by bolting add-on courses or lessons in moral, social or 'citizenship' education to a curriculum which, as in the case of the national curriculum in the UK, is built on a frame of values at odds with the kind of social cohesion and integration one is attempting to promote. If children are caught up, for example, in an education system which encourages competition, it will be difficult to convince them of the value of collaboration. If they are offered a curricular diet whose values are alien to them and in which they have little choice, they are unlikely to accept this passively or to develop satisfactorily by exposure to it. Failure to succeed in such a context must soon lead to rejection. The very nature of that form of curriculum must lead to increased alienation and thus an escalation of law and order problems (Kelly 1990; 1995).

Finally, if one adds to this dismal scene the spectre of schools excluding an increasing proportion of pupils both in response to this escalation of alienation and rejection and, worse, in the effort to compete with each other for custom, the pragmatic argument for a curriculum that is quite differently framed, and in which the focus is on the developmental needs of each child, becomes clear and compelling.

The moral argument

There is of course a moral dimension to the case we have just put, but it is important to stress its pragmatic appeal too. There are arguments of a more specifically moral and principled kind, however, and it is to a brief consideration of these that we now turn.

To offer children a curriculum whose main concern is with the economic health of society, while it may be justified in terms of training them for employment, is at root to treat them as means rather than ends, at one extreme as 'fodder for industry' and at the other as people whose prime function is to support the economic health of their society. To offer them a curriculum which is designed to discourage the development of their individuality or creativity or at least which fails to promote the development of their ability to think their own thoughts and reach their own conclusions is to be engaged in a process which is much more sinister, since it is to be concerned to condition or even to indoctrinate rather than to educate them. A developmental curriculum through its focus on the development of the individual, and perhaps especially the social and moral development of the individual, by definition is concerned to treat all children as ends in themselves rather than as means to the purposes of others.

The notion that morality requires us to treat our fellow human beings as ends in themselves has a long history in moral philosophy. It is especially associated with the moral philosophy of Immanuel Kant, who offered us a 'categorical moral imperative', one formulation of which was: 'So act as to treat humanity, whether in thine own person or in that of any other, in every case as an end withal, never as a means only'.

The debate about the status and validity of this assertion has raged since the time when Kant uttered it, and need not concern us here. What we must note, however, is that it is difficult to conceive of a moral system which does not recognise the individual value of every human being. It is also difficult to argue that our behaviour, our practices, our policies are morally acceptable if they do not satisfy this criterion of moral worth. Indeed, no one would so argue, at least not explicitly, even those whose actions, proposals, policies or ideologies at root reflect a rejection of it.

Again, therefore, we have a negative form of justification – a justification by opposites. For it is by contemplating a form of curriculum which denies the right of individuals to be treated as ends in themselves that we see more clearly both the iniquities of such a curriculum and the merits of one which is designed to achieve the opposite. History – and fiction too – has plenty of examples to offer us of societies which have not accepted this fundamental principle. There are those in present-day societies who would deny it through their educational policies and practices. A crucial consideration here, however, is the nature and constitution of the society for which such educational planning is being undertaken. And that brings us to our final point of justification.

The societies for which we are advocating a developmental curriculum are, or profess to be, democratic societies. Democracy, however, is not merely a political system; it is a moral system or, more precisely, it is a political system founded on clear moral principles (Kelly 1995). It is thus a moral – even a logical – requirement that every institution within a democratic society should conform to those moral principles encapsulated in the notion of democracy, that governments should act according to those principles and that social practices should as far as is possible be seeking to reflect them.

It has been argued (Kelly 1995) that the moral principles which are central to genuinely democratic societies include individual freedom within the democratic social context, equality of respect and treatment, treatment as an end in oneself and not as a means to the advantages of others, and equal enjoyment of that range of rights which constitutes individual entitlement in a democracy. Again there is scope for wide-ranging debate here, but it is difficult to imagine a society which does not seek to adhere to these principles being regarded as having any kind of claim to the descriptor 'democratic'. For these might be seen as the minimal sufficient conditions of democratic living.

Our major moral justification, then, for advocating a developmental curriculum is that it is a form of curriculum which is founded on these democratic moral principles and which, because it is so founded, is in a strong position to promote the development of all pupils towards a recognition of their importance.

The tension between this and other competing ideologies

There are of course, as we have noted on several occasions, other competing educational ideologies. Some of these make completely legitimate demands of the school system. We would not wish, for example, to be understood as arguing for a form of curriculum which totally ignores all considerations of an economic kind or of a vocational import. Such demands we believe not only can be reconciled within a developmental curriculum but also may be best satisfied in that kind of context. For the society of the future, to achieve economic success and viability, will need people whose education has taught them to think for themselves, to make choices and to be creative rather than automatons in whose 'education' the thinking has been done and the choices made for them and whose creative potential has been stifled through lack of opportunity for its exercise. Indeed, this constitutes a major argument for the implementation of such a curriculum.

However, there are those in all societies who are proffering ideologies, both of society and of education, with which our view of a developmental curriculum is incompatible. There are those, for example, who in effect are advocating the ending of state-provided education for all, or at least a massive reduction in the scale of provision (Lawton 1989, 1992, 1994), there being now no longer a demand for a large workforce (whether educated or not). Such ideologies are proving to be highly influential in policy-making – not least because the policies they advocate involve greatly reduced expenditure.

Our opposition to such ideologies, and our advocacy of a form of curriculum which is incompatible with them, are not based simply on the fact that we do not like them. They are grounded in our awareness that they represent not merely alternative ideologies of education but also, and perhaps more seriously, alternative political ideologies, ideologies which are inimical to democracy itself because they would deny those democratic principles we have just claimed to be the foundations of our position. They are part of that worldwide movement of recent years which has been described as a 'conservative restoration' (Apple 1990).

The subtle implementation of these policies through their influence on current policies and practices has already begun to have its effect in undermining the efforts of those who would implement a developmental curriculum. And they continue to have serious implications for the quality of educational provision, and perhaps again especially for the quality of what is available to our youngest children.

For they are leading to the imposition of instrumental forms of curricula, the inadequacies, even dangers, of which we have already noted. They are slowly but inexorably tending towards the demise of any genuine provision of education for all. They are resulting in what we have elsewhere called the death of infancy (Blenkin and Kelly 1994). But, above all, they are destroying the very foundations of democracy upon which all else is built.

Conclusion

The claims of a developmental curriculum must continue to be pressed, both in the interests of future generations of children and for the future democratic health of society. That such a curriculum costs money must be both admitted and recognised, as earlier government reports in the United Kingdom, including the Crowther Report (CACE 1959) have pointed out. For the implementation of such a curriculum has implications for levels of resourcing, staff:pupil ratios, the forms and quality of teacher education, inservice provision, and, indeed, every aspect of funding. It is our claim, however, that this would be money well spent – in economic as well as moral terms.

For, firstly, as the Crowther Report (CACE 1959: 60) said, even if we are concerned solely with national efficiency, 'we find it difficult to conceive that there could be any other application of money giving a larger or more certain return in the quickening of enterprise, in the stimulation of invention or in the general sharpening of those wits by which alone a trading nation in a crowded island can hope to make its living'.

Secondly, this economic or financial argument is further supported in respect of education in the early years by the research evidence of the High/Scope project in the USA which has demonstrated convincingly the massive savings to society which accrue when early education of high quality leads to 'lasting and better functioning in the domains of school, employment and community adjustment' (Sylva 1992: 687) and thus significantly reduces later expenditure on social services.

Thirdly, however, we must add to this economic case the moral argument we have been seeking to develop throughout this chapter. There are powerful moral reasons for recognising the entitlement of every child and young person in a genuinely democratic society to a form of educational provision which aims at supporting development towards enhanced and enriched forms of participation in a society whose health is to be gauged not only in economic terms but in social and cultural terms also.

The cost of a developmental form of education is not merely the price of economic stability and advance. It is the price of democracy itself with all that that implies for the future of humanity.

References

Apple, M.W. (1990) 'The politics of official knowledge in the United States of America'. *Journal of Curriculum Studies* 22(4), 377–383.

Barrett, G. (1989) *Disaffection from School? The Early Years.* London: Falmer.

Blenkin, G.M. and Kelly, A.V. (1994) 'The death of infancy'. *Education 3–13* 22(3), 3–9.

Board of Education (1931) *Report of the Consultative Committee on the Primary School* (The Hadow Report). London: HMSO.

Bruner, J. and Haste, H. (eds) (1987) *Making Sense: The Child's Construction of the World.* London and New York: Methuen.

Central Advisory Council for Education (CACE) (1959) *15 to 18* (The Crowther Report). London: HMSO.

Department of Education and Science (DES) (1977) *Curriculum 11–16.* London: HMSO.

Eisner, E. (1982) *Cognition and Curriculum.* New York: Longman.

Kelly, A.V. (1990) *The National Curriculum: A Critical Review* (updated edn 1994). London: Chapman.

Kelly, A.V. (1995) *Education and Democracy: Principles and Practices.* London: Chapman.

Lawton, D. (1989) *Education, Culture and the National Curriculum.* London, Sydney, Auckland and Toronto: Hodder & Stoughton.

Lawton, D. (1992) *Education and Politics in the 1990s: Conflict or Consensus.* London and Washington, DC: Falmer Press.

Lawton, D. (1994) *The Tory Mind on Education 1979–94.* London and Washington, DC: Falmer Press.

Peters, R.S. (1965) 'Education as initiation'. In R.D. Archambault (ed.) *Philosophical Analysis and Education.* London: Routledge & Kegan Paul.

Peters, R.S. (1966) *Ethics and Education.* London: Allen & Unwin.

Sylva, K. (1992) 'Quality care for the under-fives: is it worth it?' *RSA Journal* CXL(5433), 683–690.

Whitehead, A.N. (1932) *The Aims of Education.* London: Williams & Norgate.

3

THE PRIMARY NATIONAL CURRICULUM IN ENGLAND

A sociological perspective

Paul Ryan

Introduction

The relationship between school curricula and the prevailing needs and views of a society is important in considering sociological perspectives accommodating different forms of curriculum development and design. Through such perspectives, issues of accountability and responsiveness are relevant and significant to curriculum decision-making. Teachers attempt to present relevant and applicable curricula to children within the context of primary schooling which is determined by the government. Recognising society's diverse demands and influences raises questions of continuing appropriateness of different forms of curricula within periods of escalating social change and development. However, it would be a naive and simplistic analysis from a sociological perspective, if the needs, influences and demands of society were accepted unquestioningly and without some examination of their exact nature and relevance.

Current sociological perspectives in England focus on the study of contextual issues and events so as to further understanding of the relevance of the national curriculum (Whitty 1985; Halpin 1990). Figure 3.1 represents some of the contextual factors relevant to a sociological understanding of the present English primary curriculum which will be covered in this chapter. The concentric circles indicate the spheres of influence related to the curriculum. Arrows indicate the directional flow of contextual pressures and influences. This chapter argues that a balance should be drawn between the requirements of a national curriculum and an understanding of the underlying social context with its influence on the curriculum.

Significantly sociologists still regard the provision of opportunities, the degree of flexibility and the recognition of social context as important determinants of a socially relevant curriculum. The emphasis is upon

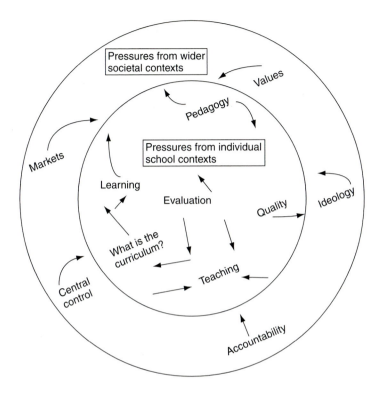

Figure 3.1 The complex and confusing social contexts for the primary curriculum

understanding the social context of schools in respect of pedagogy and the purposes underlying curriculum decision-making.

How do we decide what would be an appropriate curriculum for primary schools in relation to context and relevance? Whitty (1989: 339) suggests that instead of offering prescriptions, we should be exploring a range of mechanisms for deciding on curriculum in the first place. The implications for curricular design are that we need to adapt content, teaching style and strategy to the social circumstances of the school and, in the process, make it more relevant to the broader needs of society.

It can be argued that the curriculum should be flexible enough to allow difference in children's cultural and social needs to be accepted rather than considered a problem. The most important challenge presented by sociologists is for teachers to acknowledge, accommodate and adapt to such differences, and offer a curriculum that is still accessible, applicable, relevant and provides opportunities for all children as future citizens. Perhaps teachers themselves must rise to the challenge and focus on developing a socially relevant curriculum without lowering or narrowing pupils' opportunities and their own expectations. To begin to do this, we need to consider the wider context within which teachers and schools operate.

Societal demands and influences upon the primary curriculum

In England and Wales the national curriculum, established as a result of the 1988 Education Act, introduced a curriculum which consisted of specific subjects and associated national assessment arrangements (see Chapter 4 for a fuller explanation of the historical background). Since 1988 the rush to establish the national curriculum has meant many rapid changes resulting from content overload, unworkable assessment processes and excessive administrative tasks (Webb and Vulliamy 1996).

The implementation of any national curriculum is a complex business in which teachers have to mediate the demands of the wider political and social context, the school as a whole, and classroom practice. A variety of perspectives can be adopted, some of which are outlined in chapters constituting Part I of this book. Whilst it is not possible to consider every aspect of the sociology of a curriculum, there are particular curricular themes which address the social context issues highlighted above.

Recent trends in the sociology of education have tended to avoid attempts to establish grand theories which try to explain the relationships between schooling and curricula and societies' inequalities. One of the most recent attempts to define a curriculum relevant to a variety of contexts has been put forward by Lawton (1996). He suggests that primary schools plan on the basis of Ashton *et al.*'s (1975) model consisting of three kinds of aims – *knowledge*, *skills* and *qualities* – which are broken down into six categories for development:

1 intellectual;
2 physical;
3 aesthetic;
4 spiritual/religious;
5 emotional/personal;
6 social/moral.

Teachers in primary schools are encouraged to prioritise the aims and categories and then to plan collaboratively, incorporating the English and Welsh NC. The purpose of the approach is to enable teachers to find a less time-consuming way to integrate the ten national curriculum subjects at primary level and make them more applicable to the 'spiritual, moral, social, cultural development' of the child (Lawton 1996: 98).

Recognition of the importance to society of primary schooling and its curriculum can be traced back to the Plowden Report (CACE 1967). In a series of paragraphs concentrating on the aims of primary education, the report states: 'All schools reflect the views of society, or some section of society, about the way children should be brought up, whether or not these views are consciously held or defined' (para 493). The report goes on to discuss the purposes of primary education and identifies the need for primary schools to play their part in preparing pupils through a broad curriculum for entry into society: 'One obvious purpose is to fit children for the society into which they will grow up. To do this successfully it is necessary to predict what that society will be like' (para 494).

The overriding message of the Plowden Report is for integration within the curriculum rather than separation into subjects, it states:

> Rigid division of the curriculum into subjects tends to interrupt children's trains of thought and interest, and to hinder them from realising the common elements in problem solving. These are among the many reasons why some work, at least, should cut across subject divisions at all stages in the primary school.
>
> (CACE 1967: para 535)

Nevertheless, Chapter 17 of the Plowden Report is organised by subject. The subjects listed, in fact, provide a recognisable forerunner to the current national curriculum in England and Wales. They are, in addition to religious education, English, modern languages, history, geography, mathematics, science, art and craft, music, physical education and sex education; subjects which by implication must have been regarded as relevant to the needs of society at that time.

The importance of society in relation to the decisions about content and design of the curriculum was stressed by James Callaghan (the then Prime Minister) in 1976 when he asserted that teachers had a responsibility to explain and justify their decisions to a wider audience which included parents, employers, Local Education Authorities (LEAs) and central government (as financial providers). At that time, most curriculum decision-making rested almost solely with schools and teachers. Accountability was internal within the institutions. There are now greater difficulties in defining to whom teachers are accountable: many different people and constituencies such as national or local government agencies, parents or pupils make differing demands, depending upon their own personal, or collective social and cultural values. 'The trouble is that people understand many different things by accountability . . . [it] can be of many kinds: personal, professional, political, financial, managerial, legal, contractual' (Burgess 1992: 2).

From a sociological perspective, issues of teachers' accountability to society in general include the importance of the context within which curricular decisions are made. Teachers engage in a process of selecting appropriate texts, resources and pedagogical practices in order to implement the curriculum. They must take account of the relative merits of the influences and demands placed upon them by the social contexts of their schools and assess, on a professional basis, how these fit into a wider curriculum context. The tensions they must face in making such assessments may provide a focus for the curriculum. Tensions may be apparent in the demands and influences of groups such as pupils, parents, governors, LEAs and national government, for example. Resolution of the dilemmas created by teachers' accountability to all of these parties on an equal basis is no easy task. According to Elliot:

> In an ideal situation one might argue that a school is accountable to all those groups and agencies who have either a legal or moral right to know about and influence its work. But within any given political context the answers are not so simple.
>
> (Elliot 1979: 10)

One solution to the problem for teachers is to attempt to understand, in more depth, the nature of their work in relation to issues of pedagogy. It is to this body of work that I now turn.

What is the curriculum?

To begin to understand the primary national curriculum in England and Wales, one has first to consider the nature of 'curriculum'. Lofthouse *et al.* (1994) suggest that the study of curriculum can be approached from the perspective of a distinction between 'liberal' (academic) and 'illiberal' (vocational) studies. They argue that curriculum theory is first descriptive (concerned with what goes on) and, secondly, prescriptive (concerned with values and priorities).

In their analysis, consideration is given to the relationship between planned and received curriculum, and issues of race, class and gender. Developing a curriculum that attempts to cater for the diverse needs of pupils involves more than 'technical' activities (as Glenn DeVoogd explores in Chapter 8), as, for example, teachers must also deal with moral, philosophical, sociological and psychological considerations as crucial elements of the overall curriculum in relation to children's learning. Deciding upon an 'appropriate' curriculum by this definition involves consideration of:

- the nature of knowledge;
- the relative value of knowledge;
- the relevance of knowledge.

46

Deciding what should be included or excluded is not easy. Some would argue that in England the task of deciding what the curriculum is, has been answered with the introduction of the national curriculum (Lofthouse *et al.* 1994).

The task for primary school teachers, in this analysis, is to make the appropriate arrangements for successful implementation of the relevant NC. However, an alternative argument can be made for regarding this view of the curriculum as an abdication of teachers' and schools' responsibilities. If a version of a curriculum is accepted unquestioningly, is it possible for teachers to guarantee that the model:

- fits the values of all the teachers required to work with it;
- caters for the needs of the pupils attending the school;
- allows all pupils to have equal access to learning opportunities;
- enables children to experience achievement?

This perspective on the curriculum requires teachers to examine their own values.

Values are considered by King (1983) who talked of the curriculum in terms of the organisation of teaching and learning, and argued about the degree of autonomy at the school level. When teachers make decisions about the curriculum, they must make certain value judgements, for example:

Should we treat children the same or differently? . . .

Do we use psychological testing to gain precision in judging ability? . . .

Are some occupations more important and if so do they require specialist skills? . . .

Does our choice of subject involve social stratification, is it inevitable? . . .

What about meritocracy or equality of opportunity? . . .

Do we need to change from: 'the education your status entitles you to' to 'the status your education entitles you to'? . . .

Does the stratification of children by imputed ability match stratification of educational knowledge? . . .

Does the curriculum you offer, give the more able a wider choice and the less able a narrower choice?

(King 1982: 121–151)

King's considerations, rather than defining a contextually relevant curriculum, raise significant questions about pedagogy. Specifically, questions concerning the nature of children's learning and its relationship to teaching strategies.

Pedagogy: the nature of children's learning and its relationship to teaching

Central to considerations of the curriculum is an understanding of how pupils learn, for example, 'through making his or her own physical and mental connections with the world, through sensory explorations, personal effort . . . social experiences (Moyles 1997: 5). While it must be recognised that psychologists such as Vygotsky, Piaget and Bruner have concerned themselves with understanding the nature of learning to a greater degree than sociologists, some understanding of learning has begun to emerge with a sociological perspective.

Pollard (1990) argues that sociology has traditionally concentrated on how society has created differences in opportunities, particularly across race and gender lines. Learning processes have been a side issue to the major concerns with how different sectors of society are formed, typified, and differentiated. Little consideration was given to the sociological processes that influence the learning of concepts, knowledge and skills. Haste (1987), however, identified three factors which affect learning:

- the intra-individual: one's own understanding of the world from a personal perspective;
- the interpersonal: one's own understanding influenced by interactions with others;
- the socio-historical: one's own understanding influenced by experience of historical and cultural traditions.

Pollard (1990) integrates Haste's analysis into his social-psychological model which permits social issues to be addressed in relation to children's learning. The intra-individual and interpersonal, he maintains, cannot be fully understood without consideration of the socio-historical.

To establish a link betweeen sociology and psychology, Pollard draws on social constructivist analyses of how people make sense of things, and symbolic interactionist sociology which is concerned with the dynamics and constraints of specific contexts. Existing models of learning and related teaching are seen to be inadequate due to the lack of recognition of context in the form of social-cultural situations. Pollard (1990) considers whether teachers can bring about the social conditions of learning whereby 'high risk' and 'high ambiguity' can be coped with successfully to meet the demands of a society that is highly complex and fast changing. A relationship is expressed which advocates an understanding of the 'Individual context and learning: an analytical formula'.

48

Social control in the social situation of the primary school is seen as a product of the relationship between the self and others. It emphasises the need to create an enabling social context which will in turn foster the formation of meaning and a sense of self-identity. Children need to be able to control their social situation in order to learn, in the presence of a 'reflective agent', who, through meaningful and appropriate guidance (teaching) provides a means to extend the cognitive structuring and skill development arising from the child's initial experiences. The teacher as reflective agent is directly related to reflective teaching (Pollard and Tann 1993) which facilitates rather than controls children's learning by setting up collaborative learning tasks where the outcomes for learning may be different depending upon the social interactions of the pupils involved.

For learning to take place, appropriate adult support and instruction has to be related to children's control over their learning. An example of this is seen to be formative methods of assessment. Pollard (1990: 252) puts forward a model of pupil learning and identity (see Figure 3.2)

Adults (teachers) must be encouraged to 'co-operate, to liaise, to negotiate and to think their actions through' (Pollard 1990: 254) in respect of the teaching strategies and associated curriculum employed to bring about learning in the classroom.

Adopting a reflective stance as a teaching strategy could be included as an aspect of effective teaching. In a summary of research related to effective teaching Mortimore (1993) identified factors such as:

- curriculum knowledge;
- pedagogical knowledge;
- presentation skills
- psychological knowledge;
- sociological knowledge;
- an understanding of how learners learn;
- an understanding of how subject knowledge can be transferred;
- organisation skills;
- analytical skills;
- assessment skills;
- management skills;
- evaluative skills.

The 'effective teacher' uses all of these with imagination, creativity and sensitivity. Mortimore's work provides an illustration of how difficult and complex it is to provide a definition of 'good' or 'effective' teaching. Some would argue that it is a fruitless task with additional factors always to be found. Perhaps we should concentrate instead on the manner in which the content of the curriculum will be delivered to pupils: in other words, the teaching style. Flexibility of teaching style involves the use of a variety of

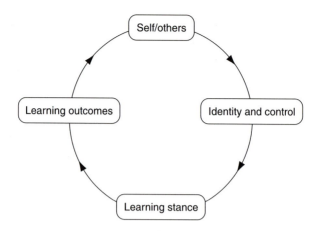

Figure 3.2 A model of learning and identity (Pollard 1990: 252)

teaching approaches to suit a variety of circumstances. Teachers adopting this perspective are required to reflect and adapt their teaching strategies to the socio-cultural background of their pupils. Part of that repertoire clearly includes some understanding of social contextual factors that might impinge upon the curriculum offered, and the teaching style(s) adopted. In line with these arguments, sociologists have avoided attempts to define 'good' or 'effective' teaching. Rather, they have examined and explored the complex and personal nature of teaching thus identifying factors that may not always be replicated. Such factors are outlined in works such as *Creative Teachers* (Woods 1995), *Changing Teacher, Changing Times* (Hargreaves 1994) and *Teachable Moments* (Woods and Jeffrey 1996).

The evidence reported by these authors concentrates on presenting teaching as it exists rather than prescribing what it should be. The authors also attempt to stress the significance of factors such as creativity, individuality and spontaneity in teaching, which they fear may be squeezed out of teaching as a result of tight control of the curriculum.

Even if we recognise that there may be a very good case for a NC, sociologists would, at the very least, urge caution. A national curriculum may provide a basis for achieving continuity, progression and a more coordinated approach to pupil learning, but it may also reduce the scope for teachers to think and act creatively, imaginatively, with sensitivity, with individuality and in relation to circumstances relevant to the social context of the school and pupils in question.

Woods and Jeffrey (1996) address this point by arguing that the imposition of the national curriculum in England and Wales has resulted in teachers negotiating a path between these poles that is an acceptance of control with little or no creativity, or a high degree of freedom and scope for creativity. They contend that teachers still have a degree of autonomy which involves deciding when, where and how creativity will feature in their repertoire of teaching strategies. Significantly, Woods and Jeffrey reject psychologically based concepts of creativity, exploring creativity from a self-actualisation perspective that considers teaching as an art.

> Artistic teaching takes risks and potentially breaks rules. It can 'question the boundaries of our existence' . . . . Exploration involves freedom to try out new ways, new activities, different solutions, some of which will inevitably fail. It is important that education provides the opportunity and disposition to play, and to take it to the limit, for 'to be able to play with ideas is to feel free to throw them into new combinations, to experiment, and even 'to fail'.
>
> (Woods and Jeffrey 1996: 5)

Hargreaves (1994) and Woods and Jeffrey (1996) explore aspects of teaching that are essential to a curriculum which is responsive, contextually relevant and involves a degree of flexibility to allow teachers to adapt the curriculum to fast-changing circumstances. Hargreaves (1988: 216) has argued that 'teachers, like other people, are not just bundles of skill, competence and technique; they are creators of meaning, interpreters of the world and all it asks of them'.

A sociological perspective of pedagogy in relation to a contextually relevant curriculum would allow children to exercise a degree of control over their own learning. The circumstances more likely to bring about this self-control would include teachers exercising individuality, creativity and reflection as crucial components of effective teaching. If, however, teachers themselves are heavily restricted, this may establish a restricted culture which is reflected in the teaching strategies adopted and may, in turn, adversely impact upon pupil learning.

Consideration of the national curriculum in English and Welsh primary schools, and the quality and applicability of it, leads also to an exploration of methods for evaluating the NC.

Evaluating the primary curriculum: the search for quality

In the past decade there has been an increased interest in standards of educational provision. Schools have been required to concentrate on the need to define and monitor the quality of educational provision that they provide. The emerging emphasis and interest in standards has been manifested through the school effectiveness (Mortimore 1993) and school improvement movements (Reynolds 1995).

Research into school effectiveness highlights some interesting indicators for evaluating the quality of the curriculum. Mortimore (1995) identifies characteristics of effective schools which are drawn from empirical research and can be used as indicators of quality in the investigation of a school's effectiveness. A corollary to the school effectiveness research is the school improvement movement which emphasises understanding, meaning based on qualitative data, openness and change. Effectiveness is concerned with *what* schools achieve; improvement is concerned with *how* they can improve their performance. Reynolds (1994) attempts to reconcile effectiveness and improvement by identifying processes in the achievement of quality, rather than focusing on norms and a body of knowledge to be acquired. Effectiveness research is useful and valid in his terms only when it contributes constructively to contextual variables and aids school development. This conception of school improvement asks not only what are the characteristics of the effective school but also how a school can become more effective (Fullan 1992).

Establishing a clear and agreed conception of quality requires an understanding of the differences inherent in the social context of every primary school. Clearly different people will use different criteria, thus reflecting those of the society as a whole. Can there be any one comprehensive, absolute definition of quality? Is this to be measured through performance on national tests? If so, it is important to keep in mind Gipps and Murphy's (1994: 173) observation that 'there is no such thing as a fair test, nor could there be: the situation is far too complex and the notion simplistic'.

If sociologists such as Ball (1994) have argued that context is crucial to understanding matters related to the curriculum and schooling in general, then one is left with the notion that difference is to be accepted not criticised nor necessarily judged in a negative manner. Angus (1993: 342) argues that 'An interactive relationship between schools, culture and society is . . . not considered in school effectiveness.'

A sociological perspective emphasises social context and differences among schools as significant factors in decisions about the quality of the curriculum offered. The many complex factors involved in making judgements of quality, coupled with the differential effects of schools' social contexts make comparison between schools very difficult. Perhaps we should be searching for strategies to improve schools from within rather than search for remedies from outside. Each school has its own specific make-up, history, tradition and culture. Importing apparently successful strategies or systems from other contexts may fail because of institutional and social contexts.

Conclusion

To provide pupils with a contextually relevant curriculum which also meets the needs of society is clearly a difficult task for primary school teachers. There are many factors to be taken into account, both inside and outside the institution. Whether the national curriculum successfully provides a curriculum that is inclusive, contextually relevant and promotes equal opportunities for all pupils is open to question. A sociological perspective provides a critique of the present curricular arrangements in English and Welsh primary schools. Implicitly it also provides some strategies that may lead to a more relevant curriculum in relation to each school's context. However, one cannot claim that the study of sociology will provide easy answers; to adopt a particular perspective mitigates against such an interpretation. What it does do is pose questions and open up lines of enquiry that should be examined when considering the contextual relevance of any form of curriculum.

References

Angus, L. (1993) 'The sociology of school effectiveness'. *The British Journal of Sociology of Education* 14(3), 333–345.

Ashton, P., Kneen, P., Davies, F. and Holley, B. (1975) *The Aims of Primary Education: A Study of Teachers' Opinions* (Schools Council Research Studies). London: Macmillan Education.

Ball, S.J. (1990) *Politics and Policy Making in Education*. London: Routledge.

Ball, S.J. (1994) *Education Reform*. Buckingham: Open University Press.

Burgess, T. (1992) 'Accountability with confidence'. In T. Burgess (ed.) *Accountability in Schools*. Harlow: Longman.

Central Advisory Council for Education (CACE) (1967) *Children and their Primary Schools* (The Plowden Report). London: HMSO.

Elliot, J. (1979) 'Self-accounting schools: are they possible?'. *Educational Analysis* 1(1) 67–71.

Fullan, M. (1991) *The New Meaning of Educational Change*. London: Cassell.

Fullan, M. (1992) *Successful School Improvement*. Buckingham: Open University Press.

Gipps, C. and Murphy, P. (1994) *A Fair Test?* Buckingham: Open University Press.

Halpin, D. (1990) 'The sociology of education and the national curriculum [1]. *British Journal of Sociology of Education* 11(1), 21–35.

Hargreaves, A. (1988) 'Teaching quality: a sociological analysis'. *The Journal of Curriculum Studies* 20(3), 211–231.

Hargreaves, A. (1994) *Changing Teachers, Changing Times*. London: Cassell.

Hargreaves, A. and Hopkins, D. (1992) 'School effectiveness, school improvement and development planning. In M. Preedy (ed.) *Managing the Effective School*. London: Paul Chapman Publishing.

Haste, H. (1987) 'Growing into rules'. In J. Bruner and H. Haste (eds) *Making Sense*. London: Methuen.

King, R. (1983) *The Sociology of School Organisation*. London: Methuen.

Lawton, D. (1996) *Beyond the National Curriculum*. London: Hodder & Stoughton.

Lofthouse, M., Bush, T., Coleman, M., O'Neill, J., West-Burnham, J. and Glover, D. (1994) *Managing the Curriculum*. Harlow: Longman.

Mortimore, P. (1993) 'School effectiveness and the management of effective teaching and learning'. *School Effectiveness and School Improvement* 4(4), 290–310.

Mortimore, P. (1995) *Effective Schools: Current Impact and Future Potential*. London: Institute of Education.

Moyles, J. (1997)'The child as active learner and meaning seeker. In R. Merry and N. Kitson (eds) *Teaching as a Learning Relationship*. London: Routledge.

Pollard, A. (1990) 'Towards a sociology of learning in primary schools'. *British Journal of Sociology of Education*. 11(3), 241–256.

Pollard, A. and Tann, S. (1993) *Reflective Teaching in the Primary School* (2nd edn). London: Cassell.

Reynolds, D. (1994) 'School effectiveness and quality in education'. In P. Ribbens and E. Burridge *Improving Education*. London: Cassell.

Reynolds, D. (1995) 'Some very peculiar practices'. *Times Educational Supplement*, 16 June, p. 19.

Webb, R. and Vulliamy, G. (1996) *Roles and Responsibilities in the Primary School*. Buckingham: Open University Press.

Whitty, G. (1985) *Sociology and School Knowledge*. London: Methuen.

Whitty, G. (1989) 'The new right and the national curriculum: state control or market forces?'. In M. Flude and M. Hammer *The Education Reform Act 1988. Its Origins and Implications*. London: Falmer Press.

Woods, P. (1995) *Creative Teachers in Primary Schools*. Buckingham: Open University Press.

Woods, P. and Jeffrey, B. (1996) *Teachable Moments*. Buckingham: Open University Press.

4

CHANGING PRIMARY/ ELEMENTARY SCHOOL CURRICULA

An analysis of the English experience 1862–2012

Colin Richards

Introduction

Benavot *et al.* (1991) argue persuasively that elementary/primary curricula the world over share a major characteristic – an emphasis on reading, writing and number. Even within those emphasised features there are many differences from country to country, in terms of the way the features are interpreted, their relationship with other curricular components, the way they are taught and learnt, the way they are assessed, and so on. Within any one country there are also differences *over time* in relation to their interpretation, teaching, learning and assessment. When other features of national curricula are considered, the differences between countries become even more marked.

This chapter explores some of the more significant curricular differences within one national 'system' – England – over a period of about 150 years. Its focus is on the 'official' curriculum promulgated by central government and, to a lesser extent, on its implementation in practice. The analysis is conducted in terms of a number of features:

(a) the nature and extent of legal prescription;
(b) the rationale (if any) offered for the curriculum;
(c) its contents in broad terms;
(d) its assessment;
(e) its monitoring/enforcement;
(f) its susceptibility to change;
(g) the extent of its implementation in practice.

Based primarily on the nature of the legal prescription underpinning the curriculum, four English elementary/primary curricula are distinguished and their main features characterised. The changes over time to the English curriculum detailed here are not to be interpreted as constituting its 'development' or 'evolution' since such a characterisation presupposes an end-point to which the changes contribute or, at the very least, a consistent direction which they embody. As the analysis will reveal, no such end-point or direction is discernible. It is hoped that the analysis will prove useful to readers in analysing the key features of their own elementary/primary curricula and in distinguishing different kinds of curricula developed over time.

A final section discusses possible options for the primary curriculum in England between the present and 2012 – the hundred and fiftieth anniversary of the introduction of the 'payment by results' curriculum, the first attempt to introduce a national curriculum for elementary aged pupils. Such options comprise three different models which may possibly be pertinent to the future of primary curricula in other countries.

The 'payment by results' curriculum 1862–1897

Until 1870 public elementary education in England was provided by voluntary agencies, very largely the churches, with some financial support from central government from 1833 onwards. In 1862 central government took direct control over the curriculum by dividing elementary education into six stages or standards and prescribing a syllabus in reading, writing and arithmetic for each standard. Those three areas, plus plain needlework for girls, were made compulsory for all schools wishing to attract government grant. All such schools had to be connected with some recognised religious denomination or at the very least provide, in addition to secular instruction, 'daily reading of the scriptures'. The government did not prevent schools from offering other subjects but neither did it require them to do so. Infant schools catering for children under 6 years were not subject to central control. In reality the government legally prescribed the totality of the curriculum in most elementary schools except for religious instruction. Its legal basis was a 'Revised Code of Minutes and Regulations of the Committee of the Privy Council on Education' (The Revised Code). This Code was passed by Parliament but did not constitute an Act or part of an Act of Parliament.

No educational rationale was offered for its introduction beyond the stated object 'to promote the education of children belonging to the classes who support themselves by manual labour'. The immediate aim of the Code was to reduce growing government expenditure on public education; in this it was initially successful. It was also introduced to make the content of elementary education more relevant to the needs of contemporary society, rather than simply meeting the needs of the churches. In the view of most educational historians it certainly succeeded in producing an orderly, civil, obedient population with sufficient comprehension to under-stand a command' (Tawney 1924), though whether this was what late Victorian society really needed is more open to question. 'Its further aim was to concentrate the efforts of teachers on the 3Rs (reading, writing and arithmetic) and in this it was partially successful, but only at the cost of forcing entirely mechanical drill methods of teaching on the schools' (Simon 1965: 115).

The initial version of the Code (Appendix A) contained a one-page syllabus setting out the material to be taught in terms of pupils' compe-tencies to be exhibited at an annual examination. No reference was made to the knowledge, understanding or attitudes to be taught to, or developed within, children; pupils were viewed simply as being able (or unable) to demonstrate a limited number of elementary skills devoid of meaning and context. Assessment of competence was assessed annually by the examina-tion of individual pupils by one of Her Majesty's Inspectors; on the result of this examination depended largely the level of grant awarded to the school and the salary paid to the teacher. No other form of assessment was prescribed, though in preparation for the visit of the inspector teachers resorted to rehearsing over and over again the kinds of procedures engaged in by inspectors. The assessment function of the inspectors was combined with a monitoring/enforcement role. Inspectors were able to monitor the effects of the Code on practice in schools through their annual visits; the latter also provided potent means of enforcing compliance given the link between the annual examination of pupils, the grant payable to the school and the salary paid to elementary school teachers from that grant. In Birchenough's (1938: 298) words, as a result of the introduction of the Revised Code, 'six cast-iron annual standards were applied to the whole country. The whole arrangement was ridiculously simple, and educational administration was reduced to a mere question of arithmetic. The school became a money-earning institution, and a place for doling out bits of knowledge'.

Though rigorously enforced the curriculum was susceptible to change. Gradually the overwhelmingly narrow utilitarian emphasis of the original Code was modified. Other subjects were made the basis of government grant so that by the 1880s in addition to the original 'elementary' or 'obligatory' subjects there were 'class' subjects such as history, geography and grammar, 'specific' subjects such as agriculture, chemistry and litera-ture, and everyday science in the form of 'object lessons' for standards I–III. Towards the end of the century yet more subjects attracted grant; these included Latin, mechanics, zoology, chemistry, gardening, singing and recitation.

The Victorians were very interested in educational developments else-where in Europe; inspectors such as Matthew Arnold reported on their visits to countries such as Prussia and France. There was some evidence of foreign influences; provision for handicrafts was informed by Prussian experience; in many schools a Swedish system of physical training was introduced; school excursions popular in Switzerland found their way into English schools. Infant education was particularly influenced by the views of Froebel – initially in independent infant schools but later in maintained schools through the employment of Froebel-trained or Froebel-educated inspectors, teachers and teacher trainers. According to Bramwell (1961) Froebelism also informed developments in the junior standards of some schools – in respect of handiwork, brushwork, nature study and local studies.

There is no doubt that the 'payment by results' curriculum had a marked influence on practice. Its rigid reinforcement through the system of annual examinations of pupils (and indirectly their teachers) ensured compliance with its demands. The system was successful in discouraging initiative and in developing habits of obedience, docility and passivity – in teachers as well as in pupils. In the words of Edmond Holmes (1911: vii, 67–68), himself one of Her Majesty's Inspectors of Schools, 'that deadly system of "payment by results" . . . seems to have been devised for the express purpose of arresting growth and strangling life, and bound us all, myself included, with links of iron, and had many zealous agents, of whom I, alas! was one'. Elsewhere he wrote of the teachers 'who had drilled themselves into passivity and helplessness'. As far as the central government was concerned there was no significant implementation problem.

The codified curriculum (1897–1926)

The withdrawal of the 'payment by results' curriculum in 1897 was soon followed by a wholesale reform of the administration of the English education system involving the establishment of Local Education Authorities. Central government still retained general oversight of the elementary school curriculum – prescribing it in general terms – but decided to leave its more detailed content sufficiently open to enable individual local authorities, schools and teachers to adapt it to local requirements. The legal basis of the curriculum was a series of Elementary Education Codes issued by the Board of Education and mandatory on all elementary schools in receipt of public funds. The 1904 Code reveals the nature and extent of government prescription of curricular content during the first quarter of this century:

> The curriculum, while allowing for local variants, should provide a training in the English language (including speaking, reading, composition, literature); handwriting taught to secure speed as well as legibility; arithmetic including practical measurement; drawing, comprising drawing from objects, memory and brush drawing; the use of ruler and compasses leading to instruction in

handicrafts; observation lessons and nature study, including the teaching of gardening to boys; geography, history, music, hygiene and physical training; for girls cookery, laundry work and housewifery; and moral instruction given both directly and indirectly.

(Quoted in Birchenough 1938)

The curricular discretion accorded schools was circumscribed partly by the background and experience of the teachers steeped in the relative passivity and conservatism of 'payment by results', partly by public opinion and partly by the publication in 1905 of the Board of Education's *Suggestions for the Consideration of Teachers and Others Concerned in the Work of Public Elementary Schools*. This publication was not intended to impose uniformity of practice but, written largely by HM Inspectors, it reflected 'effective' work as they saw it and was influential in shaping opinion, policy and, to a lesser extent, practice. Though indirectly prescriptive of content by providing detailed guidance on the subjects contained in the Code, it did stress the Board's support for teachers to determine their own teaching methods:

The only uniformity of practice that the Board of Education desire to see in the teaching of Public Elementary Schools is that each teacher shall think for himself and work out for himself such methods of teaching as may use his powers to best advantage and be best suited to the particular needs and conditions of the school. Uniformity in details of practice (except in the mere routine of school management) is not desirable even if it were attainable . . . [But] freedom implies a corresponding responsibility in its use.

(Board of Education 1905: 3–4)

For the first and only time in the history of English elementary/primary education central government provided a worked up rationale for the school and its curriculum (the Code's Appendix B) -in terms of strengthening character, developing intelligence and helping children practically as well as intellectually for 'the work of life'. It stressed the importance of skills such as observation, clear reasoning and language 'as an instrument of thought and expression'; the need for knowledge of, for example, history, literature and the 'laws' of nature and health; and the development of attitudes such as 'lively interest', industry, self-control, perseverance and loyalty. Though in large measure rhetorical this rationale did provide elementary schools with broad goals and values towards which to work.

There was one other important, and developing, influence which affected the school curriculum at this period. In 1907 the first steps were taken to permit substantial numbers of pupils from elementary schools to win scholarships to secondary schools at age 11. As a result the junior stage of elementary education, always distinct from the infant stage, became increasingly examination dominated particularly as pupils approached the scholarship examination. In Blyth's (1965: 29) words, 'Instead of the Code the Scholarship now became the tyrant'. The 1904 Code had offered a valuable opportunity for developing more consistent approaches between infant and junior stages but this opportunity was very largely missed.

Apart from the scholarship examination the assessment of pupils' attainments was conducted internally by the schools. Teachers were encouraged to build 'intelligent questioning' into their 'catechetical' teaching to ascertain how far their teaching had been appreciated and understood. Examinations, recommended as largely oral for the younger children, were held twice, three times or four times a year. HM Inspectors continued to visit, not primarily to assess the competencies of individual pupils but more to inspect teaching methods, to provide an external view of pupils' attainments for teachers and to gather information for the Board as to developments within the system. The fear and trepidation their visits used to inspire in the previous era transferred to the Codified Curriculum; inspectors remained powerful *de facto* enforcers of official policy.

There was evidence (Bramwell 1961) of slow but gradual change in curricula and syllabuses. More emphasis was given to oral work in English; practical arithmetic was gradually introduced; history became more widely taught; nature study, accompanied by gardening, developed rapidly; there was a widening in the scope of art, handiwork and physical training; a minority of elementary schools made greater use of activity methods, including drama, with older children.

Blyth (1965: 40) argues that the impact of Dewey's views 'on elementary practice was undeniable. Projects, cooperative activities and the elimination of subject divisions began to figure in the best and most fortunate elementary schools'. Foreign influences remained strongest on the work of infant departments or schools; in addition to Dewey and Froebel, Montessori had a considerable impact on a minority of schools with her emphasis on structured learning, sense training and individualisation. However, at the elementary stage at least there was less official interest in overseas developments – a stance that was to persist for much of the century.

With the removal of a detailed syllabus and the annual examination of pupils by HM Inspectors schools were free to exercise a measure of discretion but in general they did so only gradually and patchily. According to Holmes writing in 1911 the methods and attitudes engendered by 'payment by results' lingered long after its abolition in 1897. The scholarship examination also began to provide a constraining influence on practice. There was some change and development but this was a matter of degree, not any major shift. The 'Three Rs' of reading, writing and arithmetic remained the staple fare; the majority of the timetabled day was devoted to their study and practice; other subjects were regarded as far less important; the utilitarian working-class orientation of elementary schooling persisted. Elementary education remained conservative.

The unregulated curriculum (1926–1988)

1926–1967

In 1926 the existing Elementary Code was replaced by a much more compact code of regulations. The former Code had only prescribed the curriculum in general terms but its successor was even less prescriptive. It simply required that 'The secular instruction in a school must be in accordance with a suitable curriculum and syllabus framed with due regard to the organisation and circumstances of the school or schools concerned' (section 10a). As with earlier codes its issuing was soon followed by a revised version of the *Handbook of Suggestions for the Consideration of Teachers and Others Concerned with the Work of Public Elementary Schools* published in 1927. This stated that

> It is not possible to lay down any rule as to the exact number of the subjects which should be taken in an individual school. The choice, indeed, cannot in practice be absolutely free. It is in part determined by public opinion as expressing the needs of the community in which the scholars live. Every normal child must acquire the power of speaking his own language, of reading and writing it, and also some knowledge of arithmetic and measurement. Similarly, the importance of hygiene and physical training on the one hand and of moral training, formal or informal on the other, is so great that no one would propose their omission from the curriculum of an Elementary School. But in selecting other subjects the decision is not always so easy.
> (Board of Education 1927: 38)

In 1928 the government of the day accepted the main recommendations of the first Hadow Report of 1926 which was largely concerned with 'the education of the adolescent' but which also recommended the establishment of a stage or type of education termed 'primary'. Government policy to establish primary education was not accompanied by a readiness to reconsider the content of the primary curriculum. The vague prescriptions of the 1926 Code remained in place; the successor edition of the 1927 *Handbook of Suggestions* published in 1937 and reprinted in 1942 and 1944 repeated *verbatim* the words above.

It was not until the passing of the 1944 Education Act that primary education was established by statute as a recognised stage in the national system of education. There was, however, no central prescription of the curriculum except for religious instruction which had to be provided in every county and every voluntary school. The curriculum of individual schools was to be left under the control of Local Education Authorities – which in practice meant that each school was free to determine its own curriculum within the constraints of public and professional opinion and of the ever more dominant system of selection for secondary education for pupils aged 11 ('the eleven plus') at the end of the primary stage.

The only rationale offered the new primary stage and its curriculum was an indirect one – through the duty placed on LEAs 'to contribute towards the spiritual, moral, mental and physical development of the community by securing that efficient education throughout those stages (of primary, secondary and further education) shall be available to meet the needs of the population of their area' (Part II.7). What constituted 'spiritual, moral, mental and physical development' was not spelt out in the 1944 Act or in accompanying government publications.

Up to 1944 the curriculum in many infant schools consisted of activities related to reading, writing, arithmetic, dramatic play, scripture, art and craft, music, physical training and large-scale construction. In junior schools or classes catering for 7 to 11-year-olds 'the curriculum, in the narrow sense of the subjects studied remained almost unchanged (from the previous period). It included Scripture, English, arithmetic, history, geography, art, craft, music, nature study and physical training. It was rare, in the period 1898 to 1944, to find a primary school in which any of these subjects was omitted and any other included' (CACE 1967: 190). Between 1944 and 1967, and especially in the 1960s, curriculum development resulted in considerable changes to the content of the curriculum – at least as recommended by advisers appointed by LEAs, by members of curriculum development project teams sponsored by the Schools Council (established in 1964) and by HM Inspectors through their visits to schools and their publications. These changes were epitomised by changes in terminology: mathematics, religious education, science and physical education began to appear in descriptions of the primary curriculum. There were two additions to the curriculum in the period 1944–1967: one an additional subject, the other a 'pseudo-subject'. With the sponsorship of the Nuffield Foundation and the encouragement of central and local authorities a growing number of primary schools introduced the teaching of a modern foreign language – particularly during the 1960s.

The 'pseudo-subject' introduced, particularly for the oldest pupils, was 'intelligence'. With the establishment of secondary education for all in 1944 and the opening up of the grammar schools to many more pupils, there was strong pressure on primary schools to prepare their pupils very thoroughly for the selection examination at age 11. Though its actual contents varied from local authority to local authority, the examination usually involved the use of standardised intelligence tests and tests in English and arithmetic/mathematics. The coaching of older children to take such tests was widespread. The downward backwash of that preparation extended to children aged 7 to 9, or even younger, in some schools. In addition to the selection tests themselves and the practice tests leading up to them, schools used a variety of assessment methods: diagnostic tests, particularly in arithmetic and reading; standardised tests; teacher-devised tests; and end-of-year examinations. In contrast to the period 1862–1897 there was no national system for the assessment of the performance of individual pupils but in an attempt to monitor reading standards over time the Ministry of Education commissioned large-scale surveys of reading attainment using the Watts-Vernon reading test in 1948, 1952, 1956, 1964 and 1970, and the NS6 reading test in 1955, 1960 and 1970. There was no systematic monitoring or enforcement of the curriculum by HM Inspectors either; they continued to visit schools, occasionally conducting full inspections, but their role was largely an advisory one – to the schools themselves, to the Ministry of Education and latterly to the Schools Council.

Post-war thinking, but far less practice, was influenced by progressive ideas associated with a motley collection of theorists from abroad such as Pestalozzi, Froebel, Dewey, Montessori and, latterly, Piaget. Methods involving 'activity and experience', later transformed into 'discovery and experience', were more characteristic of infant rather than junior or primary schools but even they, except in extreme cases, did not prejudice the teaching of reading, writing and number. Simon (1965) points out that in junior schools in the late 1940s activity methods had 'a certain vogue' but their influence in that sector was never marked while the influence of the selection examination loomed large. Apart from the theorists mentioned above there were few direct foreign influences on English primary education during this period; it continued to be rather insular, and insulated from developments in the rest of Europe.

However, for reasons which remain unclear, by the mid-1960s the myth of a primary school 'revolution' along progressive lines had taken hold in the media. This 'myth' proclaimed English primary education to be the 'best in the world' and encouraged, in the late 1960s, a flood of educationalists from abroad, especially the United States, anxious to see 'progressive education' in action. Many were disappointed. The 'progressive' rhetoric was far removed from the prosaic nature of most practice, the author's included! In reality, primary education was only just beginning to emerge from the influence of the elementary school tradition; the curriculum remained dominated by the teaching of reading, writing and mathematics (and for some pupils intelligence), though towards the end of the period moves were afoot to widen and liberalise the content of many of the traditional subjects and to organise at least part of the curriculum around topics or themes which drew on and, at their best, interrelated a number of different subjects.

1967–1988

The year 1967 brought no change to the legal requirements placed on primary schools in respect of the curriculum. They were still required to teach religious instruction (though in practice many did not do so) and they were obliged to provide secular education under the control of the LEA. Since no LEA prescribed the curriculum to be followed in its schools, the latter were free, within the constraints of public and professional opinion, to teach what they thought was most appropriate for their pupils. However, 1967 was important for two reasons: it marked the publication of a major report on primary education (the Plowden Report) written by the government-appointed Central Advisory Council for Education, and it signalled the beginning of a major change in primary education occasioned by the move in an increasing number of LEAs to abolish the selection examination at age 11 and replace selective by comprehensive secondary schools.

Both the ending of selection and the climate of professional opinion created by the Plowden Report 'freed up' the primary curriculum in very many LEAs; 'Towards freedom of the curriculum' was in fact one of the subheadings in the report. Though government-appointed, the Council's observations and recommendations had no legal force but were influential, especially in relation to school and class organisation and, to a lesser extent, in relation to the curriculum. In respect of the latter, the Council stressed that

> children's learning does not fit into subject categories. The younger the children, the more undifferentiated their curriculum will be . . . as children come towards the top of the junior school, and we anticipate they will be there till 12, the conventional subjects become more relevant; some children can then profit from a direct approach to the structure of a subject. Even so, subjects merge and overlap and it is easy for this to happen when one teacher is in charge of the class for most of the time . . . . Yet an expanding curriculum makes great demands on the classteacher . . . . The work of the oldest children could be shared by a few teachers who, between them, can cover the curriculum.
>
> (CACE 1967: 203)

However, when it came to discuss the possible content of the primary curriculum it resorted to a traditional subject framework (albeit with two modifications) comprising: religious education, English, modern languages, history, geography, mathematics, science, art and craft, music, physical education and sex education.

Successive governments in the 1970s and early 1980s did not change the legal basis of the primary curriculum, even though HM Inspectors suggested an alternative formulation in a report *Primary Education in England* (1978) (HMI analysed the content of the curriculum in terms of skills and attitudes; language and literacy; mathematics, science; aesthetic and physical education; social studies). In the 1980s central government attempted to create an explicit consensus on the content and outcomes of both the primary and the secondary curriculum but without resorting to detailed central legal prescription. It attempted to do this by beginning to publish broadly agreed curricular objectives for the components of the school curriculum but in the event only published one agreed statement of policy, i.e. *Science 5–16* (DES 1985: 1), which stipulated that 'Science should have a place in the education of all pupils of compulsory school age, whether or not they are likely to go on to follow a career in science or technology. All pupils should be properly introduced to science in the primary school'. By the end of the period 1967–1988 the only subjects primary schools were legally required to teach were religious education and science!

Throughout the period there was no accepted rationale for primary education except for the brief statement in the 1944 Act referred to previously. The Advisory Council did tentatively attempt a rationale for the primary school and its curriculum – encapsulated in the purple prose of paragraph 505 of its report:

> A school is not merely a teaching shop, it must transmit values and attitudes. It is a community in which children learn to live first and foremost as children and not as future adults. In family life children learn to live with people of all ages. The school sets out deliberately to devise the right environment for children, to allow them to be themselves and to develop in the way and at the pace appropriate to them. It tries to equalise opportunities and to compensate for handicaps. It lays special stress on individual discovery, on first hand experience and on opportunities for creative work. It insists that knowledge does not fall into neatly separate compartments and that work and play are not opposite but complementary. A child brought up in such an atmosphere at all stages of his education has some hope of becoming a balanced and mature adult and of being able to live in, contribute to, and to look critically at the society of which he forms a part. Not all primary schools correspond to this picture, but it does represent a general and quickening trend.
>
> (CACE 1967: para 505)

The Council was mistaken; the trend was neither 'general' nor 'quickening'. Its rationale was not widely accepted.

Though progressivism was embraced by only a minority of schools and even there in such a way as not to endanger the teaching of so-called 'basic skills', the removal of selection at age 11 did leave most schools freer than ever before to determine the content of the curriculum. The evidence of the HMI primary survey (1978) strongly suggests that many schools found it difficult to know how to capitalise on their newfound freedom, especially in the 7 to 11 age range. They continued to teach English, mathematics and physical education but beyond that there was very considerable variation from school to school. It is not too much of an exaggeration to claim that a kind of curriculum lottery operated. Children received a markedly different curriculum depending on the school they attended and even, within schools, the class of which they were members. This *laissez-faire* curriculum produced at its best some outstanding work in specific areas of the curriculum, especially the arts – demonstrating the amazing potential of many primary aged children and the creativity of many of their teachers.

In almost all schools topic or thematic work was adopted as a means of transacting much of the curriculum though most aspects of English and mathematics continued to be taught separately. The content of the curriculum was influenced in some schools as a result of work emanating from national curriculum development projects and, in some cases, local initiatives. Such change tended to be idiosyncratic and localised. More generally the teaching of a modern language disappeared in most LEAs and towards the end of the period craftwork began to be replaced by craft, design and technology. The period was marked by a lack of 'curriculum consistency' (Richards 1982). By the early 1980s there was concern over this issue; central government encouraged local authorities to develop and implement curriculum policies in an attempt to provide a more consistent curriculum in their schools (both primary and secondary) but such policies were inevitably general and were not always complemented by detailed curricular guidance. Where such guidance was provided, it was never considered mandatory on schools to follow it.

For the most part assessment of pupils' progress was also left to individual schools. Testing, both formal and informal, continued but in most cases not on the scale prior to the abolition of selection. Many LEAs instigated their own programmes for monitoring performance, especially in reading, but there was no consistent pattern from LEA to LEA. Central government, in an attempt to monitor standards over time, established an Assessment of Performance Unit. Its original brief was to monitor performance across a wide area of the curriculum using light sampling of pupils nationally; in the event its main foci were, inevitably, mathematics and English, and, less inevitably, science. Its work was timely, innovative and widely respected; it was beginning to produce reasonably conclusive data when it was closed down as a result of the introduction of the national curriculum and its testing regime.

Throughout the period there was no systematic monitoring or enforcement of either local curriculum policies where they existed or national policies for religious education or science. Local authority advisers tended to advise rather than inspect. HM Inspectors continued to visit schools producing one major report (HMI 1978) on the state of English primary education and producing a variety of internal papers, most of which were not published. Inspectors' reports of the inspection of individual schools were published from 1983 but did not influence the developing national debate about the curriculum. In 1985 HMI began publishing a series of papers, *Curriculum Matters*, which were both influential and controversial but only for a short time; they were overtaken by events leading to the establishment of a national curriculum. There were no direct foreign influences on primary education during this period but towards the end of it, in the 1980s, HMI did begin to make visits to examine aspects of other educational systems, initially in the secondary sector but later in the primary stage (HMI 1987, 1989).

Viewed in retrospect the period from 1967 to 1988 was a remarkable one – remarkable for the freedom of discretion legally allowed schools in curricular matters, for the hesitant way that freedom was exercised in many schools, for the superb work of a minority and for the government's timidity and slow progress in tackling what was clearly becoming a *laissez-faire* curriculum. However, throughout one feature remained constant – the teaching of literacy and numeracy, seen as the core of the curriculum and the *raison d'être* of the primary school, as it was of its elementary school predecessor.

The national curriculum: 1988–1995

In 1988 the Education Reform Act established a national curriculum for all state primary and secondary schools. Not since the withdrawal of the Revised Code in 1897 had central government stipulated in detail what should be taught, learned and assessed in schools. It marked a 'sea-change' in government policy and, in many ways, in practice for many primary schools.

The national curriculum, promulgated in 1988 and still mandatory in English primary schools, comprises:

- three core subjects (English, mathematics, science); seven other foundation subjects (technology, history, geography, art, music, physical education and, for secondary schools, a modern foreign language);
- attainment targets – objectives covering the range of knowledge, skills

and understanding which pupils are expected to acquire as they progress through school;

- programmes of study setting out in some detail the essential matters, skills and processes which need to be covered;
- national assessment arrangements related to children's progress, particularly in the core subjects.

It was made clear at the time that 'the foundation subjects are certainly *not* a complete curriculum; they are necessary but not sufficient' (DES 1989: para 3.8).

Initially, the government encouraged the inclusion of cross-curricular issues and themes; the National Curriculum Council, the body set up to advise on, and develop, the national curriculum, produced guidance on health education, environmental education, citizenship, careers education and guidance and education for economic and industrial understanding. Promised guidance on multicultural education never saw the light of day. However, within a few years 'official' support for the curriculum beyond the national curriculum was withdrawn, partly as a result of a concern over the curriculum overload being experienced in very many primary schools but, more significantly, as a result of right-wing pressure to concentrate on the statutory elements and in particular the core subjects.

No developed rationale for the school curriculum as a whole or for primary education was provided by the government. The only semblance of a rationale was given in Section 1 of the Education Reform Act which, in a throw-back to the 1944 Act, entitled every pupil in state schools to a balanced and broadly based curriculum which:

(a) promotes the spiritual, moral, cultural, mental and physical development of pupils at the school and of society; and
(b) prepares such pupils for the opportunities, responsibilities and experiences of adult life.

In contrast to the one-page syllabus provided under the 1862 Revised Code the national curriculum comprised more than a hundred closely written pages (not all of them applicable to the primary phase!) detailing objectives and content to be covered in each subject at each stage. Though closely prescriptive in terms of content the national curriculum did not prescribe teaching texts, the way the curriculum should be organised or the teaching methods to be used. Nevertheless, it was felt to be very constraining by most primary school teachers. Concerns soon surfaced as to the impossibility of covering the required material in the time available and as to the overload placed on generalist primary teachers attempting to teach across the whole curriculum. Such anxieties led to a wide-ranging review within five years of the curriculum's introduction (NCC/SEAC 1993; SCAA 1993a, 1993b).

As with its Victorian predecessor the national curriculum had associated assessment arrangements – intended to serve a variety of purposes: formative, summative, evaluative and informative. Children's performance in relation to attainment targets (objectives) was assessed in two major ways through ongoing day-to-day assessment by teachers and, much more contentiously, by national testing arrangements at ages 7 and 11. In the event the government found it difficult to provide a reliable and valid assessment regime which was manageable by schools. Testing was pared back, assessment arrangements varied year on year and eventually the review referred to in the previous paragraph took place. The introduction of the national curriculum did lead to a considerable increase in the amount of pupil assessment and, in particular, to the development of increased teacher expertise in ongoing assessment, especially with younger primary school pupils. More generally, in line with accountability pressures the volume of testing in primary schools increased, though too often the results of this testing (and of national curriculum assessment more generally) were not used to inform subsequent curriculum planning.

The implementation of the national curriculum was enforced in law through responsibilities placed on headteachers, governing bodies and LEAs. Between 1989 and 1993 progress in its implementation was monitored by HM Inspectors, by LEA advisers/inspectors, by officers of the National Curriculum Council and by a pitifully small number of research teams. From 1994 onwards the inspection of all primary schools over a four-year period by independent inspectors operated under the auspices of the Office for Standards in Education helped to ensure compliance through the publication of inspection reports which commented in some detail on the curriculum followed in specific schools. The evidence of inspection and monitoring confirmed that schools made determined efforts to implement national curriculum requirements; deliberate non-compliance was rare; full compliance with the curriculum proved problematic because of its overload of demands; few schools felt able, or willing, to go beyond legal requirements; the provisions of the Education Reform Act concerned with setting up educational experiments were never used. For the most part primary education remained conservative. The bulk of curriculum time continued to be taken up with the core subjects (though now including science); design technology and information technology gained a precarious foothold; history and geography began to be taught more systematically; art, music and physical education were provided for legally but with reduced time allocations in some schools. Overseas influences were minimal; compliance with the national curriculum was the order of the day.

Conclusion: towards an 'enriched' (or 'impoverished') national curriculum 1995–2012

In 1993 the national curriculum and its assessment arrangements were subject to a wide-ranging review conducted by Sir Ron Dearing (NCC/SEAC 1993, SCAA 1993a, 1993b). As a result of that review the legal basis of the curriculum remained unchanged; its contents remained the same in broad terms and arrangements for its monitoring/enforcement continued as before. But the detailed contents of the mandatory curriculum for 5 to 14-year-olds were significantly pared back, especially outside the core subjects of mathematics, English and science. In addition, the testing regime was cut back – focusing national tests on 'core' aspects of English and mathematics for 7-year-olds and on English, mathematics and science for 11-year-olds. The government claimed that overall it had slimmed down what had to be taught in order to leave schools with an overall margin of roughly 20 per cent of time to use at their own discretion. Schools were, however, given a very clear steer as to how that time was to be used: 'Discretionary time should be used to support work in the basics of literacy, oracy and numeracy, and then to deepen pupils' knowledge in the other national curriculum subjects. Schools should be accountable to their governing bodies to demonstrate that the time released is well used' (SCAA 1993b).

Since the introduction of the revised national curriculum in the autumn of 1995 accountability pressures on primary schools have intensified. The government has introduced performance tables for schools based on the results of national tests at age 11 in English, mathematics and science; the Office for Standards in Education has introduced a revised inspection framework focusing on the core subjects (OFSTED 1995); the Department for Education and Employment has strongly promoted target-setting based largely on measurable performance on national curriculum or standardised tests, again in the same subjects (DfEE 1996); unfavourable comparisons have been drawn between English and overseas primary schools (particularly Germany, Switzerland, Taiwan and Japan) in relation to performance in mathematics and science (Reynolds and Farrell 1996).

The future development of the English primary curriculum over the next decade or so is unclear. It will depend on how schools respond to, first, the increasing accountability demands made on them, particularly in relation to the core subjects; secondly, the extent to which they seize on the 'discretion' accorded them as a result of the Dearing review; and thirdly, the changes resulting from any further government legislation or those resulting from the next national curriculum review scheduled for the year 2000. With no 'official' educational rationale to guide them, English schools have three major alternatives:

1   they may provide a *legal entitlement curriculum*: teaching their pupils the so-called 'basics', the nine subjects of the national curriculum and religious education (locally determined) but making no use of 'discretionary time' to add further elements;

2   they may provide *an enriched legal entitlement curriculum*: giving their pupils their legal entitlement in terms of national curriculum subjects and religious education and teaching the 'basics' but going beyond these to offer in 'discretionary time' new subjects, cross-curricular themes or extension work in existing national curriculum subjects;

3   they may provide a *neo-elementary school curriculum*: devoting more time than ever to the so-called 'basics' and providing only a rudimentary, superficial coverage of other national curriculum subjects and religious education; a curriculum similar in its broad emphases to the codified curriculum of 1897–1926.

The past history of the curriculum, analysed in this chapter, strongly suggests the likely way 'forward'. The English primary curriculum has, in line with elementary/primary curriculum the world over, *always* emphasised the teaching of reading, writing and number; the vast majority of English primary schools have *always* been subservient to outside pressures particularly from central government and from the requirements of selection at age 11; the vast majority of English primary teachers (including the author!) have *always* been hesitant to exercise the freedom or discretion they have been offered. The indications are clear: a small number of schools are likely to embrace, albeit cautiously, an *enriched legal entitlement curriculum*; a substantial number of schools are likely to opt for a *legal entitlement curriculum* but many will choose a *neo-elementary school curriculum*, less out of conviction and more out of restraint.

But with a millennium approaching isn't it time to reconsider the traditional emphases that have characterised the elementary/primary school curriculum in England and the world over? Isn't it time to develop an educational rationale for primary education in the twenty-first century? If it is, then that minority of schools adopting an enriched legal entitlement curriculum could well have a significance out of all proportion to their numbers.

References

Benavot, A., Cha,Y-K., Kames, D., Meyer, J.W. and Wong, S-Y. (1991) 'Knowledge for the masses: world models and national curricula, 1920–1986'. *American Sociological Review* 56.

Bramwell, R. (1961) *Elementary School Work 1900–1925*. Durham: University of Durham Institute of Education.

Birchenough, C. (1938) *History of Elementary Education*. London: University Tutorial Press.

Blyth, W. (1965) *English Primary Education: Volume Two*. London: Routledge & Kegan Paul.

Board of Education (1905) *Suggestions for the Consideration of Teachers and Others Concerned in the Work of Public Elementary Schools*. London: HMSO.

Board of Education (1927) *Handbook of Suggestions for the Consideration of Teachers and Others Concerned in the Work of Public Elementary Schools*. London: HMSO.

Central Advisory Council for Education (CACE) (1967) *Children and their Primary Schools*. (The Plowden Report). London: HMSO.

Department for Education and Employment (DfEE) (1996) *Setting Targets to Raise Standards: A Survey of Good Practice*. London: DfEE.

Department of Education and Science (DES) (1985) *Science 5–16: A Statement of Policy*. London: HMSO.

Department of Education and Science (DES) (1989) *National Curriculum. From Policy to Practice*. London: Department of Education and Science.

Her Majesty's Inspectorate (HMI) (1978) *Primary Education in England: A Survey by HM Inspectors of Schools*. London: HMSO.

Her Majesty's Inspectorate (HMI) (1987) *Aspects of Primary Education in the Netherlands*. London: HMSO.

Her Majesty's Inspectorate (HMI) (1989) *Education in Denmark: Aspects of the Work of the Folkeskole*. London: HMSO.

Holmes, E. (1911) *What Is and What Might Be*. London: Constable.

National Curriculum Council (NCC)/School Examinations and Assessment Council (SEAC) (1993) *The National Curriculum and its Assessment: An Interim Report*. London: NCC/SEAC.

Office for Standards in Education (OFSTED) (1995) *Guidance on the Inspection of Nursery and Primary Schools*. London: HMSO.

Reynolds, D. and Farrell, S. (1996) *Worlds Apart: A Review of International Surveys of Educational Achievement Involving England*. London: HMSO.

Richards, C. (1982) 'Curriculum consistency'. In C. Richards (ed.) *New Directions in Primary Education*. Lewes: Falmer Press.

School Curriculum and Assessment Authority (SCAA) (1993a) *The National Curriculum and its Assessment*. London: SCAA.

School Curriculum and Assessment Authority (SCAA) (1993b) *Dearing: The Final Report*. London: SCAA.

Simon, B. (1965) *Education and the Labour Movement 1870–1920*. London: Lawrence & Wishart.

Tawney, R. (1924) *Education: The Socialist Policy*. London: Independent Labour Party.

5

MAKING A CURRICULUM
Some principles of curriculum building

Maurice Galton

Defining the curriculum

The term 'curriculum' means different things to different people. For administrators, including headteachers, it often refers to the organisation of school subjects and the allocation of times when each subject is taught, as depicted upon the school timetable. For class teachers, the term embraces the content of what should be taught during each of these timetabled periods, that is a scheme of study presented in the form of a syllabus. However, even simple interpretations such as the above beg a number of questions which immediately lead us to expand our definition of the curriculum. Looking at the timetable, for example, we might observe that mathematics is allocated twice the amount of time allocated to geography and nearly four times that given to art or PE. This leads us to ask what rationale governs these decisions. Is mathematics deemed more important or are its concepts more difficult to master and therefore require a greater number of periods on the timetable? When we examine the content of what is taught in each of these subjects, more questions emerge. Why this topic rather than that one? Why do we teach x in a subject before we teach y? Decisions concerning the sequence of topics may in part be a question of logic but in some cases such decisions are influenced also by what we know about principles of learning which suggest that some topics are too difficult for pupils of a certain age or ability.

It was the attempt to address such questions whose answers could provide criteria for the selection of content, the organisation of this content to provide effective teaching and learning experiences and the development of measures to discover whether pupils had successfully mastered the content, which led to the growth of curriculum as a serious area of educational study. Beginning with Ralph Tyler's classic text, *Basic Principles of Curriculum and Instruction,* published in 1949, early curriculum theorists tended to perceive the curriculum as a 'planned and purposeful' activity. One of the first English texts, for example, divided the curriculum process into five phases:

1 the selection of aims, goals and objectives;
2 the selection of learning experiences to help in the attainment of these aims;
3 the selection of content through which certain types of experience may be offered;
4 the organisation and integration of learning experiences and content with respect to the teaching and learning process; and
5 the evaluation of the effectiveness of all aspects of these phases in attaining the goals detailed in phase 1.

Wheeler's (1967: 30) above analysis leads to a concept of curriculum which emphasises deliberate planning for a series of intended educational outcomes. Thus Jack Kerr, first English Professor of Curriculum Studies, defined the curriculum as *'all the learning which is planned and guided by the school, whether it is carried on in groups or individually inside or outside the school'* (Kerr 1968: 16). For Kerr, this definition of the curriculum involved four interrelated components in which, first, curriculum objectives are defined; second, knowledge to be taught is decided; third, learning experiences by which the pupils gained this knowledge are selected; and fourth, these processes are evaluated to determine how far the objectives have been achieved.

This view of curriculum dominated the planning of the large-scale projects of the 1960s and 1970s. In North America, projects such as the Harvard Physics Project (see Rothman *et al.*, 1969) and the CHEM Study (Chemical Education Materials Study 1963) were organised on these principles, while in the UK, the Nuffield Science Projects, in particular, adopted this objectives approach. There were, however, critics such as Lawrence Stenhouse who argued that the very term 'intended learning outcome' was itself problematic because much of what occurred and was learned within schools was unintended, as a result of what came to be known as the 'hidden curriculum'. For this reason, Stenhouse suggested a more open definition of a curriculum as 'an attempt to communicate the essential principles and features of an educational proposal in such a form that it is open to critical scrutiny and capable of effective translation into practice' (Stenhouse 1975: 4).

For Stenhouse the curriculum was like a cookery recipe; 'first conceived as an idea, then experimented upon until a satisfactory product had been made'. The recipe is then offered to the general public and their reactions and experiences become the central feature of an evaluation report on the experiment. For Stenhouse any curriculum has to be grounded in practice since it is above all an attempt to describe the way that it functions in the classroom. Just as a recipe can be varied to suit individual taste, so can a curriculum. In the last resort, therefore, the curriculum exists only in the form that it is communicated to pupils by teachers and others in the school.

Constructing the curriculum

These two views of the curriculum, known now as the 'objectives' versus the 'process model' approach to curriculum building, have led to fundamental differences in the way a curriculum is constructed. Those favouring an objectives approach tend to use what has come to be known as a 'top-down' model of curriculum construction. A team of experts is brought together to define objectives, select content and produce materials in which there are clear implications for the teaching strategies to be used in the delivery of this material. The material is then tried out in a number of selected pilot schools and data, collected throughout these trials, are fed back to the developer in order to improve the final published version. This version is disseminated widely through conferences, training workshops and is then evaluated to see whether what is happening in the classroom meets sufficient of the original criteria to justify the expense of developing the new curriculum in the first place. A recent example of this approach is, of course, the National Curriculum which was introduced into English and Welsh schools during the 1990s (Graham 1993)

The process model tends to favour what is called 'bottom up' approaches to curriculum construction. Just like a recipe, a broad specification for constructing the curriculum is devised and then a number of schools are asked to turn this framework into a reality. Such a framework will cover the areas of content but more importantly the expectations about the nature of teaching and learning required to deliver the curriculum. Thus instead of a set text the content will consist of resources and materials to support the teacher's personal interpretation of a chosen topic or theme. The trial schools are then used as a source of dissemination to other groups. Examples of the bottom-up approaches can be found in some of the curriculum developments within the Scandinavian countries as described in Galton and Blyth (1989). A most notable example is the development of the Dutch national curriculum. There, a group of *mother*-schools were asked to develop a programme. These mother schools were given additional resources with the expectation that the completed programme would eventually be undertaken within an average school budget so that over the trial period the additional funding was gradually scaled down. The programme was then introduced into the schools with the mother schools acting as a focus of help in the innovation (Van den Brink and Van Bruggen 1990).

The most striking feature of these two developments was the time scale with the Dutch bottom-up approach taking much longer. The Dutch national curriculum took nearly twelve years to embed itself satisfactorily into all primary schools, whereas in England only three years covered the implementation phase. However, the price for the shorter time scale in the English case has been that very drastic revisions were required by the end of this period. There is also considerable evidence to suggest that top-down methods of curriculum development often fail to result in the changes in practice which are deemed necessary by the curriculum developers. Sarason (1990) attributes this failure to the fact that timelines are usually unrealistic because policy-makers want immediate results and that structural solutions, such as increasing assessment and testing, are often preferred although these do not get at the underlying problems of classroom teaching and teacher development. Sarason argues also that too often support systems for implementing policy initiatives are either not provided or are inadequate. In the large-scale curriculum reforms of the 1970s, for example, the curriculum development team was disbanded immediately after the materials were completed and before the dissemination stage had commenced.

Sarason, however, goes on to argue that there are weaknesses in the bottom-up approach because often the problems facing schools are themselves very complex and time-consuming and the efforts demanded in the search for a satisfactory solution not only fail to motivate some teachers but alienate others from participating in further reform. More particularly, resistance to change in schools is, according to Sarason, a function of existing power relationships and if these relationships are left unexamined, then 'the existing system will defeat efforts at reform'. It is for such reasons that writers such as Vandenberghe (1988) urge a mixed approach in which those 'above' name the 'themes' of policy and create conditions conducive to the initiatives for those working 'below'. According to Vandenberghe, following Schön (1981) a policy theme should concern the domain in which initiatives are called for but the precise specification by which performance is to be judged should be a matter of wider debate. At the same time those 'below', that is the teachers, must be sensitive to the wider policy needs so that they respond in a thoughtful way which allows them to reflect upon the conditions and content of their own practice (Vandenberghe 1988). This mixed approach is described by Vandenberghe as 'backward mapping' which 'emphasises the importance of including the perspective of local level decision makers in the development of a policy' (Vandenberghe 1988: 152). Key people in this process of backward mapping are, therefore, those in 'middle management' positions such as local authority advisers and school coordinators whose role is to explain and relate policy initiatives to teachers while, at the same time, relaying the concerns of teachers back to policy-makers. The Council of Europe's Project No. 8, *Innovation in Primary Education* (CDCC 1988) contains a number of examples of curriculum development using this backward mapping principle.

Ideology and the curriculum

At the beginning of this chapter it was argued that even decisions concerning the selection of curriculum content involved judgements of what is worthwhile. The fact that more time is devoted to mathematics in the primary curriculum than geography or physical education is a statement about their relative importance. Judgements of this kind may appear to be largely instrumental in that the requirement to read, count and write are basic to most other educational activities and important determinants of future employment. However, even here questions of worth arise in that some kinds of mathematical knowledge are thought of as more important than others. For example, a traditional examination question for 11-year-olds might require children, given the area of a room and the cost of the carpet per square metre, to work out the cost of carpeting the floor. The pupils, however, would not be asked to demonstrate that they could measure the area of the floor. This reveals an emphasis on abstract problem-solving rather than on practical application and in cases where the examination is part of a selection process, one intellectual activity is given higher priority than the other. Writers such as Michael Apple (1979) argue that such decisions are a means whereby the powerful in our society seek to retain their power by restricting access to certain kinds of knowledge and then devising tests of this knowledge as an indicator of success.

Primary education has over the years been in the centre of this ideological debate about the system of ideas, beliefs and values which underpin the construction of the curriculum. At its simplest, this involves what Dearden (1976) terms the distinction between child-centred and traditional approaches. The traditional approach can be associated with a curriculum divided into subject areas, an emphasis on the outcomes of learning, which are mainly restricted to the intellectual sphere, a reliance on a rationalist epistemology and a view that the relative importance of subjects is independent of changing cultural influences.

The child-centred view, which in some ways is equally traditional, endeavours to construct a curriculum around a series of activities largely determined by the child's interests, attitudes and previous experiences. The process of learning *how* to learn is considered more important than the acquisition of information and the sequencing of the curriculum is underpinned by a notion of a child's development not dissimilar to the growth of plants and other natural species. In most countries the development of the elementary school curriculum has been dominated by debates about the relative importance of these two contrasting views although, in each decade, there are different justifications and variations in the way in which the principal components of these two alternative ideologies are applied to curriculum construction. For example, as the term 'culture' ceased to represent *all that was best said or thought in the world* and, instead, came to describe *a way of life*, then the criteria for selecting content required the curriculum developer to identify important elements within a society and the important features of those elements. For this reason, Dennis Lawton (1975) in his book *Class, Culture and the Curriculum* therefore elevated aspects of citizenship and learning about democracy as being of equal importance to the study of music and literature.

However, because most societies are pluralistic and as a result there is more than one value system in operation, it is often difficult to identify the ideological determinants of the curriculum, although some parts of it may be attributed to certain influences. This is because, as Kliebard (1986) argues in his historical study of the making of the American primary curriculum, one system of ideology rarely totally replaces another, except in totalitarian countries. Instead, teachers graft some parts of the new curriculum on to the older parts of the other so that a 'hybrid' form emerges. Thus, for example, despite the influences of progressivism across most Western European countries, the primary curriculum continues to be dominated by the teaching of basic skills in mathematics and in the mother tongue. In most countries this central feature of the early twentieth-century 'elementary' curriculum tends to be taught in the morning rather than in the afternoon period. This reflects the view that children are at their best at the beginning of the school day and indicates the high value placed on these basic skills compared with that given to the arts and humanities within the primary curriculum.

The primary curriculum and the millennium

As the Council of Europe Project No. 8, *Innovation in Primary Education*, noted, a major change confronting primary education results from rapid technological advances bringing about the development of global economic systems. At the same time, the knowledge explosion and the capacity of computers to store this knowledge places less emphasis on memorisation. So-called procedural knowledge now has less to do with *knowing what* and more to do with *knowing how* to access and use information. For example, children carrying out project work in primary school may well use CD-roms and even personal contacts through e-mail to access relevant data. They will also require the skills of being able to download, extract, edit and then transfer this material to a new file for inclusion in their project book. Looking to the longer term, those countries within the Pacific Rim, who were in the first wave of industrial development, are in the process of transferring their manufacturing industries to neighbouring countries where labour is cheaper. They are increasingly appropriating the servicing role that is currently largely the prerogative of the advanced Western countries in Europe and the United States. Currently, for example, the entire ticketing operation of one of the world's biggest airlines is being transferred to India where labour costs are much cheaper. In another development based on the English and French colonial settlements of the last century, the Singapore government is establishing schools for the children of Singaporeans working abroad in countries where new factories have been built so that, on their return home, their children will not be disadvantaged in terms of educational aspirations.

As Berliner and Biddle (1995) argue, these economic changes present great challenges forcing us in the developed world to question the premise that we will only maintain our current economic advantage by increasing the amount of education for all children. Berliner and Biddle suggest that within a global economy there may be greater emphasis among the least able, as recent American employment surveys indicate, on qualities of reliability, perseverance and cooperation. Already within the United States and the United Kingdom there has been a shift in employment patterns so that graduates are now filling occupations which ten years ago would have been filled by school-leavers. Less well-qualified pupils will be driven towards the caring services and retailing as major sources of employment, areas where communication and personal skills rather than intellectual ones are essential requirements.

Faced with these huge changes, curriculum developers have still to solve some of the fundamental problems within the existing schooling system that would make it possible for schools to adapt more quickly to the consequences of globalisation. Among these obstacles to change (referred to by Galton in Kitson and Merry 1997) is the inherent conservatism of teachers and the remarkable stability of existing cultural patterns of schooling, particularly the relationships of teachers with other groups in society such as parents. Coupled with this conservatism, the result of devolved administrative power to schools has been a greater degree of *managerialism*. This has resulted in the demise of the collegiality which was an important characteristic of most primary schools in the past and enabled them to preserve a degree of individuality. It would appear that current attempts to address such developments are over simplistic. Countries which previously adopted top-down approaches are now rapidly decentralising, while those with decentralised systems are seeking to reintroduce centralised bureaucratic structures. In the last decade, the study of curriculum theory has largely been neglected. Given the immense problems facing our civilisation as we approach the millennium, there is now an urgent need to advance the study of both the theory and practice of curriculum development within the context of rapid technological advance.

References

Apple, M. (1979) *Ideology and the Curriculum.* London: Routledge & Kegan Paul.

Berliner, D. and Biddle, B. (1995) *The Manufactured Crisis: Myths, Fraud and the Attack on America's Public Schools.* Wokingham: Addison Wesley.

Chemical Education Materials Study (CHEM) (1963) *Chemistry: An Experimental Science.* San Francisco: W.H. Freeman.

Council for Cultural Cooperation (CDCC) (1988) *Innovation in Primary Education: Final Report* [DECS/EGT 987 23] Project No. 8. Strasbourg: Council of Europe.

Dearden, R. (1976) *Problems in Primary Education.* London: Routledge & Kegan Paul.

Galton, M. and Blyth, A. (1989) (eds) *Handbook of Primary Education in Europe.* London: David Fulton Publishers for the Council of Europe.

Graham, D. (with Tyler, D.) (1993) *A Lesson For Us All: The Making of the National Curriculum.* London: Routledge.

Kerr, J. (ed.) (1968) *Changing the Curriculum.* London: University of London Press.

Kitson, N. and Merry, R. (eds) (1997) *Teaching in the Primary School: A Learning Relationship.* London: Routledge.

Kliebard, H. (1986) *The Struggle for the American Curriculum 1893–1958.* New York: Methuen.

Lawton, D. (1975) *Class, Culture and the Curriculum.* London: Routledge & Kegan Paul.

Rothman, A., Welsh, W. and Walberg, H. (1969) 'Physics teacher characteristics and student learning'. *Journal of Research in Science Teaching,* 6 pp 59–63.

Sarason, S. (1990) *The Predictable Failure of Educational Reform.* San Francisco: Jossey-Bass.

Schön, D. (1971) *Beyond the Stable State.* London: Temple Smith.

Stenhouse, L. (1975) *An Introduction to Curriculum Research and Development.* London: Heinemann.

Tyler, R. (1949) *Basic Principles of Curriculum and Instruction.* Chicago: University of Chicago Press.

Vandenberghe, R. (1988) 'School improvement: a European perspective'. In F. Parkay (ed.) *Improving Schools for the 21st Century: Implications for Research and Development.* Gainsville: University of Florida.

Van den Brink, G. and Van Bruggen, J. (1990) 'Dutch curriculum response in the 1980s'. *The Curriculum Journal* l(3) 275–289.

Wheeler, D. (1967) *Curriculum Process,* London: University of London Press.

Part II

PRIMARY CURRICULA: INTERNATIONAL CONTEXTS AND PERSPECTIVES

INTRODUCTION

Janet Moyles and Linda Hargreaves

Having examined the development of the national curriculum for primary education in England and Wales in Part I and having explored the relationships and tensions in schooling between children's needs and societies' demands, in Part II we outline how others have approached, and are currently operating and debating, similar issues worldwide. As the countries involved – Africa, Japan, the United States of America, Australia, Hong Kong and China – are so culturally, politically and socially diverse (and some so geographically vast), authors have usually focused upon one specific geographical area of that country to apply as the basis for their discussions. Differences in perspectives within and across countries are also acknowledged.

That said, it is equally illuminating to see how many similarities exist particularly between thinking about education and schooling in post-modern societies and the common factors which are determining each country's current approach to the advancement of primary curricula. All those issues raised in Part I surface again in Part II with concepts of childhood, social and political systems all vying for dominance within educational thinking. Nowhere is this more evident than in the discourses on primary education and schooling in South Africa and China.

To enable some general comparisons to be made across countries and systems authors were given an overall framework around which to structure their contributions related to the three strands already identified within the book: those of *childhood*, *curriculum* and *classroom practice*. In addition, authors were asked to contextualise for readers how children's daily lives and their schooling occur in practice in that country through offering scenarios of primary age children in homes and classrooms. A general picture of the structure of society and schooling in each country is given, with statistical information where this is realistic, together with information regarding the ages of children and phases of schooling represented within the 'primary' dimension. Some of these relate particularly to the education of children before formal schooling, labelled generally as 'kindergarten', and usually relating to children in the 0 to 6-year-old age range.

Childhood (family and society)

Writers focus on how childhood is perceived in each country, not only in considering the society's rhetoric but the reality of life for a 'typical' child of primary age. As different societies have very specific ways of socialising children into the culture, these are also included, together with the society's perceptions on the role of the family and gender and equity issues. Parental rights, responsibilities and influences over the education of their children have offered different perspectives on 'consumerism' in various societies.

Curriculum (systems, policies and training issues)

Who determines educational policy and to whom the education system is accountable are just two of the issues raised by authors under this heading. As we saw in Part I, the nature of the curriculum and who has been involved in its determination both have a significant influence on its final manifestation, with industrial and commercial considerations frequently overriding issues of what is developmentally appropriate for children at different ages. This also raises perspectives on what is the purpose of education for primary children, with some countries such as Africa still concerned with basic literacy and numeracy and other countries returning to this as of major concern in technologically advanced societies. Being competitive in world markets has raised the focus of educational evaluation in many developed and developing countries which has meant all levels in the educational hierarchy coming under scrutiny and having to be accountable each to the other. The particular impact on teacher education is a focus in each chapter.

Classroom/school practices and processes

A final, but certainly not insignificant aspect for each author, is how classroom practice is influenced by those who develop the broader policies, from politicians, through district and local authorities, to heads and principals and thence to classroom practitioners. How the curriculum is perceived and implemented by educationalists, and the dilemmas they face, are all raised and discussed. Examples of weekly timetables and curriculum content highlight again the similarities and differences across and between countries, as do pedagogical matters. The impact of curriculum implementation on the school and wider community engenders further issues warranting discussion.

In Chapter 6, Anthony Pell outlines the situation to be found in South Africa, where control and rote learning are still the primary means by which the curriculum is implemented. He examines the life of a rural

African child and the impact of apartheid on education and the primary curriculum in policy and practice. Curriculum change and teacher development are explored from the example of a particular project on science development (Gazankulu) in which Pell was engaged earlier this decade and outlines the implications this has had for primary education generally. As in other chapters, the issue of teachers as 'professionals' or as 'workers/technicians' is raised and what this is likely to mean for the future of teacher education.

The two writers in Chapter 7 offer different but related perspectives on primary curriculum issues in Japan. Hidenori Sugimine takes a historical/political approach to exploring changing concepts and ideologies of home, school and society before and after the Second World War and how this has affected Japanese liberalism and perceptions of academic performance. He points out that the Japanese competitive approach to education has had a profound effect upon policies and practices related to the 'schooled' society and the conflict between traditional and 'progressive' styles of classroom practice including those based in a humanistic perspective. Kazumi Yamamoto, on the other hand, writes about education systems, curriculum and teacher training in Japan, offering a particularly clear outline of curriculum regulations and requirements imposed across kindergarten and elementary schooling. She offers insights into the background to Japan's primary education system at national and local educational administrative levels including the framework of schooling, the curriculum and codes of practice. Kazumi Yamamoto also describes the training and certification of teachers across the 3 to 12-year-old age range.

Glenn DeVoogd, in Chapter 8, gives a wide overview of education in the United States of America, using the state of Texas and its education system as a general example and relating this outwards (on a 'large lens' principle) wherever possible. He discusses the diverse social, cultural and economic forces that push a lively debate from different perspectives concerning a vision for, and the schooling of, kindergarten and elementary age children in the US. He points out the competing impacts of postmodernist practices, with the focus on individuality versus homogeneity of culture and the political agenda based on capitalism and consumerism. Teaching as a profession or technical activity is discussed in some detail as is the use of texts and software in potentially deskilling teachers. Glenn also explores teacher training at inservice and initial level and points out the difficulties for teacher educators of a system which is outcome-based and heavily accountable to state government.

The current situation in the state of New South Wales as representative of some aspects of Australian primary education is outlined in Chapter 9 by Les Regan. He details aspects within the three main headings above, dwelling particularly on the difficulties faced in primary education through budgetary cuts at national and local government level. As in other chapters, this one raises the issues of the purpose of primary education and the links with secondary and tertiary education.

Chapter 10 is a retrospective and prospective discussion by Paul Morris and Ben Adamson on the unique situation existing in Hong Kong as it moves from a British territory to being part of the vast political system of the People's Republic of China. The authors explore the differential status and validity accorded to the curriculum in Hong Kong primary schools and its relationship to the secondary subject-based curriculum. The writers argue that the primary curriculum in Hong Kong, which essentially emerged in the early post-war period, is one which contains those features associated with closed systems, disciplinary modes of conceptualising knowledge and a focus on public knowledge despite government attempts over the last two decades to move to a curriculum displaying opposite features. It is conjectured what will happen under Chinese rule.

Finally, in Chapter 11, Martin Cortazzi outlines some of the features of the primary curriculum particularly in China but also offering reference to Taiwan, Malaysia and the Lebanon. He makes the relationship between these countries and the system in England and critically examines the question of whether it is possible to transfer primary approaches, methods and techniques from one country to another given the vast cultural, social and political situations which prevail.

By retaining similar foci across each chapter, readers will be enabled to make their own comparisons. More importantly, those from different countries, using the English curriculum as a basic example, will be able to reflect upon, analyse and evaluate the current situation in their own country and make more informed decisions and choices regarding curriculum policy and practice particularly at the current time. The thoughts expressed by the Norwegian Ministry of Education as it approaches unparalleled changes in its education system in an attempt to address society's current and future needs, are thought-provoking:

> We are standing at the threshold of a new millennium. There is an explosive demand for technology, knowledge and information. This imposes new challenges, and new demands on society and on each one of us. The most important challenge may become: Will we be able to shape the development of society ourselves or will we allow the development to shape us?
>
> (ODIN 1997)

Reference

ODIN (Ministry of Education, Research and Church Affairs) (1997) *The Compulsory School Reform*. Available on http://odin.dep.no/kuf/publ/GR97/96nr04e.html.

6

PRIMARY EDUCATION FOR THE RURAL BLACK SOUTH AFRICAN CHILD

Anthony Pell

Introduction

During the last decade of South Africa's turbulent history, common remarks often heard from teachers and administrators were 'politics should be kept out of the school' and 'children should not be used to fight political battles'. This belief, which was particularly strong among the white population, would of course be widely supported in Britain, but in the reality of South Africa and Africa generally, the political dimension in even primary education is much too strong to ignore. Elsewhere, Hawes (1979) has referred to the changes that occurred in primary education as the colonial powers left Africa in the 1960s. In the countries of the British Commonwealth, the nature of the curriculum continued to reflect its British origins with opportunities being widened by the new governments to move towards free primary education for all. In Ghana and Tanzania, in particular, the strong socialist political direction of the new nation states reshaped goals for the primary schools, but in other countries where the transition to self-government was less severe, British and American influences through the respective aid agencies were to have a continuing impact.

The stability of all African governments has come under threat in the intervening period to the present. The complete breakdown of order, endemic warfare, autocratic and dictatorial regimes, corrupt governments: all have affected most of the countries in Africa at one time or another. South Africa was uniquely able to resist the forces of change on the continent for some forty years. The cost was great, however: the imposition of a separate development policy of 'apartheid' on the black population by the white Afrikaner government. Eventually, Dr H.F. Verwoerd's grand, socially engineered design was to collapse with South Africa's first multiracial elections in 1994, but today the legacy of apartheid remains in the stunted educational growth of a generation of black Africans, who have the daunting task of responding to the needs of the 'new' country.

In this chapter, rural African primary education is seen as a South African experience. Inevitably, the imposition of the Afrikaner value system on black schooling has such a dominating effect that there is a temptation to believe that Afrikaner apartheid alone is responsible for the impoverished state of African primary education in the country, but once the apartheid factors have been allowed for there is still much remaining in common with the other countries of Africa. The problems caused by large classes, lack of resources, didactic teaching and power-coercive syllabus or curriculum change are pervasive on the continent (Hawes 1979). Levy (1992), however, reports a curriculum development scheme operating in the Northern Transvaal region of South Africa which provides a curriculum building strategy which may be readily transferred to other similar African national contexts.

The remainder of the chapter is structured as follows. The first section will provide a description of the social and domestic environment within which most young black rural African children grow up. In the second section the education system for primary children during the apartheid years is described and discussed. In the next section background information and statistics for pupils, teachers and schools will be presented with an emphasis on the contrast between educational conditions in rural and urban areas, and for black and white sections of society. The fourth section will then examine classroom practice and the nature of teaching and learning. The chapter will end with reference to a particular teacher development project, and the possibilities and potential for change.

Day-to-day life for the young rural African child

The typical rural African pupil will live in a thatched hut in a village settlement of several hundred dwellings (see plates 6.1a, 6.1b, 6.1c).

An increasing number of villages have access to electricity with street-lights on the main pathways between the huts, and an electricity supply in the few homes of brick construction. Roads and paths will be of simple dirt: only the main highways between towns will be of tar. The water supply will be via stand-pipes with perhaps only one tap for each hundred dwellings. During a particularly dry spring and summer, the water supply may be rationed daily or interrupted for months when the daily routine becomes dominated by the search for and collection of water, sometimes from a tap over 10 kilometres away. A further daily necessity is a long trek to collect a supply of fuel, usually wood, for cooking, and heating, where night-time temperatures can be as low as 8 degrees centigrade.

The family will keep goats and chickens, to provide milk and food, and more well-to-do residents might keep cattle in a 'kraal' on the edge of the

Plate 6.1a Village settlement – pupils welcome

Plate 6.1b Village settlement – thatched house

Plate 6.1c Village settlement – the shop

settlement, and any houses belonging to the Tsonga-speaking Shangaan will have neat gardens and hedges with a large vegetable patch to supplement food purchases. Each village has at least one general store, which will receive daily deliveries of bread and newspapers, and will have a telephone link for the village. A few residents might own a car but, for most, transport to the nearest town, 50 kilometres away, will be by a daily bus. There being little local employment, men who do have a job spend most of their time away from the village in distant towns and cities. Women are left at home to raise a family, maintain the house and provide for the family financially often by taking any employment possible. It is common to see gangs of women engaged in construction work on roads, bridges and buildings. Families tend to be very large to provide security in old age and to support others who have no income. The family is 'extended' and a child will have numerous brothers and sisters, aunts and uncles.

A strong Christian ethic runs through family life, which is a reflection of the original missionary schooling background of the society's elders. The settlements will probably have several 'church groups', which meet on Sundays often in the open air. The advent of satellite technology and the microwave link means that television might be available at the 'beer parlour' adjacent to the general store to bring current international news and sport to compete with traditional values. There will be a small health centre or nurse in the settlement, or in the next village 10 kilometres away. Generally, modern medical techniques are respected, but some, including educated professionals, will seek advice and comfort from magicians and witchdoctors. A particularly brutal development in recent years has been the mob pursuit and killing of 'witches' who have given offence, perhaps by 'directing lightning to strike and destroy a family in its hut'.

Within this community the African child will grow up, socialisation and play taking place among peers, animals and the routine of the home. In an environment that is poor in technical resources, there will be some inhibited development of motor skills and coordination between hand and eye, as for instance in the need to press a button, operate a switch or turn a screw. (Yet a few minutes demonstration with a group of preschool children allowed them to master a screw-vice and position an object in three-dimensional space (see plate 6.2), an achievement beyond some mature primary teachers.)

The primary school in the rural African community

It is within the settlement primary school that the child's awareness and perceptions should be structured and meaningfully channelled. Each settlement has at least one primary school, depending upon its size, and a few even have preschools taking pupils from the age of 3 years.

Within the primary school, teachers start to 'lead the child towards adulthood'. They see children as empty vessels to be filled with the culture, beliefs and expectations of their society. There is an understanding that certain areas of human life and aspiration are not open to the black child: for example, a secondary pupil who returned to his village at the end of term with the electronic project he had constructed, only to be greeted with severe criticism for daring to attempt 'white man's work'. In the event, this youngster went on successfully to study electrical engineering at the most prestigious of the country's universities. The family's reaction can be understood, however, since they were much too poor to pay the fees for higher education and so would prefer to deflect the child's ambition into a more mundane, practical direction that would benefit the family financially in the short term rather than penalise it.

Upon entering school, the child is expected to learn, above all, how to conform to the limited, prescribed goals of black schooling: the child is to listen, remember and obey. Corporal punishment is widely used, despite being banned by the authorities after pupil protests in the early 1990s. The order and structure of school life is respected by parents and families whose own home environments are affected by so many problems – water, fuel, sickness, absent men, etc. – that are difficult to solve.

91

Plate 6.2 Preschool pupils learn motor skills

This, in turn, makes the teachers a respected body within the community, although this is not a close partnership because of the mismatch of objectives of the two groups. Teachers would like the pupils to pass the annual tests (in order to move to the next standard) while parents want to see their children become more valuable members of the extended family; and may withdraw the child from school for various periods to help with family chores, such as driving cattle or fetching pensions. The only formal interaction a parent is likely to have with the school is to receive the four-termly reports on the pass/fail tests, and if summoned, to explain a poor attendance record. Although it is a national goal to have all children in the primary schools, in some areas perhaps only 50 per cent will be attending.

For the child, the purpose of primary school is to acquire the skills of reading and writing, and to be able better to follow the instructions of elders, become successful in the community and a credit to the family. Although there are pupils who are inquisitive and want to explore ideas through active learning, they are restrained by the mental straightjacket of low-order, telling-method teaching.

The end of the apartheid years gave renewed hope to all black South Africans. More primary pupils and their families have seen the possibilities of going on to complete secondary schooling so as to enter a much wider, black job market. This means that there is a strong motivational drive in the average child to complete primary schooling as soon as possible, despite large classes and prescriptive lessons.

Apartheid and education

The origins of apartheid lie in the 1930s among Afrikaner intellectuals who perceived conflict in Africa as essentially tribal: to ensure stability for South Africa in the long term, separate development for blacks should be planned (Davenport 1977). A Native Affairs Commission called for education that differentiated sufficiently between blacks and whites to enable the former to undertake the limited tasks in adult life as prescribed by the latter. In particular, it was intended that the language education of the child should be sufficiently oriented towards the vernacular or mother tongue to maintain tribal loyalty and culture at the expense of becoming a competitive participant in the Afrikaans-English-speaking, white-controlled economy.

By 1953, the leading Afrikaner social engineer, Dr H.F. Verwoerd, had introduced the legislation for 'separate development', including separate education in separate black 'homelands'. In planning and economic terms, the establishment of regional governments and services, often in remote 'bush' areas, was a mammoth undertaking. The human cost in the forcible movement of large segments of the black population from their existing homes to designated tribal areas was incalculable. Education was controlled by the Afrikaner Department of Native Affairs. Schools for black children run by missions were taken over; mother tongue instruction imposed throughout the primary school with English and Afrikaans compulsory in the senior primary school. The primary curriculum was then to become almost set in stone and to remain static for twenty years.

From 1971, the new tribal 'homelands' were given a wide range of administrative powers including the responsibility for education, which they could either exercise in full or relinquish the control of curriculum matters to the Afrikaner central government. Where homeland regions, such as Gazankulu and Bophutatswana, took control of the curriculum, all manner of reforms became possible during the 1980s with the central government meeting the financial budget.

The creation of the homeland policy showed the application of the traditional scientific problem-solving method to the solution of the perceived difficulties of operating a multi-racial society did not extend to an awareness of the fallible nature of scientific 'solutions'. The philosopher Karl Popper (Magee 1973) has pointed out that the conclusion of the inductive thinking process is not final but provisional: never can all evidence be assembled to eliminate error in the conclusion. This is such

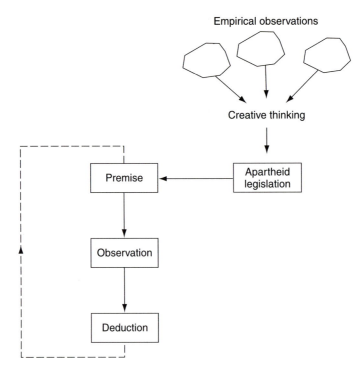

Figure 6.1 A model for a static society driven by deductive logic

an important point in the perception of South African education that change in the post-apartheid society could well flounder if it is ignored. Figure 6.1 shows a model of deductive logic that seemed to support the structures of apartheid in a static society, while Figure 6.2 shows the inductive model of Popper leading to a dynamic, progressive society where outcomes are continually monitored to become the fuel for further action.

For example, according to the deductive thinking model (Figure 6.1) the (mistaken) initial premise that 'the black child is incapable of deep mathematical thought' would lead, after 'observation' of the child's skin colour, to the logical deduction that that child should be sent to an impoverished primary school to learn elementary number work by rote. The 'Popper-type' analytic thinking model (Figure 6.2), however, is cyclical and so provides for a feedback stage after a deduction from the original provisional or temporary premise. Thus, if the black child's capabilities were found subsequently to have been grossly underestimated, this real evidence can become a new provisional premise to be applied in the creative, inductive thinking stage to set up a modified curriculum scheme.

Popper saw no future for authoritarian societies based upon the static model. Yet, for black South Africans in the apartheid years, their daily

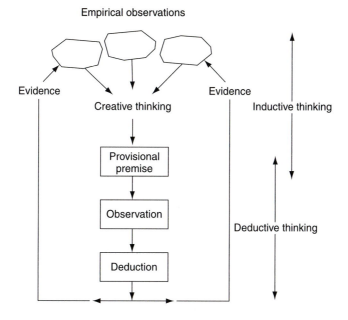

Figure 6.2 A model for a dynamic society driven by 'Popper-type' logic

tasks were prescribed by unyielding, non-negotiable, unjust premises. In addition to limiting the educational opportunities of black children, pre-scribed book-learning by rote, recitation methods ensured that they would develop few thinking skills beyond taking orders. Even in the newly created black universities, book-learning predominated with both the large numbers of BA students, and the few BSc students of engineering acquir-ing degrees by the memorisation of approved texts. The creation of black graduates with poor quality degrees had two planned outcomes: it would establish a black middle class able to manage other black workers, while at the same time minimising any thoughtful, concerted challenge to the apartheid system by black thinkers. In education, the appearance of black graduates with few skills to impart to their pupils, other than those of book learning, mitigated against change and innovation.

Education statistics in South Africa: implications for classroom practice

School population figures

Statistical data in South Africa traditionally have been arranged by racial group. New geographical provincial regions were established in 1994. Consequently, data from a number of education departments have had to

Table 6.1 Pupil enrolment for 1991: all race groups

Region		School type			
		Primary %	Secondary %	Combined %	Total all pupils
	Non-urban	62	19	18	5,789,169
	Urban	55	33	12	4,310,045
Northern Transvaal					
	Non-urban	67	31	2	1,500,542
	Urban	53	42	5	141,875
Gazankulu					
	Non-urban	NA	NA	NA	311,110
	Urban	NA	NA	NA	27,501

Source: EduSource 1994, Table 1.

Note:

   The school year runs from January to December. Statistics for Gazunkulu not available (NA).

be aggregated to provide a basis for planning in each of the new provinces. For the most part, figures for African pupils are given with subdivisions into rural (non-urban) and urban areas. From the information in Table 6.1, pupils from non-urban areas are seen to make up a majority (57.3 per cent) of the school population. In the Northern Transvaal, non-urban or rural pupils constitute 91.4 per cent of the total population. This region is also considered to be the poorest in South Africa, having virtually no industry and an agricultural output heavily dependent upon erratic rainfall.

The system of standards and classes

In Figure 6.3, we can see how black pupils are distributed across class levels within schools from the lowest class, Sub-Standard A (SSA), through to the highest, Standard 10 (ST10). The reasons for the apparent drop-out between the lowest and highest levels will be explained below.

   It is a surprise to many outside Africa to find a vast disparity in the ages of pupils at the various class levels. Figure 6.4, constructed from data for 8,100,000 black pupils at school in 1991 (EduSource 1994), shows the age distributions for the lowest primary class (SSA), the highest primary class (ST5), and for the most senior secondary school class (ST10).

   With 9 per cent of pupils in the highest primary class being aged 17 years or more, and over a thousand being aged more than 21 years, it is clear that African primary teachers have to address issues of maturity quite foreign to their colleagues in Europe.

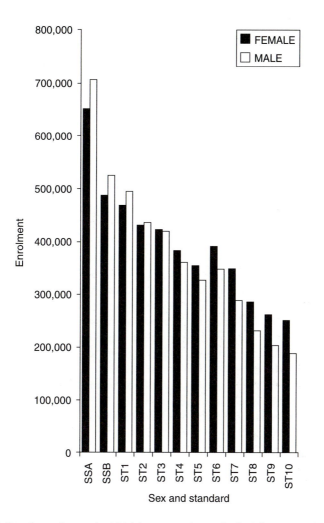

Figure 6.3 Pupil enrolment in 1994 by sex and standard (African pupils) (Strauss *et al.* 1994)

The school assessment system

The wide age distribution can be explained largely by the rigid application of pass/fail throughout the whole school system which is typical of the South African approach to education as a Christian battle between right and wrong: a moral absolutism adopted in the nineteenth century by the Afrikaner to oppose the perceived British 'liberal' approach to education (Davenport 1977; see also Chapter 4).

Table 6.2 illustrates the numbers of 'repeaters' (pupils repeating a year because they did not 'pass' the first (or second) time). Hence, as shown in Figure 6.4 (p. 99), 17–year-olds in the primary school still attempting to work through the maze of Standards. Even the 6-year-olds in SSA can 'fail' at the end of their first year and be held back for another year, or more.

Some of the pupils, however, will have started school late, often to help a lone mother. Others will have left school for short periods, or even full years to satisfy family domestic needs. Many pupils, unable to cope with the system, leave permanently at some point, later to announce that they 'have Standard Three', or more proudly that they 'have reached Standard Seven'.

Schooling *has* to be completed to get a certificate at the conclusion of Standard Ten as an essential prerequisite for job-seeking. With no job there would be no money, and, possibly, the family would go without food. The criteria for pass/fail, however, are often quite arbitrary: so many marks on a rote memory test to get a pass; so many subjects to be passed, and so on. Assessment is exclusively by written tests, pitched at Bloom Levels 1 and 2 (Bloom 1956) in the secondary schools, and simply at Bloom Level 1, the recall of knowledge, assumed to be meaningful, in the primary schools. Teachers who achieve high pass-rates, by drilling the pupils in rote learning, will be marked out for promotion. Inspectors, principals, heads of department and classroom teachers have been known to succumb to the temptation to adjust marks to produce more favourable outcomes to all. When the Gazankulu regional government introduced strict objective examination standards in 1989, appalling levels of achievement were identified which had been concealed by elevating pupils' marks by up to 60 per cent.

Thus, for both the child and the school, there could be a disturbing lack of continuity in education with movement into and out from a system which itself was malfunctioning.

Pupil:classroom ratios and class sizes in rural African schools

Table 6.3 shows the pupil to classroom ratios for the country as a whole, and for African and coloured pupils in the Northern Transvaal, based on the 1991 figures for schools and classrooms (see Appendix) and overall pupil numbers (Table 6.1).

Table 6.4 shows pupil:teacher ratios for black African pupils. (Strauss *et al.* 1994) report that 81 per cent of the school population in 1984 was black African. The pupil:teacher ratio of approximately 37:1 in Table 6.4, is a convenient administrative figure which does not take account of the more important practical pupil:classroom ratio in the Northern Transvaal of about 53:1 averaged across primary and secondary schools. In fact, even this ratio would be extremely conservative. In the Gazankulu region until

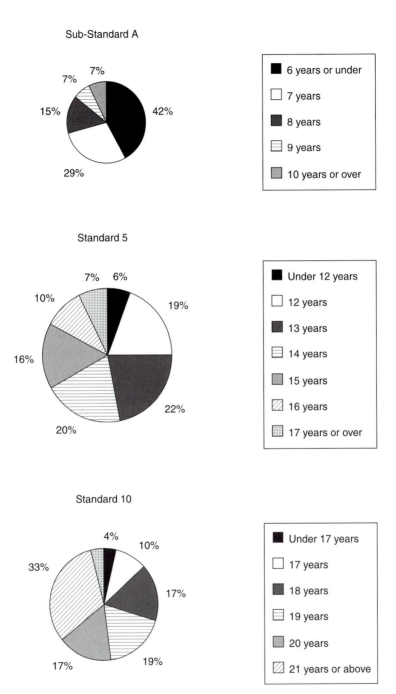

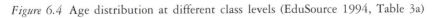

Figure 6.4 Age distribution at different class levels (EduSource 1994, Table 3a)

Table 6.2 Repetition rates for African pupils by Standard (1991)

Region	Percentage of pupils repeating the year											
	SSA	SSB	ST1	ST2	ST3	ST4	ST5	ST6	ST7	ST8	ST9	ST10
Non-urban	17	15	15	12	15	12	12	19	24	23	24	35
Urban	18	16	15	11	15	12	11	23	23	23	24	29
Northern Transvaal												
Non-urban	12	12	16	14	16	13	11	22	26	26	27	44
Urban	13	11	14	12	12	10	8	26	32	28	32	43

Source: EduSource 1994, Tables 4 and 4a.

Note:
EduSource report that these statistics are possibly *underestimates* of the true situation.

Table 6.3 Pupil to classroom ratios, 1991

Region	Number of African and Coloured Pupils	Number of classrooms	Ratio of pupils to classroom
All	8,957,180	203,285	44:1
Northern Transvaal	1,610,692	30,566	53:1

Source: EduSource 1994, various tables.

Note:
 Classroom ratios have always been difficult to isolate and this breakdown is the only one possible from available data.

Table 6.4 Pupil to teacher ratios, non-whites, 1991

Region	Number of pupils	Number of teachers	Ratio of pupil to teacher
All	9,199,985	247,996*	37:1
Northern Transvaal			
Non-urban	1,498,759	40,160	37:1
Urban	112,972	3,150	36:1

Source: EduSource 1994, various tables.

Note:
* Includes 319 unclassified Indian teachers.
 Data for white teachers and schools are not readily comparable but a pupil to teacher ratio of less than 17:1 is estimated for 1991.

late 1994, for example, classes of over 70 were quite common with the pupils sitting three or more to an old-fashioned double desk, or even sitting on the floor. Where there were too few classrooms, the pupils sat on bricks under a tree that shaded them from the hot African sun (Plate 6.3).

Teaching and learning in rural African classrooms

The figures above reveal the daunting obstacles which face rural African teachers when attempting to put into operation a coherent learning scheme for the pupils. For historical reasons, the pupils are to be drilled and tested in classes of fifty or more, where some pupils are twice the age of the others, and the approved teaching method will be that of 'telling' the pupils. Even if the teacher has acquired somehow an expansive view of the learning process, realism must dictate that the teacher remain trapped, with the pupils, in a closed system. It says much for the resilience of the African teacher that schooling continued as it did during the apartheid years, even in areas such as the Gazankulu region, which were relatively untroubled during the 1980s, unlike the more urban areas to the south.

101

Plate 6.3 Outdoor lessons

The teacher training system

By 1987 there were two main routes to qualify as a teacher. A university graduate could follow a one-year postgraduate education course, or a school-leaver with a certain matriculation 'score' in the Standard Ten examination could enter a college of education for a three-year course in educational theory and practical teaching. Table 6.5 shows the qualifications of African primary teachers (see also Tables 6.A3 and 6.A4 in the Appendix to this chapter). The large number of *under-qualified* teachers is due to the preponderance of two-year-trained teachers, many of whom are now taking the 'third-year' course part time to become 'qualified' again. Unqualified, recent Standard Ten matriculants with little teaching experience make a significant contribution to the primary teacher force. They will be given a book and a large class and will use the prescriptive, didactic, 'telling' approach practised by the other 'qualified' teachers and the school principal.

Black colleges of education prepare teachers for the schools along the rigidly prescribed lines originally laid down by what was to become the Department of Education and Training (DET), and which ceased to exist in 1995. Until recent years, educational theory taught to the student

Table 6.5 Qualifications of African primary teachers, 1991

| Region | Teacher classification | | | |
	Unqualified	Underqualified	Qualified	All
All				
Non-urban	17,476	57,343	7,327	82,146
Urban	1,068	29,726	1,802	32,956
Northern Transvaal				
Non-urban	3,646	21,198	504	25,348
Urban	79	1,290	71	1,440

Source: EduSource 1994, Table 8a.

Note:
  'Unqualified' means non-graduates with no professional training;
  'underqualified' means less than the approved length of professional training (one year
  for a graduate: three years for a non-graduate).

teachers was firmly oriented towards the one-dimensional Afrikaner perception of education as a book-revealed truth. Practical teaching emphasised the mechanics of the job: preparing schemes of work, setting tests,
preparing mark schedules and following correct procedures. Academic
studies consisted of working through approved school textbooks to ensure
that the teachers knew what they had to teach the pupils. Primary teachers
were made familiar with all the subjects of the primary curriculum but
specialist courses are offered in preschool education and higher primary
physical science. In its later years, the DET appeared to modiy its curricular schemes for the colleges to bring them more into line with modern
thinking overseas. For instance, activity methods were to be introduced to
allow pupils to learn by direct involvement in their tasks (e.g. practical
science work and investigations). Unfortunately, these new ideas were
introduced to student teachers as more 'book-learning' but on a new topic
for their pass/fail examinations. They then returned to the 'old' approach
upon entering the real world of the classroom.

In conclusion, the young African primary teacher of today faces the task
of inspiring learning in a school system characterised by:

- very large classes;
- classes with a wide age range;
- classes which contain significant numbers of 'repeating' pupils;
- rote learning, drill-lessons;
- pass/fail testing, on a monthly basis;
- 'irregular' mark adjustment in tests,
- minimal resources in a deprived environment.

Yet, despite these difficulties, many primary teachers are making valiant efforts to operate as professionally as possible.

The primary curriculum at work

The Northern Transvaal ceased to exist administratively from 1995, but the only real change so far has been the phasing out of Afrikaans as a compulsory language. Table 6.6 shows the content of the primary school curriculum operating in the Gazankulu homeland region.

All primary school pupils have ten thirty-minute periods per day. This gives a weekly tuition time of twenty-five hours, a figure comparable with those in other African countries at the level of the higher primary school, but excessive for the youngest pupils in the lower schools (Hawes 1979). Like most other countries with British traditions in education, English is the medium of instruction in the higher primary school. Only Tanzania uses the mother tongue, Swahili, throughout the whole primary phase.

The primary school day will be over by 1.00 p. m. Lessons start as early as 7.30 a.m. at the coolest time of the day. Afternoon temperatures commonly reach the mid-thirties and even in winter it can be very hot. Probably because of these climatic conditions, shift systems, where a second group of pupils arrives later in the day for lessons, have never operated in the Northern Transvaal although they were used in the past in areas where temperatures were not so excessive.

In the lower primary school, which extends to Standard Two, teaching will be the responsibility of a general subjects class teacher. Specialist teachers appear in the higher primary classes for general science, mathematics and other subjects according to availability. Whole-class is the only practicable classroom proposition: also the teachers are unfamiliar with alternative methods. Primary classes are always all-ability: there is no setting, no selection and no streaming. Subject material is taught rigidly as laid down in the approved textbooks. Subjects are not integrated, nor is there any discussion as to whether they should be. To a degree, the learning appears superficial to an outside observer: a teacher will assess progress not as the rate at which linked topics are mastered but by the simple 'completion' of chapters, as in 'we have just finished Chapter 3 and will start Chapter 4 next lesson'.

The child's cultural roots are reflected in programmes of study in the home language, Tsonga in this case. In music, agriculture and the craft subjects, the central government would have commissioned a local official to provide appropriate cultural material for the syllabuses and schemes of work. Due to the lack of resources, even the craft subjects can retreat to an exposition of textbook information. Indeed, even at the senior secondary level in 'token' vocational subjects for blacks, only the 'theory' of woodwork, metalwork, butchery need be mastered to achieve certification.

Table 6.6 Primary school curriculum: Northern Transvaal (Gazankulu)

Class level	Curriculum	Number of periods
SSA	Mother tongue language (Tsonga)	30
	Mathematics	10
	Health education	2
	Environmental studies	2
	Art and craft	2
	Music	2
	Physical education	2
SSB	As above with the introduction of 10 periods of English	
ST1	As above, but until 1995 Afrikaans joined the other two languages in an equally shared 30-period allocation	
ST2	As above	
ST3	General science and agriculture replace health education and environmental science	
ST4	As above	
ST5	Tsonga	10
	English	10
	Afrikaans	10
	Mathematics	10
	General science	4
	Art and craft	2
	Agriculture or homecraft	2
	Music	2

One reason why the static curriculum of South African primary schools was able to last so long without the innovative input common in some other African countries (Hawes 1979; Farrant 1980) was the lack of involvement of university education departments at the essential curriculum development stage. The model of the apartheid education strategy (Figure 6.1) has no place for university input into the school curriculum unless it reinforces the philosophy of the prescribed premises of the 'system'. Visits to higher education institutions revealed that education departments were limited to the study and application of education as a distinct discipline without subject context, which was the province of other respective, academic departments. The universities' organisational structure, therefore, inhibited the development of practical curriculum ideas for the schools, although in recent years, some institutions – for example, the University of the Western Cape – have developed intervention and support programmes for local schools while acting as facilitators for curriculum schemes originating elsewhere, such as Britain and the USA (Levy 1992). Indeed, during the apartheid years, this latter route provided a valuable means of access to the black population for overseas aid agencies. Resulting from this link, primary programmes in English, mathematics and science have appeared in some parts of the country.

For example, in the Northern Transvaal (Gazankulu) curriculum scheme, the author observed over a hundred primary science lessons using a purpose-designed observation schedule (Eggleston *et al.* 1975; Pell 1983). To give a flavour of what happened in a typical science classroom, here is a report on a relatively enthusiastic teacher at the start of the Gazankulu project having received only perfunctory inservice training.

A typical primary science lesson

The large class is seated in rows facing the teacher in very cramped conditions. The teacher has a number of items of apparatus on the table at the front of the room, which have been brought from a store cupboard in the staff-room. A teacher-made poster is the only adornment to the bare walls. The pupils have notebooks and possibly some text books, but these will be hidden away under the desks. A chalk board of dubious quality rests against the front wall.

The topic for the day is introduced: the name written on the board. Pupils are asked to identify the items of equipment: names are also displayed on the board.

The equipment needed is arranged by the teacher, helped by one or more pupils in the form, and an 'investigation' takes place with pupil assistance. Low-order factual questioning interspersed with 'telling method' teaching brings about the intended outcome. The pupils are passive observers as the experiment proceeds. The teacher writes conclusions on the board, and possibly draws a detailed diagram.

The teacher summarises what has been seen, and promptly removes with the duster all the valuable information so painstakingly prepared on the blackboard.

Now, for the first time the pupils become active. They are instructed to take out notebooks for a test on what they have 'learned'. After a few minutes of general disturbance as 60 to 70 pupils search for books, pencils, etc., the class then sees five or six Bloom level 1, recall-of-knowledge questions being written on the board.

1   What are the names of the poles of a magnet?
2   Like poles . . . ? Unlike poles . . . ?
3   Magnets attract?
4   Where can you find a magnet in the school office?

The pupils now work in their books and the teacher tries to move around the crowded class marking the answers.

The lesson ends: the specialist teacher gathers up the equipment and leaves. The pupils are left with a notebook containing answers (right or wrong) to invisible questions:

1   North √ and South √
2   repel, √ attract √
3   Five X
4   Telephone √

Later that day, this same notebook will display other 'valuable' lists of learning from maths, Afrikaans and Tsonga lessons. At the end of the month, the pupils will be tested on pass/fail criteria according to the amount of information they have remembered. At the end of the year, if they have not remembered enough they will have to repeat the year and the teachers will be heavily criticised for 'poor results'.

Primary school organisation: teachers as 'workers' or professionals

From the historical and statistical perspectives described earlier, it is clear that the school curriculum is 'teacher-proof' and non-negotiable. Ngobeni (1995), who was a school principal in the Northern Transvaal, has described the work of the class teachers, delivering the contents of the national curriculum, didactically, from the approved texts, to children in a very crowded and passive class. The deputy principal and heads of department (HoD) have purely administrative roles, collecting registers etc. The principal and the senior administrators, as graduates or students of the prized, book-learned BA degree will have qualifications as a 'safe pair of hands' to guide the prescribed curriculum as its makers intended.

Ngobeni (1995) sees class teachers allocated to 'cells' (Figure 6.5), acting independently of each other. Communication takes place on matters of curriculum delivery between the principal and the teachers, but although the teachers will chat informally at breaks and end-of-school, little time will be spent discussing curriculum matters. The only staff development recognised by the system is that of higher level, approved certification, which will enhance promotion prospects. The obvious effect of the cellular organisation is that the isolated teachers withdraw from having any

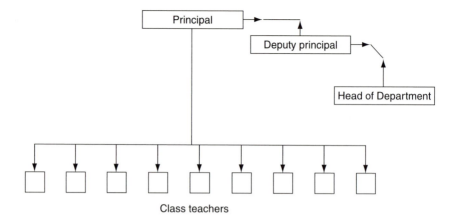

Figure 6.5 Primary teachers in their 'cells' (Ngobeni 1995)

responsibility for the school as a whole, leaving the principal or his deputies to relate and be accountable to the community outside.

Not all rural primary schools receive the same level of funding from the regional government. It has been a festering problem for the duration of the apartheid years, that most primary schools are designated 'community schools' and have to find the first 20 per cent of the cost of any new buildings. At 1994 prices, £10,000 would build a traditional four-class-room block. It is hardly surprising, therefore, to see classes having to sit under trees when a deprived rural community is asked to collect £2,000 before a start on building will be considered.

The new government in South Africa led to the establishment of parent–teacher–pupil associations throughout the country to contribute to the discussion on school organisation. Such democratic input was previously unheard of, although early reports of progress indicate the expected difficulties as the participants accommodate to the new freedoms. There has also been input from area meetings in the Northern Transvaal to discuss publicly the *medium* of instruction, so real change has now begun. It is to be hoped that central government will soon permit regional variations within a broad framework of objectives. Furthermore, the major black teachers' association, the progressive South African Democratic Teachers Union, has called for full teacher participation in curriculum development, so the days of the cellular primary school organisation might well be numbered.

The impact of a teacher-led curriculum programme in South Africa: the Gazankulu Development Project in Science

In Britain, Hoyle (1973) classified teachers into the self-explanatory categories of the 'restricted' and 'extended-professional'. South African primary school teachers might be thought of as a more basic group of 'worker teacher' (Pell 1988), achieving limited external objectives in exchange for remuneration to support their own extended families. Yet among the 'worker teachers', there would be some capable intellects who could act as 'change-agents' in bringing about meaningful curriculum change (Hoyle 1971; Bolam 1975). The attempt to do this was tested practically in the Gazankulu project, an inservice programme set up to improve the quality of learning in secondary and primary science (Levy 1996).

The Gazankulu Development Project in Science 1987–1994

In 1987, the writer was invited by the Chief Minister of Gazankulu to conduct an evaluation of the mathematics and science needs in the homeland of the Shangaan in the Northern Transvaal. The Chief Minister was of the opinion that if black pupils could be shown to be successful in curriculum areas effectively barred to them, a major pillar of the apartheid structure would be destroyed.

Plate 6.4 The science centre at Giyani

109

Plate 6.5 Computer room at Mhala science centre

After an evaluation of the existing situation, a twenty-four-point development plan was approved by the regional government and the writer was asked to implement the proposals. To support the thrust of teacher-led curriculum development, teacher-pupil resource centres for science education and inservice training were built, comprising laboratories, workshops, libraries, tutorial rooms, computer rooms. (Walker, 1994; Plates 6.4 and 6.5). Three mobile units (Plate 6.6) brought resources to bush schools. A secondary science intervention programme was begun to improve the quality of learning which required the designation of eleven schools as 'science high schools' with new, air-conditioned double-laboratories.

The key factor, however, was the introduction of an in-house Science Education Diploma (SED) for the intended change-agents of the primary and secondary schools. By 1994, two-hundred-and-fifty teachers had passed through the part-time SED course, with the re-educated teachers of 1988 re-educating their colleagues.

Plate 6.6 Mobile unit in the 'bush'

A *typical primary science lesson — after the Science Education Diploma*

The science lesson described earlier (pp. 106–7) was performed by a teacher who had attended an in-service content course on primary physics. Later, having spent a year on the SED course, the teacher's grasp of the learning process has advanced significantly, as shown in the observational account below.

> The science teacher arrives in the classroom with equipment in a box, and, taking out a magnet and several rock specimens, immediately starts a question-and-answer session with the class to explore the depth of their knowledge of the magnetism concept.
>
> After several minutes, the teacher writes the topic on the chalkboard together with simple diagrams of what had been seen. The pupils start to copy the information, thus beginning to acquire the ability to record observations for later analysis and problem-solving. The teacher, meanwhile, sets up the equipment without undue pressure.
>
> The teacher claps hands when ready to proceed. The pupils stop writing, knowing that there will be other writing periods later in the lesson. The teacher leads the pupils in an investigation on the magnetic properties of a range of materials. There is only one set of apparatus, it being impracticable to organise any group activity with a class of seventy. The teacher involves as many pupils as

possible in questioning/answering, adopting the procedure of always asking the first question of a girl. Both lower and higher order questions are employed, matched to the pupil who is called upon to respond. Several pupils will be called on to assist in the investigation, and girl 'assistants' are likely to be in the majority because the teacher will have learned that positive discrimination in favour of girls in the science classroom will challenge the common African cultural role of the subservient female.

Key observations in the practical investigation are briefly noted by the teacher on the chalk-board as they occur. This is especially important in what is a hybrid Tsonga-English delivered lesson, in which scientific and technical words without any Tsongan equivalent, are given in English so that the new 'foreign' words and sounds can be seen, heard and related together.

The main investigatory phase takes ten minutes whereupon the pupils return to their notebooks. The majority complete their initial, unfinished task and then join the others who are copying the table of results, sentences in English, which describe what was done, and the conclusion.

The teacher can now circulate to some degree around the closely packed classroom, offering praise, advice, and criticism as appropriate.

With a few minutes remaining, the teacher draws attention to the record of the lesson on the board and summarises what has been observed, interspersing this with questions for pupils to take away for reflection.

Finally, the teacher invites any pupils who wish to repeat the experiments for themselves to return at the end of the school day (1.00 p.m.). By this means, extra 'hands-on' learning is available to self-selected pupils from the class of seventy. This strategy ensures that the class as a whole acquires scientific concepts by concrete observation, while the most motivated pupils have access to the individual or group learning more familiar to European teachers.

In comparing this lesson with the earlier one, it is apparent that the teacher does not cover as much content in the new 'mode', but the quality of learning is much enhanced. There is no attempt to impose 'politically correct', organisational models in the primary African classroom (Farrant 1980) because such models are impracticable in this context. The previous obsession with 'drill and test' has been replaced with 'see-record-think-understand'. However, to be realistic, even with new types of teaching, the testing and accountability dimension remains strong, and is flourishing worldwide, so after a coherent set of lessons on magnetism, the teacher would be able to test the pupils on concept acquisition, knowledge and higher thinking skills during a specific lesson set aside for that purpose. The effectiveness of the methods used by the re-educated teachers was conveyed informally to the neighbouring regions but, unfortunately, efforts of formal expansion were frustrated by the administrative inflexibility of the old Verwoerdian system.

Conclusion

This chapter will conclude with a list of the positive implications of the Gazankulu project for curriculum development not only within South African rural primary education, but also with the potential for application in other rural African countries. The success of the project showed that change was possible even within the then hostile political environment, given a sufficiently strong will among key political figures. It showed:

- a pool of potential change-agents within the primary teaching force, currently hidden by restrictive laws and a flawed higher education selection system;
- the need to reconsider the amount of practically related curriculum theory in inservice courses, if teachers are to become 'extended professionals';
- the potential for an active network of teacher-researchers whose work could be disseminated to teachers' centres in other African countries;
- the need for in-depth content-related courses for teachers at the pre- and initial teacher training stage in technical subjects;
- the vital role of primary principals, actively involved in the change process, as key conduits for change both in schools and in their communities;
- and finally that continuous evaluation should be built into all curriculum projects to enable decisions on the next cycle of development to be made on the basis of all the evidence.

The skills of evaluation are considerable and, while the SED teachers were aware of the dimensions of evaluation, they lacked the experience of the professional evaluator. In the Gazankulu Programme at primary level, success was measured by 'take-up' and end-of-year test results that unsurprisingly were always in favour of the project schools. This is a possible role for NGOs: African governments might appoint contracted evaluators to report on their teacher change-agent projects. By this means the resources of benevolent donors might be put to profitable use while allowing African teachers the national pride of contributing to the lasting, indigenous change in their country's development.

Appendix

Table 6.A1 Numbers of Schools, 1991

Type of school	Number of schools in region			
	All non-urban	All urban	All Northern Transvaal	All regions
Primary	13,605	4,388	2,477	17,993
Secondary	2,218	1,655	962	3,873
Combined	2,398	900	85	3,296
All	18,221	6,943	3,524	25,164

Source: EduSource 1994, Table 5a.

Note:
These statistics apply to schools for *all* race groups.
Strauss *et al.* (1994) report that 82 per cent of all schools in 1994 were to be found in the black sector. In the three years since 1991, there had been a 4 per cent increase in the total number of all schools.

Table 6.A2 Numbers of Classrooms, 1991

Type of school	Number of classrooms in region			
	All non-urban	*All urban*	*All Northern Transvaal*	*All regions*
Primary	75,230	44,859	20,120	120,089
Secondary	22,865	27,081	9,658	49,946
Combined	20,864	1,238	788	33,250
All	118,959	84,326	30,566	203,285

Source: EduSource, 1994 Table 6b.

Note:
These statistics apply to schools for African and Coloured pupils only.

Table 6.A3 Qualifications of all South African teachers, 1994

Teacher classification	Number of teachers	Percentage of teachers
Unqualified	25,410	7.5
Underqualified		
Graduates	2,869	0.9
Non-graduates, no school leaving certificate	24,368	7.2
Non-graduates, less than three years' professional training.	66,692	19.8
Qualified		
Non-graduate, three years' professional training	102,167	30.3
Non-graduate, four years' professional training	31,481	9.3
Graduate, one year's professional training	84,030	24.9

Source: Strauss *et al.* 1994, Figure 10.

Table 6.A4 Number of teachers, 1994

Region	School type			
	Primary	Secondary	Combined	All
Non-white				
Non-urban	84,903	32,398	24,351	141,652
Urban	54,169	37,198	14,628	105,995
Northern Transvaal				
Non-urban	25,349	14,132	679	40,160
Urban	1,462	1,486	202	3,150
Gazankulu	–	–	–	8,453
White	29,834	24,204	–	54,038

Source: EduSource 1994, Table 7a.

Acknowledgements

The author would like to thank the following teachers from the Northern Transvaal for providing valuable background material: M.J. Chauke; Mrs R.H. Chauke; Miss L.P. Kotelo; Miss M.L. Mabunda; N.L. Manganye; S.T. Mbhanyele; P.G. Ngobeni.

References

Bloom, B.S. (ed.) (1956) *Taxonomy of Educational Objectives, Handbook 1, The Cognitive Domain.* London: Longman.
Bolam, R. (1975) 'The management of educational change – towards a conceptual

framework'. In V.P. Houghton, G.A.R. McHugh and C. Morgan (eds) *Management in Education Reader 1: The Management of Organisations and Individuals*. London: Ward-lock Educational/The Open University.

Davenport, T.R.H. (1977) *South Africa: A Modern History*. London: Macmillan.

EduSource (1994) *EduSource Data News*, No. 6, June. Johannesburg: The Education Foundation.

Eggleston, J.F., Galton, M.J. and Jones, M.E. (1975) *A Science Teaching Observation Schedule*. London: Macmillan Education.

Farrant, J.S. (1980) *Principles and Practice of Education*. Harlow: Longman.

Hawes, H. (1979) *Curriculum and Reality in African Primary Schools*. Harlow: Longman.

Hoyle, E. (1971) 'The role of the change agent in educational innovation'. In J. Walton (ed.) *Curriculum Organisation and Design*. London: Ward-Lock Educational.

Hoyle, E. (1973) 'Strategies of curriculum change'. In R. Watkins (ed.) *In-Service Training: Structure and Content*. London: Ward-Lock Educational.

Levy, S. (1992) *Projects Speak for Themselves*. Johannesburg: Sharon Levy.

Magee, B. (1973) *Popper*. London: Fontana/Collins.

Ngobeni, P.G. (1995) 'In-service education for primary schools in South Africa'. Unpublished MA dissertation, University of London Institute of Education.

Pell, A.W. (1983) 'Paths towards success and failure in physics at GCE Advanced level; a longitudinal study of pupils attitudes'. Unpublished PhD thesis, University of Leicester.

Pell, A.W. (1988) 'Science teachers' attitudes: why they matter'. *Spectrum (Pretoria)*. 26(2), 61–64.

Strauss, J.P., Plekker, S.J., Strauss, J.W.W. and van der Linde, H.J. (1994) *Education and Manpower Development*, No. 15. Bloemfontein: University of the Orange Free State.

Walker, A. (1994) 'Centres of hope for a new tomorrow'. *Times Educational Supplement*, 30 December.

7

PRIMARY CURRICULUM
Two perspectives from Japan

Part I Hidenori Sugimine
Part II Kazumi Yamamoto

Introduction – Kazumi Yamamoto

Japan lies off the east coast of the Asiatic continent, with the Japan Sea to the west and the Pacific Ocean to the east. The population of Japan is about 123 million people who occupy a land area of some 378,000 square kilometres, hence an average population density of 332 people per square kilometre (1990 figures). It is often said that Japanese society evolved from an agrarian life-style (as distinct from a hunter-gatherer life-style) in which most people lived relatively close together in the fertile plains between mountains, leading to an emphasis on social conformity.

The first modern education system in Japan was enacted by the government in 1981 and it showed very strong Western influences. Educational and socio-political changes went hand-in-hand, and Japan achieved rapid economic growth.

In the two parts of this chapter, Japanese contributors give their respective views on some aspects of the Japanese primary curriculum. Part I, by Hidenori Sugimine, who is a professor and headteacher of a middle school, outlines the historical, philosophical and political background of education in Japan, with particular reference to primary education. In Part II Kazumi Yamamoto, a professor of early childhood education, deals with curricula, systems of education evaluation and teacher training in Japan.

PART I – HIDENORI SUGIMINE
The background of education in Japan

In 1871 the first Japanese modern public education plan was enacted by the government. The Minister of Education announced this legislation with pride and aimed for the immediate achievement of a modernised Japan where individuals gained success in society. However, there was disagreement between the dominant political parties with one insisting on such important domestic reformation being given time for consideration and the other insisting on promulgating a public education system without delay. However, change was enacted swiftly and thus began the demise of the traditional, male-dominated, feudalistic way of life. Equality, particularly of women, was targeted in the reforms which followed, together with other 'modern' ideas on securing worldly success and social advancement, based mainly in Western ideas.

The Fundamental Code of Education ('Gakusei') represented a victory for the liberal view, but the costs of elementary (primary) education had to be borne by the people and the system quickly proved unworkable. By 1879, the Gakusei was replaced by a new educational ordinance (Meiji Restoration) but the former remains as a great historical document: a statement of liberal views that, despite later attacks and reverses, continued to represent an important standard in Japanese educational thinking.

Confronted, however, with external pressures from Western powers, Japan adopted a unique 'industrialisation strategy' for ensuring independence, security and freedom from poverty. Importing advanced technologies from Western countries, Japan strived rapidly to Westernise, modernise and industrialise. Thus two goals for education – to 'enrich the nation' and to 'strengthen the nation's arms' continued to be emphasised throughout the successive years to the start of the Second World War.

The background to the war period

The basic principles and ideals of the pre-war education system were carried into the 1930s when the proclaimed goal of 'strengthening the nation's arms' gradually gained emphasis. In the same period, the nationalist movements rose in Japanese society. Agrarian reformers, communitarians, imperialists, Asian liberationists, militarists and national socialists all shared common ground in the conception of Japan as a unique nation-state ruled by an Emperor directly descended from divine ancestors in a line 'unbroken for ages eternal' (Ministry of Education 1980) with a distinctive national mission. In 1937, the Ministry of Education issued 'The Principles of National Polity' which stated:

> The Emperors become one in essence with the Imperial Ancestors
> through the religious rites and, responding to the august spirit of
> the Imperial Ancestors, rear their people and cause them to
> prosper . . . the Emperors hand over the august injunction of
> the Imperial Ancestors and thereby make clear the great principle
> of the founding of the nation and the great Way which the people

should follow. Here lies the basic principle of our education . . . united with the religious rites and government.

(Hall 1949: 73)

The result of this thinking was a mistaken war and a miserable defeat. This defeat led to a great change in Japan's social conditions, as well as the people's way of thinking. Concentration was focused upon the goal of 'Enrich the nation and the people'. Subsequent changes brought about a high rate of economic growth in post-war Japan.

The background to post-war educational thinking

With a new Japanese Constitution, the basic legislation governing post-war education was 'the fundamental law of education' which is a statement of general policy and objectives important for the construction of a democratic Japan. It states:

> Having established the Constitution of Japan, we have shown our resolution to contribute to the peace of the world and welfare of humanity by building a democratic and cultural state. The realisation of this ideal shall depend fundamentally on the power of education. We shall esteem individual dignity and endeavour to bring up people who love truth and peace, while education which aims at the creation of culture, general and rich in individuality, shall be spread far and wide.

(Ministry of Education 1947: passim)

Both militarism and nationalism were rejected in the new constitution and education law. This recognition represents a clear discontinuity between pre-war and post-war education.

The post-war reconstruction of Japan was facilitated by the atomic bombs on Hiroshima and Nagasaki. The 1945 atomic bomb did more than physical damage. Half a century later the Japanese still have a clear picture of the bombing and people continue to die from associated illnesses: the bomb is not a thing of the past.

Children and childhood

Prior to the war, Japanese families could be said to be characterised by traditional parental roles and responsibilities with some over-protection of children based on maternalism. During the war, children born in the cities had to move to the country to Buddhist temples or small inns for safety and many children found it hard to adjust to being without their parents. After the war, children returned to the cities only to find their home towns and houses destroyed by air raids. Life was very difficult and many children fell into a frightening state of hunger. Parents and teachers were somewhat bewildered by the new democracy and were so busy trying to rebuild their own lives that family values appeared to decline (Sugimine and Sugimine 1993). Without toys or learning materials children had to amuse themselves with physical games. Boys especially were enthusiastic about the new game of baseball imported from the United States. Defeat in the war also weakened paternalism which had been exemplified, according to some, by the excessively formalistic and trivial control of children by school principals and teachers.

In those circumstances, the daily occupations and ordinary aspects of life were more in need of interpretation than ever before. To study physics, literature, Japanese history and so on were more or less useless from the standpoint of daily life and survival. In fact, it was from this kind of political and social situation that the idea in the US of a 'core curriculum' had been developed in the 1930s. The core curriculum model placed children at the centre of education and this gained overwhelming support from teachers in the post-war democratisation. This reflected methods which had been introduced in Japan after the First World War but which had been abolished in the atmosphere of ultra-nationalism prior to, and during, the Second World War. Individual subjects such as history and geography were integrated into social studies which appeared to have greater relevance to the post-war lives of children and their families.

Whereas children themselves perhaps changed little, the social and economic conditions influencing children's post-war lives changed dramatically. Firstly, the birth-rate went into decline. Despite a baby boom in 1949 (2.7 million) when the family average was 4.32 children, and another in 1973 (2.09 million), the birth-rate fell steadily over the post-war years and by 1993 it stood at 1.19 million, with an average of 1.46 children per family, insufficient to sustain the population. The birth-rate has dropped by a staggering 40 per cent over the last ten years.

Secondly, the instability of family life generally had put many strains and stresses on relationships and children often found themselves in unstable interactions with parents, especially unstable mother–infant interaction. Many families found it difficult to provide children with sufficient opportunity to acquire good discipline, self-restraint or basic routines for everyday life. Parents either over-protected their children or were found lacking in basic care regimes.

Thirdly, in 1953 television was introduced into children's lives. By 1963, the television 'animation boom' had spread all over Japan. This has successively and rapidly grown to include television games, cassette recorders, CD players, personal computers and, now, cellular telephones. The children's worldly experiences have become wider using network communications but it is a world maintained mostly by indirect experience. Children have to learn in an abstract way and have tended, it seems, to lose a basic grasp on reality. Whereas information technology generally is very motivating, it does not provide children with a way of gathering direct information such as through manual play and their opportunities for choice are limited by what is available in the media. It seems there has been a tendency for them to lose their powers of imagination, to contextualise and they have become very functional in their thinking.

Children and schooling

The level of children's education is now considered highly important. Most Japanese people are expected to complete higher education and the name of the alma mater is valued. One could argue that schools have become fact-grinding and knowledge-based institutions even at elementary level. In 1976, 26.6 per cent of primary school children attended after-school classes ('Juku') and by 1993 the figure was 41.7 per cent (Sugimine 1992). Such attendance is felt by parents to offer a better chance of passing examinations for entry into famous high schools by attempting to get ahead of other students – individualism in action. The view appears to be that school studies are not enough for individuals to get better jobs in society or have personal happiness.

There are many confusions about education and schooling which are leading to something of a crisis in Japan. The school is no more a central organisation which has a monopoly over the knowledge explosion, the information society: the lifelong learning society has eroded the position of the school. The stability of knowledge is lost in rapid social changes and we cannot forecast what knowledge will be valuable in the future. The function of the school in forming a national and individual identity in children has become opaque under the changing social structures and the diversification of culture. Schooling has become privatised, industrialised and strongly geared towards competition and entrance examinations. The state system is being dismantled. The value of education to the formation of individuality has become subordinate to the value of examinations and schools are criticised if they do not 'produce' the desired examination outcomes. This has created many conflicting views about the value of education and schooling and the processes of child-oriented learning versus curriculum delivery. Some serious problems in relation to school-refusal by children have been the inevitable consequence.

Education and modern Japanese society

The high rate of economic growth in post-war Japan has created economic mechanisms of mass production, mass distribution and mass consumption through the process of industrialisation and modernisation as well as of scientific and technological development. Values associated with affluence, convenience, peace, welfare, stability and safety have made possible the realisation of the people's long-cherished dreams. Freedom from poverty, the improvement of living standards and level of welfare and education, and longer life expectancy have served, in many ways, to 'enrich the nation and enrich the people'. Adverse factors such as inconvenience, oppression and inequality have either disappeared or have significantly decreased.

The quantitative expansion in the national economy during rapid growth from around 1955 to 1970, paralleled the quantitative expansion and popularisation of further and higher education. Rapid economic growth has, however, raised serious problems in the lives of children. Like other industrialised nations, Japan has suffered a variety of physical and psychological 'pollutions' and more and more people share concerns about the characteristics, limitations and weak points of modern society. These pollutions extend from the breakdown of the ecological systems of nature and of urban environments to the deterioration of the physical and mental health of the people, as well as breakdown in human relations. Specifically, they are manifest in the forms of:

- environmental problems, which are the negative side effects of affluence;
- resources and energy problems;
- decline in people's morale as workers;
- decline in family and community life;
- increase in new types of crime;
- an overflow of vulgar, mass culture.

This deterioration threatens the mental and physical health of Japanese children. They have much less contact with nature, much more mediated experience and there is an unacceptable gap between school and their experiences in daily life. They tend to choose convenience in all things, rather than using their own minds and bodies, and certain human qualities are bound to degenerate, particularly social factors and stress-related conditions. Such qualities as self-reliance, self-restraint, perseverance, a sense of responsibility and solidarity, consideration for others, gratitude, reverence for one's ancestors and older family members, reverence for nature and religion have led to people becoming 'poorer in their hearts' (Sugimine 1996). The decline in the forces supporting social unity has led, for example, to school bullying and other symptoms of 'desolation' in education such as children's suicides and general violence (Sugimine 1996). In turn, these have caused a decline in public confidence in schools and teachers and in the education sector as a whole which is now commanding full attention.

Clearly reforms, or rather 'revisions', are necessary to adapt to the changing circumstances. The basis on which this will be done is outlined by Kazumi Yamamoto in the second part of this chapter.

PART II – KAZUMI YAMAMOTO
Education systems, curriculum and teacher training in Japan

The current situation in Japanese education

In Japan, there have been many changes in education since 1989. The following account describes some of the changes of the last decade and gives details of both nursery and primary education (the latter starting at age 6 in Japan), allowing comparison with systems in the UK and elsewhere. Recent changes in Japan include the following:

- revision of the Courses of Study for Schools (school curriculum), and of the Courses of Study for Kindergarten (Kindergarten Education Guidelines 1989);
- revision of the Care of Children at Day Nursery Syllabus (1990);
- revision of the Evaluation Forms (the Record of Registration and the Record of Child Guidance 1992);
- revision of the Educational Personnel Certification Law (1989);
- revision of the Nursery Nurse Training Curriculum (1991);
- revision of Official Requirements for Establishment of Universities and Colleges (1991).

The basic aim of these and other revisions was to adjust to those changes in society, scientific and technological progress, material affluence, and changes towards an 'information-oriented' society, increasing 'internationalism', diversification of value-systems, smaller numbers of children, increased life expectancy, and changes in family dynamics. It is expected that many of these trends will continue and accelerate. Changes in education are intended to prepare pupils for the society into which they are expected to enter in the future. Although the changes in Japan have been called 'reformation', they are more a cumulative series of slight adjustments, and so the term is 'revision', as distinct from the major changes of 'reformation' in the UK in the 1988 Education Reform Act.

The present system of school education in Japan: background

The modern system of formal education in Japan was inaugurated in 1872, in the fifth year of the Meiji era. Geographically, Japan is a group of islands off the eastern coast of the Asiatic continent, and the people of Japan were strongly influenced by their continental neighbours for many centuries. However, increasing travel and communication since 1867 have introduced Western cultural influences, including influences on education. The basic principles of formal education in Japan are laid down in the Constitution of Japan (1946), the Fundamental Law of Education (1947), and the School Education Law (1947). The Constitution specifies the basic national education policy as follows:

> All people shall have the right to receive an equal education corresponding to their ability, as provided by law. The people shall be obligated to have all boys and girls under their protection receive ordinary education as provided for by law. Such compulsory education shall be free.
>
> (Article 26)

School (education) system

The Fundamental Law of Education, in accordance with the spirit of the Constitution, defines the purpose and rules of education in detail, such as equality of access, nine years of compulsory education and coeducation. More specific provisions relating to the school system, educational administration, financial support, and other matters are specified in various laws and regulations, including the School Education Law. These established a formal 6–3–3–4 system on the principle of equal educational opportunity. The 6–3–3–4 system is as follows (see Figure 7.1):

- six years for primary (elementary) schools ('shogakko');
- three years for lower secondary (middle) schools ('chugaku');
- three years for upper secondary (high) schools ('koko');
- four years for universities ('daigaku').

All children are required, from the age of 6 years, to attend an elementary school, which is intended to give children between the ages of 6 and 12 a general education appropriate to their mental and physical development (School Education Law). A further term of three years in a lower secondary school is also compulsory (to the age of 15), for a total of nine years of compulsory education. In principle, it is necessary to pass an entrance examination to enter a high (upper secondary) school, and further examinations to enter a junior college or university.

Preschool education

Kindergartens ('yochien') accept children aged 3, 4 or 5 years for periods of three, two, or one years respectively, and they are intended to offer non-compulsory preschool education, providing a suitable environment for

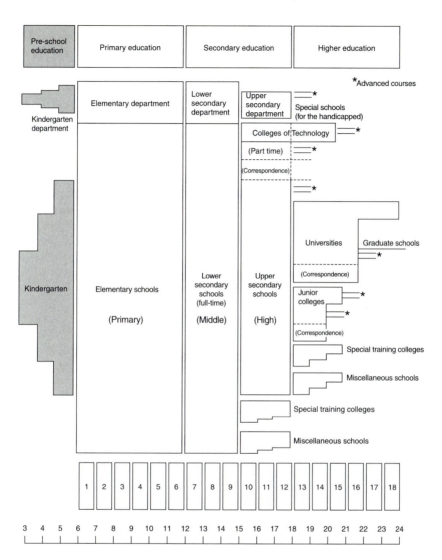

Figure 7.1 Organisation of the present school system in Japan (Ministry of Education 1995)

physical and mental development (School Education Law). The first kindergarten in Japan was founded in 1876, in the ninth year of the Meiji era, thirty-six years after Froebel opened a kindergarten in Germany. The first deputy kindergarten teacher in Japan was a German woman who had studied Froebel's philosophy in Germany. Froebel's 'gifts and the idea of play' were introduced and influenced kindergarten teachers in Japan.

In the 1910s and 1920s, in the Taisho era, a Liberal Education Movement started, and began to introduce ideas of education and psychology from Europe and the United States of America: kindergartens and schools have continued to develop under Western influence.

Day Nurseries are another institution for younger children. These are under the aegis of the Ministry of Health and Welfare, as distinct from the kindergartens supervised by the Ministry of Education ('Monbusho'). The prescribed intention (under the Child Welfare Law) of day nurseries is that children, whose families cannot look after them by reason of work, illness or other cause during the day, may be entrusted by their parents to the day nurseries, which accept children of ages up to and including 5 years. Originally the commonest reason why parents could not care for children was that both parents had to work for economic reasons, but recently an increasing number of mothers have been advancing in society.

In 1963 the Ministry of Education and the Ministry of Health and Welfare specified that the contents of education for children aged 3 to 5 years should be the same throughout the nation.

The primary curriculum

Curriculum standards in schools and kindergarten

In Japan, in respect of elementary and secondary education, in order to maintain a uniform standard of education throughout the country, and to secure substantially the equal opportunity of education which is guaranteed under the Constitution of Japan, the Ministry of Education, Science and Culture set 'Courses of Study' as the national standards of school curricula in compliance with the provisions of laws and regulations. These provide national standards for the objectives and contents of the teaching of each school subject and each school prepares to implement the concrete details of its curricula in accordance with those standards.

The Courses of Study, first prescribed in 1947, were revised in 1951, 1955, 1958, 1968, 1977 and 1989, so these revisions have been repeated at about ten-year intervals since 1958. The revised Courses of Study issued by the Ministry of Education, Science and Culture in 1989 went fully into effect in elementary schools in April 1992, and the Ministry's revised Courses of Study for Kindergarten (Kindergarten Educational Guidelines 1989) which are the national standards for kindergarten curricula, went into full effect in kindergartens in April 1990.

As for the revision of Curriculum Standards, the Ministry sets Courses of Study for schools and for kindergartens on the basis of recommendations from the Curriculum Council, which is composed of teachers, researchers and others with an interest in education.

Under the responsibility of the headteacher, each school organises its own curriculum on the basis of the Courses of Study, taking into consideration the actual conditions of the school and the community it serves, together with the developmental level and characteristics of the pupils. A local board of education will produce 'curriculum guidelines' on the basis of the Courses of Study.

Presently in elementary schools, the three fields of subjects, moral education and special activities are to be covered in the curriculum. Subjects include:

- Japanese language;
- social studies (for Grades 3–6);
- arithmetic;
- science (for Grades 3–6);
- life environmental studies (for Grades 1 and 2);
- music;
- art and handicrafts;
- homemaking (for Grades 5 and 6);
- physical education.

Special activities include classroom activities, student council, club activities, and school events. The basic unit of time is the school 'hour' of forty-five minutes.

In each kindergarten, the curriculum is arranged by the headteacher in accordance with the standards shown in the Courses of Study for Kindergarten, taking into consideration the actual situation of the kindergarten and the community. The current contents of Courses of Study for Kindergarten have been rethought in the 1989 revisions according to various aspects of children's development, to include five areas:

- health;
- human relationships;
- environment;
- language;
- expression.

The minimum period for kindergarten education is thirty-nine weeks a year, at a standard of four classroom hours per day, in consideration of the developmental level of the minds and bodies of this age of children.

Revised curriculum standards in schools

The Courses of Study are revised with the intention of adjusting education to cultivate the qualities anticipated to be required of people coping with the demands of a future society. With a view to cultivating the basis of lifelong learning in consideration of anticipated changes in society and in

127

the consciousness of pupils, and with the basic aim of fostering in the pupils the capability of coping independently with social change, revised Courses of Study were drawn up in line with the following principles recommended by the Curriculum Council:

- to encourage the development of young people with richness of heart/ spiritual welfare and strength of mind;
- to attach more importance to nurturing children's capacity to cope positively with changes in society. Children's willingness to learn independently is also to be stimulated;
- to place more emphasis on the essential knowledge and skills required of every citizen of our nation, and to enhance educational programmes that enable each child to develop his or her individuality fully;
- to put more value on developing in children an attitude of respect for Japanese culture and traditions, as well as an increased understanding of the cultures and histories of other countries.

In accordance with the above four guidelines, the Curriculum Standards in primary (elementary) schools have been revised to improve seven points (Daiichihouki 1989 8–19):

- to improve education for lower school classes;
- to enrich the content of moral education;
- to place more emphasis on the essential knowledge and skills required of every citizen of our nation;
- to improve the contents of education to correspond with changes in society;
- to develop children's individuality fully;
- to improve teaching techniques;
- to introduce a five-day school week.

A brief discussion of the above points now follows.

1 IMPROVEMENT OF EDUCATION FOR THE LOWER SCHOOL CLASSES

Three changes have been made to achieve this:

- the creation of a new subject called 'life environment studies' for Grades 1 and 2.
- improved teaching of the Japanese language.
- the pursuit of a more holistic approach to combining subjects, reducing 'pigeon-holing'

The creation of this first item has attracted particular attention. This new subject includes materials previously taught separately as science and social studies; with the addition of elements designed to encourage self-reliance and self-awareness. Science and social studies were largely taught by the 'transmission' style and it is hoped that the new combination will improve learning through increased experience. Although the Courses of Study have been revised many times, this is the first example of creation or abolition of any subject since 1947. Discussions of the changes took some twenty years and centred particularly on how to adjust the teaching of subjects for lower classes appropriately to the children's stage of development. Previously, primary schools used almost exclusively textbook-centred, desk-based study methods for studies in this field but now the intention is to foster fundamental abilities and attitudes to living and learning through concrete experience and activities by the children themselves in such ways as to encourage self-reliance (Ministry of Education, Science and Culture 1989). Hitherto, typical classes involved pupils sitting at desks to learn from textbooks and listen to teachers, but the life environment studies course leads to learning by experience (for example, by observing, enquiring, making, searching, playing, and self-expression). 'Learning through play' or 'learning by doing' is adopted, and the new learning style involves outdoor experience, learning in the community and classrooms without desks. In kindergarten, texts and desks are rarely used, so the increased practical emphasis in primary schools brings them somewhat more into line with kindergarten experiences.

2 ESSENTIAL KNOWLEDGE AND SKILLS AND CHILDREN'S INDIVIDUALITY

In primary schools, pupils are required to master the essential knowledge and skills of each subject through educational programmes. In England, core and foundation subjects are established in the national curriculum but, in Japan, essential knowledge and basic skills are prescribed for each subject. In the case of Japanese language, the essential knowledge includes sound, pronunciation, letters and grammar, and essential skills include understanding and expression. These standards specify some fundamental contents which all primary school children have to study. They also specify the allotments of time for study, for example the hours for composition. In England, there are four key stages between the ages of 5 and 16, and attainment targets are set for each of those four stages, but in Japan there are objectives for every grade of every subject. Each child's individuality is nurtured in every subject. Though there are many methods of teaching, it is considered most important to suit the teaching to the child.

3 OTHER CHANGES

To cope with the information-oriented society, children must be educated in the uses of computers. In 1994, the proportion of schools with computers available to children was 77.4 per cent of primary schools and 99.4 per cent of junior high schools. At present, schools in Japan operate alternate six-day and five-day weeks, making every second and fourth Saturday a holiday, but this is due to change to a standard five-day week, which will be a novelty in Japan. At the moment, the first and third Saturday of each month are school days, giving children something to do while their parents are not available, as many companies and organisations are still in the process of reducing working hours towards a five-day week, and other playgrounds are scarce.

The main points of revision of curriculum standards for kindergarten

The Course of Study which defines curriculum standards for kindergartens is issued by the Ministry of Education, Science, Sports and Culture. That Course was revised in 1989 to cope with changes in children's social environments among other developments. In order to deepen teachers' understanding of kindergarten education, to ensure educational activities appropriate for infants, it is specified that the basic idea of kindergarten education is to conduct it through environment. To this end, teachers must build a relationship of trust with their pupils and create a good educational environment in cooperation with the pupils. Also, the following three points should be emphasised in kindergarten education:

- that a lifestyle be developed which is suitable for infancy;
- that objectives be achieved in an integrated manner centred on instruction through play;
- that instruction be adjusted to suit the developmental characteristics of individual infants.

The objectives written in the Courses of Study for Kindergarten are:

- to encourage basic habits and attitudes for a healthy, safe and happy life, and to nurture the foundations for a healthy mind and body;
- to encourage love and trust for people, and to cultivate an attitude of independence, cooperation and morality;
- to encourage interest in nature and in society, and to cultivate sensitivity and a capacity to appreciate one's surroundings;
- to encourage interest in language in daily life, to develop pleasant

attitudes in talking and listening to others, and to cultivate a sense of language;
- to encourage broad mindedness and creativity through various experiences.

The Courses of Study for Kindergarten also indicate 'aims' (which are the concretely specified objectives of kindergarten education) and 'contents'. Before the 1989 revision, 'aims' and 'contents' were divided into six areas according to the aspects of child activities which are to be experienced at the infant stage: health, society, nature, language, art and crafts, music and rhythm. Sometimes in kindergarten education, such 'areas' were confused with subjects for elementary school and teacher-centred education was practised. In order to clarify the points of view from which teachers should regard their work in conducting integrated instruction, the aims and contents have been rethought into five areas in the 1989 revision as mentioned above: health, human relationships, environment, language and expression.

The aims describe the feelings, attitudes and desires which are expected to be developed by the time the infants graduate from kindergarten. The contents are the specified material to be taught in order to achieve those aims. The areas interact with each other and should be achieved through children's experiences in kindergarten. The contents should be taught comprehensively through their activities. These revised five 'areas' focus on the figure of the developing infant and are designed to suit various aspects of development which are to be fostered at the infant stage. It is now reconfirmed that children's spontaneous activities and play and work integrated through the entirety of their living are very important in kindergarten education.

Evaluation – a new view to encourage the urge to study

If the performance of an education system may be discussed in terms of input and output, then in Japan, the system works as follows:

1 the input is prescribed in the Courses of Study, which specify the educational contents (that is, the required input by teachers);
2 (a) the output (in terms of learning achievements and development) is assessed according to an established system of evaluation; and
   (b) that assessment is entered in the Record of Guidance. This record of evaluations of children can be used to assess performance and provide feedback to assess performance.

In 1989 a new set of Courses of Study was produced and a new system of evaluation was produced in 1992. Since the 1992 revision, the New

Evaluation Form has been divided into the 'Record of School Registration', which is the school equivalent of the civil registration lists, and the 'Record of Guidance', which is a compilation of evaluations of children's performance like a collation of school reports and notes for guidance, with entries made every year.

The new system of evaluation emphasised three points:

- to be useful, teaching and learning depends on a new view of learning ability;
- to evaluate each child's potential as well as possible;
- to choose the contents of child records carefully and to shorten the period for which the Record of Guidance is to be kept. The period for which the Record of School Registration is to be kept available has remained unchanged at twenty years but since the 1992 revision the period of retention of the Record of Guidance has been shortened to five years.

In the Record of Guidance the entries for each pupil are classified as the:

- record of study for each subject;
- record of special activities;
- record of behaviour;
- articles which may be referred for guidance;
- record of attendance/absence.

The Record of Study for each subject is made up of 'absolute', 'relative' and 'personal' assessments), composed of:

1 viewpoints of subjects', which is assessed by an 'absolute' method, in which there are 'viewpoints' for every year (or grade) of subject, and those 'viewpoints' have four attainment goals (in the national curriculum of England, there are four key stages for students aged from 5 to 16, with targets for each stage, whereas in Japan there are targets for each year or grade of each subject);
2 'assessment/evaluation', which is a relative method (a three-grade system is used in higher school grades, but not in lower grades);
3 the 'teachers' view', by the 'personal' method, in which teachers' personal opinions of individuals' development are recorded.

The new system of evaluation is intended to emphasise the value of the pupils' inherent willingness and talents to study and learn, to think, to do and to exercise a sense of judgement: the revised system is designed to reflect such qualities. To make this assessment, teachers observe children's activities and their practice paper tests. Each school either sends a Grade

Report to parents, based on the Record for Guidance, at the end of every term (three times in each academic year), or arranges meetings between parents and teachers to the same end.

Kindergartens have their own system of Records of Kindergarten Children's Guidance, and this too consists of the Record of Registration and the Record of Guidance. In the latter the 'absolute' assessment system is used (checklists), each achievement being ticked off in the record and notes on the process of guidance are to be written freely. Kindergarten staff keep contact with parents through meetings held every term to improve mutual understanding.

As to the implementation and evaluation of the curriculum, each school designates its own plans for educational guidance and the school's self-evaluation – in terms of the extent to which the school has been accomplishing its targets – is submitted to the Board of Education.

With the new ideas about learning ability, schools across the country are promoting various improvements such as strengthening the guidance for each individual, learning through experience, 'problematising' tasks to promote active involvement, and team-teaching. Considerable attention is also being given to such matters as morality education to help broaden the mind, practical exercises to promote experience of traditional culture, encouraging the scientific mind, pursuing environmental studies, solving problems such as bullying, and the guidance of students.

Numbers of schools and children

Table 7.1 shows the numbers of schools, children and teachers by establishments (national, local public and private).

State schools make up 99.3 per cent of all primary schools and 94.5 per cent of middle schools, so relatively very little compulsory education takes place at private schools. On the other hand, 58.2 per cent of kindergarten schools are private and they are not compulsory. This is a dramatic difference.

The enrolment rate for compulsory schools in Japan has always been nearly 100 per cent. About 94 per cent of all 5-year-olds receive educational care in Japan, with kindergarten enrolment being 63.7 per cent for children aged 4 and 5 years. The enrolment rate for day nurseries is 30.4 per cent for children aged four and five years. Some 56.3 per cent of teachers in primary schools are female, as are 34.6 per cent in middle schools. Most kindergarten teachers and day nursery nurses are female.

Class size and organisation

The national government has set standards for class sizes and organisation. Classes in kindergartens, primary schools and middle schools are, in

Table 7.1 Number of institutions, students and teachers

Type of institution	Number of institutions				Number of students				Number of full-time teachers			
	Total	National	Local public	Private	Total	National	Local public	Private	Total	National	Local public	Private
Day nurseries (aged 0–6)	22,784	0	13,462	9,322	1,763,399	0	990,902	772,497	176,796	0	–	–
Kindergarten (aged 3–6)	14,901	49	6,195	8,657	1,852,183	6,786	370,736	1,474,661	103,014	287	24,918	77,809
Elementary (primary) schools (aged 6–12)	24,635	73	24,390	172	8,582,871	47,248	8,468,014	67,609	434,945	1,782	430,044	3,119
Lower secondary (middle) schools (aged 12–15)	11,289	78	10,568	643	4,681,166	34,575	4,415,185	231,406	273,527	1,682	260,695	11,150

Source: Schools information (May 1994), Ministry of Education, Science, Sports and Culture 1994.
    Day nursery information (October 1989), Moriue 1989.

principle, to be composed of pupils of the same age, except for special cases when students from several grades can join in one class.

The Standards for the Establishment of Kindergartens set the maximum class size at forty children. According to statistics for 1992, kindergarten class size averaged 26.4, with an average of 19.1 children per teacher. For local public primary (elementary) schools the class size limit is set by prefectural boards of education, subject to the upper limit set by law (currently set at forty, since 1980). Most classes have around thirty-one to thirty-five pupils per class (the actual average being 31.1). A six-class school (one class per year) is the most common, the next most common being that with thirteen to eighteen classes (two or three classes per year). The typical class is of the same age group, and teacher-centred, but there has recently been a trend to increasing experimentation in teaching, for example reorganising, reducing the number of children per class, and 'opening up' the classroom. All this has been facilitated by the recent fall in numbers of pupils, making more space available in schools.

School terms and vacation schedules

In Japan, school terms differ from those in Western countries, as the school year starts on 1 April and ends on 31 March the following year, which matches the Japanese financial year. All kindergarten, primary, middle and high schools have three terms per academic year, which are from April to July, from September to December, and from January to March, with vacations between terms. All educational institutions are closed on Sundays, on national holidays and (since 1992) the second and fourth Saturday in each month. All pupils join new schools in April, for which occasion each school has one entrance ceremony per year.

Teacher training and teacher certification

Teachers in kindergartens, primary (elementary) schools and middle (secondary) schools are required to have relevant certificates, which are awarded by prefectural boards of education as provided for by the Educational Personnel Certification Law. Teacher training for regular teacher certificates is provided at universities and other institutions of higher education.

Since the revision of the Educational Personnel Certification Law, there have been three classes of educational certificate: Advanced, First Class and Second Class:

1   teachers holding an Advanced certificate have earned a Master's degree, or its equivalent of 30 credits obtained by a period of study lasting at least one year in an advanced university course;

135

2   those holding a First Class certificate have earned a Bachelor's degree;
3   those with a Second Class certificate have earned a title of Associate, through completion of a course in a junior college.

Teachers with a Kindergarten or Elementary School Teacher Certificate are qualified to teach all subjects, whereas those with certificates for upper and lower secondary schools can teach the subjects for which their certificates were awarded. To obtain such a certificate, a student teacher must gain the prescribed number of credits for teaching and for professional subjects in courses approved by the Ministry of Education, Science, Sports and Culture. For example, students who want a First Class Elementary Teacher certificate need eighteen credits for teaching subjects and forty-one credits for professional subjects in courses given at universities or colleges approved by the Ministry. For a Second Class kindergarten teacher's licence, eight credits for teaching subjects and twenty-three credits for professional subjects are required.

In the revision of the Educational Personnel Certification Law, which is intended to improve the standard of teacher training, the required number of credits for professional subjects was increased, but now there is some discussion as to whether there should be more teaching practice in schools, and training in counselling for such matters as bullying among children.

Training of nurses at day nurseries

Nurses (the equivalent of UK nursery nurses) at day nurseries are qualified when they graduate from a two-year training school or college, before which they must have graduated from a high (upper secondary) school approved by the Ministry of Health and Welfare, or when they pass an examination for day nursery nurses given by their prefectural government. Since the revision, students have been required to complete at least two years in an institute of higher education.

Inservice training of teachers

The law on Special Regulations Concerning Educational Public Service Personnel requires teachers to pursue consistent inservice training. Prefectural boards of education are responsible by law for planning and encouraging daily inservice training in local public schools.

In May 1988 a system of one-year work experience/inservice training was prepared for *beginners* and this has been fully active since 1990. It was prepared at the level of national, prefectural and local boards of education, for teachers who have finished a year of training for beginners. There is also a wide range of programmes of continuing professional development (CPD) at all school levels.

Conclusion

We are looking forward to the twenty-first century, in which we believe societies will be increasingly information-oriented, increasingly 'international' or global and with increasing diversification of value systems. The many reformational changes in education in Japan, particularly since 1989, have been intended to prepare pupils for the society which we expect in the next century. Teaching techniques are being developed to address various goals: for example, to encourage the development of children's individuality. However, there are many difficulties yet to be resolved, such as bullying, and the Ministry of Education is already working on ways to address those difficulties in the educational reforms scheduled for the early part of the next century.

References

Daiichihouki (ed.) (1989) *Contents and Highlights of the Revised Course of Study for Primary Schools*. Tokyo: Daiichihouki.

Early Childhood Education Association of Japan (eds) (1979) *Early Childhood Education and Care in Japan*. Tokyo: Child-sha Press.

Hall, R.K. (ed.) (1949) 'The principles of national polity' (*Kokutai no Hongi*) (trans. J.O. Gauntlett) Cambridge, MA: Harvard University Press.

Kondou, S. and Fukushima, T., (eds) (1991) *Commentary Regarding the Revision of Evaluation Forms*. Tokyo: Gyousei Press.

Konishi, K. (1989) *Life Environment Studies and Teaching Plans*. Osaka: Osakashosedi.

Koya, N. (1991) 'The new view of learning ability and evaluation'. *Monthly Journal of Education* 11, 8–10. Tokyo: Gakken Press.

Ministry of Education, (1947) 'The fundamental law of education'. Government paper, 31 March.

Ministry of Education (1980) *Monbusho*. Tokyo: Kyiokuchokugo.

Ministry of Education, Science and Culture (1989) *An Outline of Revision of the Courses of Study in Japan*. Tokyo: internal document.

Ministry of Education, Science, Sports and Culture (1991) *Outline of Education in Japan*. Tokyo: UNESCO ASIA Center Press.

Ministry of Education, Science, Sports and Culture (1994) *Education in Japan*. Tokyo: Gyousei Press.

Ministry of Education, Science, Sports and Culture (1995) *Educational Policy in Japan*. Tokyo: Gyousei Press.

Ministry of Education, Science, Sports and Culture (1995) *Monbushou*. Tokyo: Kyiokuchokugo.

Moriue, Shobou (ed.) (1989) *New Material and Data in Early Childhood Education and Care in Japan*. Kyoto: Minerva (Supplement, p. 17).

Sugimine, H. (1992) 'Fundamental problems of school education'. *Education for the Lives of Children*. Gakujyutsutosyo.

Sugimine, H. (1996) 'General moral principles of primary/secondary education'. *Education for the Lives of Children*. Kyodo: Syuppan.

Sugimine. H. and Sugimine, F. (1993) *Doctors' Testimonies of Hiroshima*. Kizu, Hyoto: International Human Network.

8

RELATIONSHIPS AND TENSIONS IN THE PRIMARY CURRICULUM OF THE UNITED STATES

Glenn DeVoogd

Introduction

The United States of America is shaped partly by its history as a immigrant country. Americans' distaste for a strong central government was formed as immigrants left different countries in Europe in search of new opportunity, freedom of religion and freedom from government oppression. After independence from Europe in 1776, the framers of the constitution ensured local control of government by giving more powers to the states and local governments and fewer powers to the central government. Local control of government as well as differences in values that existed between immigrants from different nations allowed for diversity of goals in education. Soon these immigrant pioneers broke out of the eastern cities towards the expansive yet wild west on foot, on horse and wagon train to claim land. In general they found good, cheap land to farm and those who worked hard were successful. The promise of America is that any individual employing pioneer values of hard work, innovation and self-sufficiency has the opportunity to succeed. These values have been translated in the present age to provide great rewards for those who excel with observable results and few rewards for others. Our obsession with positive results is summed up by a famous football coach, Vince Lombardi, who said, 'Winning isn't everything, it's the only thing'.

These values of hard work, innovation and the pursuit and rewarding of excellence have guided America's educational system and are exemplified by Texas. Since its secession from Mexico in 1836, the Lone Star State has cherished the pioneer values of hard work, the pursuit of excellence, innovation and independence. These societal values not only assist teachers

139

in their work, but also create tensions that exist between society's demands on an educational system and children's needs.

Society's views of children, what we know about them and what we want them to be, determine how we provide for children's education in society. The diverse range of American societal attitudes provides the teacher with points of assistance and conflict with which they struggle every day. In this chapter we examine how American and Texan viewpoints specifically relate to:

- how and what information children learn;
- the health and well-being of all children;
- the diversity and mobility of its population;
- competing ideas and tensions in the primary curriculum;
- the professional nature of teaching.

Issues of a society's views of children and the corresponding policies and practices are often so closely related that, in this chapter, I have dealt with them by describing typical American scenes of educational contexts and analyzing these by relating them to the five themes mentioned above.

A typical day in the life of a child

Although the following scenarios are mostly made up of a composite of Texan educational contexts, a range of American activities and routines that distinguish the American character is included. The following is a typical day in the life of a boy named Tony who is in Miss Kate's class.

Tony's routine

Since Tony goes to bed rather early, he doesn't mind waking up at 6.30 a.m. to watch *Rug Rats*, his favourite comic show on television, while he eats his morning cereal and milk. Sometimes his father and 11-year-old brother join his television watching but he must be mindful of time because he has to wash, dress and brush his teeth so he can meet the school bus by 7.30 a.m. at the corner near his house.

After school at 3.15 p.m., Tony takes the bus to the neighbour's house, where Miss Molly runs a preschool in her home for five 3- and 4-year-olds and an after-school care for children like Tony whose parents don't finish work until after five. Sara and Antonio, Tony's parents, have left instructions that their children are to finish their homework first and then play outside, without watching television, so they get some exercise. Sara picks up the children after work about 5.00 p.m. and starts preparing dinner while the children watch television or a movie on video cassette.

The family eat together just after 6.00 p.m. and get a chance to discuss the day with each other for the first time. After dinner everyone pursues their own agenda such as watching television, playing 'Nintendo', playing on the computer, a quick shopping trip or playing board games. On Wednesday night (and Sunday morning) the family goes together to church where the children and adults attend separate Bible studies from 7.00 to 8.00 p.m. Twice a month Tony goes with his brother and father to Boy Scouts where adolescents learn the value of self-sufficiency and 'proper moral values'. In the spring and part of the summer, Tony will play in a soccer team which will meet each week on Monday after school until 5.00 p. m. and on Saturday for games. Tony usually gets ready for bed at 8.30 p. m. when his mother or father will usually listen to their children read or they will read a story to their children.

A proliferation of information

As a 6-year-old, Tony has more information available to him than children have had previously. In the last ten years, the proliferation of information for children started with a rise in the popularity and affordability of children's books. Large sections of book stores became reserved for children. Bookstores and mailorder book clubs exclusively for children sprang up as parents began to develop large book collections for their children and teachers boasted of their children's collections. So popular are they now that teachers rely on parents to teach their children a great deal about books and their contents. A rich literacy environment and educationally oriented parents like Tony's are important reasons why reading achievement is relatively high among young American school children (Elley 1992).

Tony is also socialized into the culture by watching video cassette movies and commercial and public television for between ten and twenty-five hours a week (Anderson et al. 1981; Clements 1985). Recently lowered prices of movies such as new Disney releases make a large video library a possibility for most children. Through his repeated viewing of videos, Tony is able to quote much of the movie script and replay the storyline in play times. Compared to earlier days when children had to be read to to access information, electronic media allows children more access to factual information, such as the *Magic School Bus in the Human Body* (a software program, television show and video) and *Bill Nye Science Guy* (a television show and web site), than ever before. Like the proliferation of books, the availability of video potentially also allows for increased cognitive development of children outside the classroom.

Wider accessibility of electronic media can also expose children to events heretofore censored in the mass media which can negatively affect children's social and emotional growth. Children may watch violence on television or sexually explicit and illicit material on the worldwide web. Unguided, children may come to experience life in a junk culture, where unnecessary violence, randomness and commercial seduction stunt a child's social and emotional growth (Giroux 1994). Tony's parents, being conscious of the possible detrimental effects of unchecked electronic media viewing, are careful to monitor and limit their children's usage by establishing a prohibition on television watching immediately after school. Instead of simply watching whatever is shown on a limited number of commercial networks, Tony's parents have a cable hookup which allows their television to receive about a hundred channels – greater availability and selection of electronic media has also enabled parents and children to discriminate in their usage of media.

Likewise, teachers can no longer just view a film and call that 'instruction'. Though the proliferation of information has benefited knowledge acquisition, it has also challenged teachers to concentrate studies beyond the mere memorisation of facts. Society's ready acquisition of information and materials has pushed students to do something meaningful with the knowledge to which they have access. This has in turn led to a more constructivist approach (discussed later in the chapter) where children use what they know in meaningful projects and a variety of applications (DeVoogd 1995).

Further socialisation and education of children especially in areas of moral development and sports occur outside primary schools as evidenced by Tony's family's participation in church, the boy scouts and soccer leagues. In church and scouts children are encouraged to broaden their understanding of the world in learning activities outside school with art, songs, stories and memorisation of moral passages. Again, children who are fortunate enough to have these experiences broaden their general understanding of the world, which provides teachers with more knowledgeable children.

The health and well-being of all children

Although these eight- to ten-hour days away from parents reflect the American society's expectation of hard work and high cognitive expectations for students in schools, they often ignore the children's emotional needs (Wieder and Greenspan 1992), social needs, and physical needs previously provided by mothers at home. In years past, children of normal nurturing families received support and comfort with more hours at home and less at school. Also, children commonly went home for lunch and did not often have day care outside the home. Young families now have many stresses which negatively impact a young child's social emotional health at a critical period in the development of self-esteem and motivation for learning. Major stresses for young families include, but are not limited to, long days away from each other and double shifts by mothers who go to work and also work hard at home with little time to meet their own social, emotional or cognitive needs or those of their children. The consequences may mean poor nutrition, poor sleep, poor finances, poor health and inadequate child care.

Both child and parents have long days away from home, often nine hours a day, and chores to do once they get home. In a fifteen- country study of Western European nations by the Organization for Economic Co-operation and Development (OECD 1993), teaching occurred over 1093 hours per year in comparison to a European average of 825 hours per year for 9-year-olds and a low of 748 in Italy. So children spend a great deal of time not only in school but also in managed care after school. America's belief that personal fulfilment is acquired through work (Olmsted and Weikart 1995), greater accessibility to a variety of jobs and sinking and stagnant real income for middle- and lower-class work has pushed the number of mothers in the labour force with children under 6 years of age to 62 per cent in 1994 (US Bureau of Labor Statistics). Though children are at home for shorter periods of time, schools are increasing their demands for parent participation in learning. Tony, like most children, is expected to complete an increasing amount of homework during the primary school years. Parents are also expected to read to, listen to, and even teach their children to read (Stevens *et al.* 1992).

Resource and neglect

America represents more extremes of wealth and poverty than comparable countries in the rest of the world, the burden of which falls disproportionately on the children (Berliner and Biddle 1995) and even more disproportionately on the youngest children. As a country, the United States is arguably world leader in health technology but eighteenth in infant mortality. It has more millionaires and billionaires than any other country, but it is also eighteenth in terms of the width of the gap between the rich and the poor (Edelman 1996). America produces more than any other country, but the 21 per cent childhood poverty rate in 1990 was twice that of the UK and four times that of Sweden and Finland (Smeeding *et al.* 1990). American scientists are skilled in medicine, space travel and military hardware and yet overall student scores lag behind student scores in other countries in mathematics and science achievement.

The largest reason for this difference is poor students living in states where school funding is low. Students in equitably and well-funded schools, for example in Iowa, achieve scores comparable to the highest scoring countries in the world in mathematics and science (Westbury 1992). Per capita spending can range as much as four to one in states such as Texas where some districts spend $2000 per student per year and others spend $8000 per student per year (1995 figures) (Berliner and Biddle 1995).

In the vital first years of life when a baby's substantial first impressions are being made of the world, the law allows only 55 per cent of America's first teachers – the parents – to take three months unpaid leave to take care of the newborn (Jones 1996). Children need excellent health care and education to develop strong bodies and minds, but the United States is often indifferent when it comes to the education and care of its youngest citizens (Brazelton 1997).

In 1994, of the 19 million children under 5 years in the United States (about 7 per cent of the population), 10 million needed child care while their mother worked. Of that group, 48 per cent found a relative to care for their child (Casper 1996b). Of the 51 per cent who paid for care by non-relatives the average cost was $74 a week. Poor families feel the cost of child care disproportionately by paying 18 per cent of their income compared to families above poverty who pay 7 per cent of their income (Casper 1996a). Such costs are difficult for families who are often young and earning significantly less than older, more established workers. The stress for poor working families is particularly hard felt because while federal assistance for the unemployed comes with medical insurance, low income work often comes without it (43 million people or 17 per cent of the American population has no health insurance). As a result of the lack of benefits many poor families avoid taking their children to doctors, which leads to generally poor health care for young poor children.

In the 1960s and 1970s the purpose of early childhood education, within the programme called Headstart, was to provide cognitive support for children of economically disadvantaged homes so they could enter school on an equal footing with their peers. Unfortunately, even in 1995, Headstart was only able to fund programmes for 752,000 3- and 4-year-olds, with just 36 per cent of the children eligible to receive the programme (Edelman 1996).

Recent reports in popular media reflect the attitude that 'good, afford-able day care is not a luxury or a fringe benefit for welfare mothers and working parents but essential brain food for the next generation' (Nash 1997). Even though demands on quality day care are high, the National Child Care Staffing Study (NCCSS), including interviews and observations of child care sites in five representative cities in the United States, describes a relatively low level of care for young children, average wages lower than the poverty threshold ($9,363/annually compared to $22,226/average annual pay for similar educational level (US Census Bureau 1996a)), and an unsurprising 41 per cent turnover (Whitebook et al. 1993).

In general, teachers feel unprepared and incapable of providing ade-quately to meet the social, emotional and physical needs of all children. Rarely do early childhood pre-service students learn about children's social, emotional and physical needs in depth. For example, a teacher who unwittingly teaches with a very structured approach in which children's actions are limited to a very narrow range of behaviours, does not allow the child to construct and learn how to learn (Wieder and Greenspan 1992).

The long hours also affect teachers' effectiveness on the job and as parents. At the end of a busy eight-hour day, seven of which have been worked with twenty-five children, teachers have very little patience or energy to go to inservice courses, take university classes or personally pursue professional development. Teachers' ability to compile portfolios, meet in groups to consider the needs of children or the class in general or to make plans is limited by their lack of time. In addition, teachers who often choose their profession so they can be with their own children after school and on vacations, resist attempts at lengthening their time away from their family.

While guiding children socially and emotionally is difficult for any teacher in the present system, for teachers of children who are socially and emotionally needy it is overwhelming. Teachers who work in certain poor rural and poor inner-city populations share a disproportionately high percentage of children whose parents are socially and emotionally deprived. Such parents often teach their own children those disadvantaged habits or neglect their children's needs using oppressive methods of behaviour management. Teachers in these contexts are overloaded with the social and emotional needs among children in their classrooms.

A diverse and mobile society

In the United States, the tensions and relationships between children's needs and society's demands are as complex and diverse as the population in which it exists. Cultural influences such as ethnic background and religion all play roles to define teachers' relationships to children and schools. These social, cultural and economic forces generate lively debate from different perspectives concerning the vision and education of children. Though there is much common ground, differences are often confusing as people move beyond their homes to teach in different neighbourhoods, cities and states. Let us take, for example, a young teacher named Kate who has moved to the economically and socially poor suburbs of north Houston. Kate is one of a number of new teachers in kindergarten and elementary schooling (see Table 8.1).

Kate's mother, some fifteen years previously, had established her own pre-school in the northern suburbs of Chicago. Her mother had taught Kate that it is just as, if not more, important to focus on the emotional, social and physical aspects of a child's early life as well as the cognitive. As she was growing up, Kate watched her mother talking with children to help them construct strategies for social relations such as encouraging children to 'use their words' instead of physically chastising them as a

GLEN DEVOOGD

Table 8.1 New teachers in US schools

US elementary students and teachers	Nursery school (public)	Nursery school (private)	Kinder-garten (public)	Kinder-garten (private)	Elementary (public) kindergarten (6th grade)	Elementary (private) kinder-garten (6th grade)
Students	1,940,000	2,319,000	3,278,000	585,000	28,109,000	3,378,000
Teachers	97,000	116,000	149,000	26,000	1,873,000	225,000
New teachers from one of 900 univer-sities	11,000*	13,000*	17,000*	3,000*	206,000*	25,000*

Source: US Census Bureau 1997. Otherwise US Census Bureau 1996b.

Note:
* Calculated by taking 11 per cent of new first-year teachers, which is the turn over rate in the United States.

solution to problems. Kate's mother observed students carefully noting their progress and then planned lessons to fit the children's needs. She had resisted attempts on the part of a few parents to focus interactions on memorizing letters and numbers.

Kate married and moved to Houston, Texas where work is plentiful, albeit poorly compensated. After going to college for four years and being with her mother in the preschool, Kate was brimming with ideas about what to do in her all-day kindergarten class. In her first day at work, the principal, who had hired her, brought her the teacher's manuals and materials of six different programmes including teachers' manuals which script teacher activity down to the questions you ask, texts, and sometimes workbooks. The children in her class were from the low socio-economic levels, many speaking Spanish and many receiving free lunch from the government. Her heart sank when she discovered that doing all of the six commercially published programmes during the school day did not allow her to use any of the ideas she had learned about in college or with her mother. What is worse is that she did not believe the programmes were meeting the children's English language or social needs, but she did not want to offend the principal so continued with all the programmes required.

She had tried out programmes of constructive social development, children constructing their own rules. Kate was frustrated to discover that she had a hard time getting children to generate rules, which was not the norm in other classes or in the homes she had visited. Although Texas has a law to limit class sizes to twenty-two children, Kate has

146

twenty-five. Her district applied to be exempt from that law and to compensate Kate the district has provided a quarter-time aide. Unfortunately, the principal assigned the aide to office work instead of to the classroom.

Differences between Kate's and her mother's classrooms are indicative of:

- the region of the United States;
- the part of the city;
- socio-economic class (labour versus manager class);
- perceptions of teaching as a professional versus technical job.

In Kate's mother's school, there is a good deal more respect for the individual teacher and the need for the teacher to determine curriculum. In contrast, Kate is required by her principal to act as a technician following the script provided by curriculum publishers. Although in most northern states, teacher unions protect teachers' rights and professional expectations, non-union private schools like Kate's mother's also reflect that norm in society. Teachers are expected to make their own plans and use observation to adjust instruction to meet the needs of the student within certain broad limits of acceptable behaviour. In the south, pay is about 20 per cent lower and teachers are expected to comply with principal's wishes for evaluation, planning, and even when aides are allocated to their classroom.

Each region of the United States reflects different and diverse educational outlooks. Kate's school, in a working-class Mexican-American suburb, reflects the working-class and ethnic values of the community (Anyon 1980). Teachers are authorities to be obeyed or there is punishment. In other schools where professionals send their children in Houston, the focus of misbehaviour becomes an opportunity for students to explore and construct moral development (DeVries and Zan 1994). The principal in Kate's school views the teachers as technicians who implement programmes written by experts and not professionals who make unique decisions based on the teacher's professional understanding of the diverse abilities of children, the curriculum and the context of instruction (Schwab 1978). That context is contrasted with Kate's mother's school in upper-middle-class Chicago where the teacher, as a professional, is responsible for constructing her or his own curriculum to meet the needs of each child. Kate's mother's programme focuses more on Piagetian concepts of construction through play, whereas Kate's kindergarten reflects more direct instruction and teacher control.

Language and culture is another tension for Kate. Although Kate has no preparation in the area of English as a second language, bilingual education, or multicultural education, she is working with many Hispanic children and their parents. Those parents have chosen to place their children in a non-bilingual class hoping English immersion will help them to learn English faster. Kate feels that children might be able to read some words in Spanish, but she has no time or authority to teach in Spanish. The norms and procedures in the two areas provide a contrast of language (English/Spanish), social norms (obedience and respect as social norms versus constructive sense-making), and also of the economic resources of the parents.

Competing ideas and tensions in the curriculum

Early education in America was established by communities and local consortiums. The federal government has hitherto resisted matters of social policy believing that state and local government as well as community organisations who had a more personal understanding of the problems that face the community would be better at solving local problems (Olmsted and Senninger 1995). Though changes may occur in the future, the federal government has provided money to fit specific categories of special education such as grants for any student at any level who is slow in reading and mathematics and 3- and 4-year-olds at risk of failure because of their poverty or because English is not their first language. Also, the federal government has provided money for states to establish statewide goals. They have pledged to provide national standards and tests to all the districts who want to use them (Mathis 1997).

Instead, local school districts in every town run by elected local school board members, have been establishing curricular and teaching programmes to try to ensure student achievement. Local school boards, knowing that an important element in any programme is that the teachers are personally devoted to making it a success, have asked schools to set up a committee of teachers, staff and the principal to manage their own school. This site-based management (SBM) usually makes decisions on how to spend inservice money, but rarely decides important issues such as school budget, staff meeting agendas or school policy.

State control began as local school boards established some basic rules about schooling and instituted licensing of teachers through the university. By state law, schooling is compulsory through to at least the age of 16 although schooling continues to be free until students receive their high school diploma regardless of their age. In Texas teachers must take at least twelve course credits in early childhood education to teach the approximately 15 per cent of the total 5 million 3– and 4–year-olds who are eligible to attend public schools and almost all 5-year-old children who attend kindergarten. The state provides elementary certification for children aged 6 years (first grade) through to age 13 (eighth grade). (Although there are various arrangements for schools, most school districts offer elementary schools which include Kindergarten through to grade five, middle schools for grades six to eight and high school for grades nine to twelve. Elementary and middle school is composed of approximately 35 million students or 13 per cent of the nation's population. The remaining four years' free education at the high school numbers 15 million students or 6 per cent of the population. College students are also a large group with 12 million attending at least part time (5 per cent of the population: US Census Bureau 1996b). In most states, newly certified teachers must renew their teaching certificate every five years or so by attending a teacher development inservice programme.

In the last ten years, states have increasingly become involved in establishing an annual assessment and a state curriculum. In most states, the assessment test started as a simple reading and mathematics test in third or fourth grade (8- to 9-year-olds). The test was originally designed to assess minimum standards for schools and soon high school students were required to pass a tenth grade test to receive a diploma. By the late 1980s, the assessment test was being published in the newspaper by school, grade and percentage of students who had passed the minimum standards, broken down into those of European descent, African-Americans, Hispanics and Native Americans. Realtors (estate agents) know the schools which score well on the state assessment and house buyers are willing to pay top dollars for houses in neighbourhoods where schools score well (Markley 1996).

In 1996, hundreds of Houston administrators signed an agreement to be willing to resign if the state test scores of students under their authority declined. They also agreed to accept a bonus if their school scores increased. All academic subjects and curricular material are chosen by whether they align or not with the state assessment test. For example, few schools teach writing in any other structure than the traditional 'five-paragraph essay' with an introduction, three supporting paragraphs (each containing a topic sentence) and a concluding paragraph. The five-paragraph essay is also the criterion for the writing portion of the state assessment test. Although teachers complain about doing state assessment-related work, it is unclear after years of teaching under threat of state assessment that teachers would teach any differently. In this case, the teacher perception that a tension existed within children's need to write in different genres has been considerably dulled by the loss of practice in teaching writing any other way.

Diverse modes of pre-service and inservice teacher education

While teachers at different levels are obliged to attend to state objectives, assessments and district administrators, university programmes are not so tightly aligned to state and local curricula. Universities are accredited by a national organisation and are much more likely to suggest that teachers pursue diverse philosophies of education. In the last ten years, scholarly journals have explored constructivist forms of early childhood education with American adaptations of preschools in Reggio Emilia (Hendrick 1997), project approaches (Chard 1997), reading and writing workshops (Avery 1993), dramatic storytelling (Cooper 1993), moral development (DeVries and Zan 1994), use of technology (DeVoogd 1995) and assessment (Mindes *et al*. 1996). However, since such constructivist approaches do not always score as high in the short term on standardized assessments and since they require knowledge and skill on the part of the teacher, these approaches are discouraged by administrators and eventually forgotten by teachers.

Competing curriculum standards

Of all of the areas of schooling perhaps the most battled ground is that for control of the curriculum. Teachers are often faced with inconsistent and contradicting advice from state government and school district level officials, as well as recommendations from professional organisations, other teachers and parents, all of whom wield authority in education and children's lives. To what degree and from which sources do teachers accept authority? Those at the university who have scholarly expertise studying particular subject areas should determine the direction of instruction for students. Parents have the ultimate responsibility for their own children and yet the government gives out money, legislations and mandates which also carry the full force of the law. To get a feel for the conflicting opinions of different authorities' groups, imagine Kate's perspective, as a beginning first-grade teacher, in the following scenario as an example of conflicting authority from literacy research.

Conflicting views on methods for teaching beginning reading surround Kate at the state government level. In a recent press conference, the governor of Texas, George Bush, cited research indicating the helpfulness of phonemic awareness and promptly asked teachers to commit fifteen minutes a day to phonics instruction. Private groups and committee members are proposing alternate literacy objectives for the Texas Essential Knowledge and Skills (TEKS: Garner 1997).

Kate also notices different views expressed in scholarly places. After studying beginning literacy at the University of Houston, Kate concludes, after much reading of research in the area of phonemic awareness, that the latter can be achieved in the context of reading meaningful words. Her opinion is shared by many professors at the state university. Yet parents of her students in the teacher's class have asked that children work more on worksheets and isolated letter recognition.

Kate looks to the national level of professional organisations and to the national government in the hope of finding a consistent message about ways to teach beginning reading, but she remains disappointed. The International Reading Association (IRA) and National Council for Teachers of English (NCTE) has published a national standards for language instruction (Greer *et al.* 1996) that places the importance of letter–sound relationships only in the context of words of the children's choosing and at a much lower importance than the Texas state officials. The national curriculum was elicited and endorsed by US Department of Education. This same US Department of Education had published, a decade previously, a book on effective teaching recommending generative phonics (Bennett 1986), an approach quite different from the IRA/NCTE document.

The school district and her principal have requested all lower elementary teachers to teach a generative phonics instruction each day. In addition, Kate was asked to teach five other commercial programmes, two of which focus on literacy skills. Kate does not agree with them all or all of the activities, but she has to submit her lesson plans weekly and she is afraid the principal might disapprove if she does not schedule times for all five programmes in the class day. She has heard of another teacher who taught a rhyming lesson in a method that deviated from the programme and was reprimanded. Kate also feels a sense of responsibility to the students to present them with a consistent programme that meets their needs instead of simply pacifying all of the groups which have authority over the education of the young children.

So Kate starts her career as a first-grade teacher. Although some first-grade classrooms have desks off to the side of the room and focus more on a centre-based approach to classrooms, in her class rectangular tables for two children with compartments for books fill the centre of the room. She thinks the principal will like that. Every space on the wall is covered with brightly coloured pictures, numbers and letters children will study during the year. Two bulletin boards have student drawings and pictures hanging. Student mobiles are hanging from the ceiling. Around the edges of the room, Kate has a learning centre for every subject area: a literacy centre with a bookcase of books and tapes for children to listen to; a mathematics centre with games; a science centre with pictures of flowers and real flowers for children to pick apart. In social studies she plans for children to write their own 'rules' and illustrate them on a bulletin board.

Kate starts the day by reading a story to the children and then teaches from the phonics programme given to her, focusing on sounding out words since all children have learned letters in kindergarten. Typically, Kate reviews the letter sounds with the students with a song or by making the shape with their bodies. Most of the time is spent in whole-group blending letters and reading controlled vocabulary books with a reading partner. Children have a fifteen-minute recess and then work in their mandatory spelling and handwriting books. Pupils can either buy a hot lunch for a dollar or bring their own. The following social studies lesson focuses on 'being friends'. Children listen to a hand-puppet play given by the teacher about a situation in which friends learn to work through a conflict. Following the story, children practise in groups of four with their own puppets, working out scenarios listed in the teacher's manual. For mathematics children use cubes to represent numerical problems on paper at centres Kate has set up all around the room. After recess children examine with magnifying glasses and pick apart wild flowers they have collected during recess. At 3.15 p.m. Kate gives the children a short spelling activity and books for homework.

In this scenario (made up of bits and pieces from class activities of different but typical teachers in the Houston area), Kate wants to teach the 'right way', but feels tremendous conflict over how her conclusions about appropriate reading instruction challenge various authorities in her school. Teaching reading by using a portion of each programme seems to be equally conflicting and troubling to her. What is perhaps more distressing is that by choosing any one clear, consistent course of action she could easily alienate herself from any of the many authorities or, indeed, the pupils themselves. If she uses the phonics kit given her by the principal she fears that she might bore and alienate the children as readers. If she teaches the way she believes is most efficient, the principal may reprimand her. Regardless of the course of action she takes, she knows she will probably remain in conflict and dissatisfied in her goals for teaching beginning readers. In the end, Kate complies with the principal for the sake of keeping her job, but she hopes to convince her principal the following year to make some changes that more appropriately meet the needs of the children. In the meantime, Kate's weekly timetable continues along the lines shown in Table 8.2.

The professional nature of teaching

Differences in the views of the professional versus technical nature of teaching define the positions which also cause tensions for teachers. In this section, we see how the teachers' inadequate compensation as well as their inability to determine curriculum and to provide for appropriate materials, all indicate ways in which society presently tends to relate to teachers as technicians and not as professionals.

In Texas, the educational society has high expectations for teachers. They are asked to excel in a number of examinations and learning ordeals to achieve the status of teacher. There is a general elementary certificate as well as bilingual and early childhood endorsements, all of which require the student teacher to take a state examination. A fourth exit examination tests knowledge of English. Also, there is an examination to enter university, various examinations in classes to maintain a good grade point

Table 8.2 Typical weekly classroom schedule

School time	Monday	Tuesday	Wednesday	Thursday	Friday
8.15–9.45	Reading	Reading	Reading	Reading	Reading
9.45–10.00	Recess	Recess	Recess	Recess	Recess
10.15–11.15	Writing, spelling and handwriting	Writing, spelling and handwriting	Music time with music teacher	Writing, spelling and handwriting	Writing, spelling and handwriting
11.15–12.00	Lunch and recess	Lunch and recess	Lunch and recess	Lunch and recess	Lunch and recess
12.00–1.00	Mathematics	Mathematics	Mathematics	Mathematics	Mathematics
1.00–2.00	Science	Physical education	Science	Physical education	Science
2.00–2.15	Recess	Teacher reads a story	Recess	Teacher reads a story	Recess
2.15–3.15	Social studies	Social studies	Art time with art teacher	Social studies	Social studies

average and, if the teacher is applying for a Master's degree, another examination to exit the programme is also required. Teachers are cognitively well screened.

Yet in spite of these rigorous standards, teachers once qualified are treated as if they are irresponsible and unworthy of public trust. As illustrated in the above example, Kate wanted to form her curriculum to meet the unique circumstances of her knowledge, the pupils' knowledge, the curriculum and the context of the learning situation (Schwab 1978). Instead, she was provided with a number of scripted programmes to follow as if she were merely a technician and incapable of determining the needs of students. Over the course of the years, teachers using such scripts tend to become over-reliant on such rigid methods and lose their ability to teach without them.

Funding for materials is also inadequate: teachers are most often provided with no choice of materials and are even expected to pay for supplementary resources out of their own pay or ask students to contribute materials themselves. In Texas, the state provides a school building with a series of textbooks for each subject area from a list of five textbooks. If teachers want, or feel they want, to use the money spent on textbooks on trade books, software or other more appropriate media, they must proceed through a long series of bureaucratic approvals and even then they may eventually be denied their choice of materials.

Finally, public elementary school teachers are poorly compensated for their efforts. In the United States teacher pay averages $36,400 (Fullerton 1996) compared to $37,224 mean salary for other types pf work with a four-year college degree requirement and $56,105 for alternative occupations requiring advanced degrees (US Census Bureau 1996a). In addition to their modest remuneration teachers are asked to pay for their own required university inservice education and contribute towards the cost of their own health insurance.

Conclusion

Of all those in our land of 'liberty and justice for all', children are the least powerful and most deserving of our protection and educational guidance. Children deserve professionals who seek to meet the needs of students in a fair and equitable manner. Their teachers deserve a market place of competing educational ideals on which they can draw to meet their needs. In many ways, parents, as the primary guardians of children, do their best to provide what they can. In most cases, parents best is excellent, but for 21 per cent of the children at risk of hunger in America, more needs to be provided to allow to children to feel secure, fed, cared for and healthy.

The dynamic nature of American society has provided new challenges for American and Texan educators of young children. Many experience the land of plenty while others experience neglect. Divergent views of the work of teaching as a profession or a technical skill sometimes provide conflict and other times support for teachers. The mobility and ethnic diversity of its population also creates tensions and relationships between society's demands and children's needs. Different levels of government, school officials and professional organisations have unloaded goals and purposes of schooling to teachers, which are too many in number and too conflicting in nature. All of these challenges require our inbred pioneer values of hard work, innovation and self-sufficiency to resolve. And though individual solutions will provide high quality care for many, providing quality care for all children will take the effort of all Americans. For we know that the promise of America's future rests in the quality of education of all its young children.

References

Anderson, D.R., Lorch, E.P., Smith, R., Bradford, R. and Levin, S.R. (1981) 'Effects of peer presence on preschool television viewing behavior'. *Developmental Psychology*, 17, 446–453.

Anyon, J. (1980) 'Social class and the hidden curriculum of work'. *Journal of Education* 162(1), 67–92.

Avery, C. (1993) . . . *And with a light touch*. Portsmouth, NH: Heinemann.

Bennett, W. (1986) *What Works*. Washington, DC: GPO.

Berliner D.C. and Biddle, B.J. (1995) *The Manufactured Crisis: Myths, Fraud and the Attack on America's Public Schools*. Reading, MA: Addison-Wesley.

Brazelton, T.B. (1997) 'Stresses and supports for families in the1990s'. Unpublished paper. Houston, TX, January.

Casper, L. (1996a) *What Does it Cost to Mind our Preschoolers?* Current Population Reports. (Census Bureau Publication # P70–52). Washington, DC: US Department of Commerce.

Casper, L. (1996b) *Who's Minding our Preschoolers?* Current Population Reports (Census Bureau Publication # P70–53). Washington, DC: US Department of Commerce.

Chard, S. (1997) *Engaging Children's Minds: The Project Approach*. Norwood, NJ: Ablex. Available http://www.ualberta.ca/~schard/projects.htm

Clements, D.H. (1985) 'Technological advances and the young child: television and computers'. In C.S. Mcloughlin and D.F. Gullo (eds) *Young Children in Context: Impact of Self, Family and Society on Development* (pp. 218–253). Springfeld, IL: Charles Thomas.

Cooper, P. (1993) *When Stories Come to School: Telling, Writing, and Performing Stories in the Early Childhood Classroom*. New York, NY: Teachers and Writers Collaborative.

DeVoogd, G.L. (1995) 'New roles and routines for elementary teachers and students: a staff development project using computers to teach the revision of writing'. Unpublished PhD dissertation. East Lansing, MI: Michigan State University.

DeVries, R. and Zan, B. (1994) *Moral Children, Moral Classrooms*. New York: Teacher's College Press.

Edelman, M.W. (1996) *The State of America's Children Yearbook 1996*. Washington, DC: National Association for the Education of Young Children.

Elley, W.B. (1992) *How in the World do Students Read?*. Washington, DC: IEA Press.

Fullerton, H. (1996) *School Teachers; Kindergarten, Elementary, and Secondary. Occupational Outlook Handbook*. Washington, DC: US Bureau of Labor Statistics. Available http://stats.bls.gov/oco/ocos069.htm.

Garner, D. (1997) *Alternative Document Draft for English/Language Arts/Reading*. Available http://www.htcomp.net/tad/.

Giroux, H.A. (1994) 'Doing cultural studies: youth and the challenge of pedagogy'. *Harvard Educational Review* 64(3), 278–308.

Greer, M., Smith, R.S. and Erwin, L. (eds.) (1996) *Standards for the English Language Arts* (National Council Teachers of English and International Reading Association). Urbana, IL: NCTE Press.

Hendrick, J. (ed.) (1997) *First Steps Toward Teaching the Reggio Way.* Upper Saddle River, NJ: Prentice-Hall.

Jones, R. (1996). 'New family leave law has a price'. *Houston Chronicle Interactive,* May. Available http: //www1.chron.com/content/chronicle/business/96/05/02/family.2–0.html.

Markley, M. (1996) 'Search for quality education'. *Houston Chronicle Interactive'.* October. Available http: //www.chron.com/content/chronicle/metropolitan/96/10/13/schools/quality.2–1.html.

Mathis, N. (1997) 'Clinton calls for "crusade" on education'. *Houston Chronicle Interactive,* February. Available http://www1.chron.com/cgi-bin/auth/story/content/chronicle/page1/97/02/05/sou-main.html.

Mindes, G., Ireton, H. and Mardell-Czudnowski, C. (1996) *Assessing Young Children.* Boston, MA: Delmar.

Nash, M. (1997). 'Fertile minds'. *Time* 149(5), 3 February. Available http://pathfinder.com/@@vpb3fgUAnnxRavzN/time/magazine/1997/dom/970203/special.fertile-minds.html

Olmsted, P.P. and Senninger, M.M. (1995) 'A nation-by-nation look at the findings'. In P.P. Olmsted and D. P. Weikart (eds.) *The IEA Pre-primary Study: Early Childhood Care and Education in 11 Countries.* Tarrytown, NY: Pergamon.

Olmsted, P.P. and Weikart, D.P. (1995) *The IEA Pre-primary Study: Early Childhood Care and Education in 11 Countries.* Tarrytown, NY: Pergamon.

Organization for Economic Co-operation and Development (OECD) (1993). *Education Statistics 1985–1992.* Paris: Organization for Economic Co-operation and Development.

Schwab, J. (1978). *Science, Curriculum, and Liberal Education.* Chicago, IL: University of Chicago Press.

Smeeding, T.M., O'Higgins, M. and Rainwater, L. (eds.) (1990) *Poverty, Inequality, and Income Distribution in Comparative Perspective: The Luxembourg Income Study (LIS)* Lanham, MD: University Press of America.

Stevens, J.H., Hough, R.A. and Nurss, J.R. (1992) 'The influence of parents on children development and education'. In B. Spodek (ed.) *Handbook of Research on the Education of Young Children.* New York: Macmillan.

US Census Bureau (1996a) *Mean Earnings of Workers 18 Years Old and Over, by Educational Attainment 1955–1994* (Education Attainment in the United States: March 1995 # P20–489). Washington, DC: US Census Bureau. Available http://www.census.gov/population/socdemo/education/table19.dat.

US Census Bureau (1996b) *School Enrolment of Persons 3–34 years old by Level and Control of School, Race, and Hispanic origin 1955–1994* (Current Population Reports # P20–487). Washington, DC: US Census Bureau. Available http://www.census.gov/population/socdemo/school/tablea-1.txt.

US Census Bureau (1997) *National Population Estimates for the 1990s.* Washington, DC: US Census Bureau. Available http://www.census.gov/population/www/estimates/nat-90s-detail.html#PACK4 or pop @ census.gov.

US Department of Labor, Bureau of Labor Statistics (1997) *Maternal Labor Force Participation of Married Women with Children under Six* (Table A4). Washington, DC: GPO.

Westbury, I. (1992) 'Comparing American and Japanese achievement: is the United States really a low achiever?'. *Educational Researcher* 21(5), 18–24.

Whitebook, M., Phillips, D. and Howes, C. (1993) *National Child Care Staffing Study Revisited: Four Years in the Life of Center-based Care*. Oakland, CA: Child Care Employee Project.

Wieder, S. and Greenspan, S.I. (1992) 'The emotional basis of learning'. In B. Spodek (ed.) *Handbook of Research on the Education of Young Children*. New York: Macmillan.

9

PRIMARY EDUCATION

An Australian perspective

Les Regan

Introduction: the broad context

Australia is a large island continent occupying a total land-mass of almost 8 million square kilometres, approximately thirty times the area of the British Isles. Its population is around 18 million, 80 per cent of whom live on narrow coastal strips covering less than 4 per cent of the total land area: it has, therefore, a high level of urbanisation (Boss *et al.* 1995: 2). The rural population is considerably scattered, although very few people live in the large arid 'heart' of the continent. The indigenous Aboriginal and Torres Strait Islander people constitute about 1.6 per cent of the total population. Immigration has accounted for one-quarter of Australia's population growth since 1913. The vast majority of immigrants have settled in the larger cities rather than in rural areas.

The political system includes an elected federal government and elected governments of six States and two Territories. Australia does not have a national system of schooling so each of these eight local governments is separately responsible for the primary and secondary schooling which occurs within its boundaries.

Formal schooling takes place in preschools (at which attendance is voluntary), primary schools and secondary schools. Children spend six or seven years at primary school, depending on the State or Territory, until around 12 years of age. Education is compulsory for students between the ages of 6 and 15 years (16 years in Tasmania). However, minimum ages for admission to primary schools differ across the various States/Territories (ranging from 4-and-a-half to 6 years).

Most primary schools are relatively small (average 220 children) with those in cities and larger towns having enrolments of between four hundred and eight hundred students. Average class sizes differ somewhat across areas from around twenty-four to twenty-seven pupils (Boss *et al.*

1995: 232). The scattered nature of the rural population has required the establishment of many one-teacher and two-teacher government schools.

Schools are usually classified as government or non-government schools. Non-government schools consist largely of Roman Catholic and, to a lesser extent, Anglican schools. All government primary schools and almost all non-government primary schools are coeducational. Most primary students would attend a school located in their immediate neighbourhood. Of the total full-time equivalent teaching staff (200,345 in 1994), 63 per cent were female and 37 per cent were male (*Australian Bureau of Statistics* 1996: 276). There is a higher proportion of female teachers to male teachers in primary schools and a higher proportion again in preschools.

The extent of provision of pre-compulsory education varies widely across the six States but nationwide approximately 39 per cent of 3–year-olds and 77 per cent of 4-year-olds attend preschool and/or day care programmes (Boss *et al*. 1995: 223). Of the primary school population of some 1.82 million children (approximately 10 per cent of the nation's total population), about 75 per cent attend state schools.

Childhood and society

Perceptions of childhood

Childhood in Australia would be regarded in much the same way as in any other developed societies, as representing a time of exploration and play during which the child is inculcated into the values and principles of the society, in the context of a safe and secure physical, social and psychological environment provided primarily by the family. However, significant changes have occurred in the family structures in the last twenty years, including the following trends (Boss *et al*. 1995: 25–32; Foster and Harman 1992: 116–118):

- there has been a transition from the nuclear family to a wide range of family and non-family types;
- the numbers of *de facto* relationships have increased markedly;
- the average number of children per family has decreased;
- many children now live in a family where their mother or father has been married before and where consequently there may be step-siblings or half-siblings within a blended family;
- the number of single parents has increased significantly.

These changes have affected the nature of childhood. The current downturn in the economy has severely depleted families' finances and in many cases has forced both partners to work long hours in full-time jobs (if available) out of economic necessity. Along with their contemporaries from other developed countries, many parents now have less time to carry out their expected nurturing role and the stresses and strains of modern living are creating domestic environments in which children cannot be given the attention they deserve.

From the basis of the immediate family and friends, for most children socialisation continues through the informal and semi-formal interactions which they have with adults and other children at various preschool and compulsory schooling contexts. Foster and Harman make the observation that:

> Socialisation within the family seeks to initiate (if not complete) the learning of behaviours appropriate to segments of society outside the family. The family has the task of transmitting culture to the young, and in that sense it helps to keep the culture alive. [One particular interest is] the overlap between the socialisation that occurs in the family and that which is attributed to the education system.
>
> (Foster and Harman 1992: 113)

Some sociologists have been interested in examining the relationship between the 'cultural capital' (Bordieu 1977) which the child brings to the school and the extent to which the school recognises and builds on that capital. This notion of 'cultural capital' is particularly relevant to Australia's multicultural situation, where mismatches may exist between the language, attitudes, values and behaviours which children acquire through the process of socialisation into their particular culture and that which the school defines as legitimate.

Some children will find themselves caught between two cultures – the culture of the home and the culture of their formal schooling. Conflicts may arise, escalating in their effects as the individuals grow older and become increasingly susceptible to peer-group pressure. These cultural differences may be related to social class, ethnicity, race or regional divisions, or a combination of these factors

Elements of the mass culture are also acquired through radio, cinema, television and videos. Australia has one of the highest proportions of home-ownership of video-machines in the world and some surveys have shown that many primary school children spend as much time watching television and videos each week as they spend at school. Concern has also been expressed in some Aboriginal and Torres Strait Island communities that the watching of videos and satellite television by old and young people alike is hastening the destruction of traditional culture and values contained within the 'old ways'.

Women's roles in society

The following composite picture describes the various roles which many children would observe females and males 'typically' enacting in a 'typical' Australian home and in 'typical' pre- and primary schools.

In the home the children would tend to see their mother in the role of chief childrearer and as a domestic worker with the father responsible for 'outside' jobs such as mowing the lawn, washing the car and general home maintenance. Shopping would tend to be the mother's job. At their pre-school (to which they would usually be taken by their mother), the children would see mostly female teachers/carers and assistants and few, if any, males.

At primary school, children would see mostly female teachers, particularly in the lower primary classes. However, the principal would probably be male. All of the clerical assistants and the librarian at the school would be female. If parents came in to help, they would be likely to be female. If the children caught the bus or train home after school, the driver would most likely be a male. If the children were collected after school, it would be more likely to be by the mother because the father would have a 'full-time' job.

At meetings of the Parents' and Citizens' Association or the School Council during the evening, if anyone from home attended, it would be more likely to be the mother. Similarly, when teachers wished to meet with parents at the school for occasional reports, the mother would most likely be the parent attending.

This generalised description illustrates Foster and Harman's (1992: 136) assertion that 'Fathers might well be invisible in at least the early years of the child's schooling'.

Equal opportunities

In 1989 the Department of the Prime Minister and Cabinet issued a statement about social justice which emphasised 'the right of all Australians to equality of treatment and opportunity, and the removal of barriers of race, ethnicity, culture, religion, language, gender or place of birth'. Also in 1989 the Australian Education Council announced ten National Goals for primary and secondary schooling, one of which was: 'To promote equality of educational opportunities, and to provide for groups with special learning requirements'.

However, despite this, educational inequalities persist. These are not the obvious ones which exist between private schools and government schools (and described in earlier Australian research, such as that undertaken by Connell *et al.* 1982) but rather are to be found within the government-school systems. For example, Hatton *et al.* (1994: 4) observe that 'families in poverty [are] excluded from educational decision making, their skills undervalued and their children often seen as innately less intelligent'. Foster and Harman (1992: 222) assert that 'structured inequality in society is reflected in similar structured inequality in education' and Connell *et al.* (1991: 23) claim that 'class inequalities in education (measured by a range of outcomes from school progression to test results to secondary retention to tertiary entry) persist on a massive scale in contemporary Australian education'. Connell *et al.* (1991: 32) also assert that many do not accept that 'the education system is one of the education structures that historically generate social inequalities' but instead believe that 'it is poverty which causes educational disadvantage and that the education system is simply registering the effects of such poverty'.

Policies and provision for certain subgroups remain inadequate. For example: Blackmore *et al.* (1996) argue that enactment of the equal opportunity policy for girls has not taken full account of structural differences associated with race, class, ethnicity and regionality; while Long (1995) points out that, despite governmental urging to develop Australia as the 'clever country', there is no federal government policy for children with high intellectual potential.

In writing about education the previous more liberal notion of 'equality of opportunity' (i.e. 'positively discriminating for disadvantaged groups of students in society, with the aim of redressing environmental and social inequality') has been replaced by the notion of 'equity' in education (i.e. 'educational justice or fairness as measured by equality of outcomes') in recent times (Foster and Harman 1992: 241–242). These writers also observe that once 'equity' is defined in these terms, notions of 'effectiveness' and 'efficiency' are introduced into the equation, bringing with them instrumentalist and managerialist approaches.

Parental rights, responsibilities and influences

Technically, in all Australian States and Territories *education* is compulsory for children between the ages of six and 15–16 years but *schooling* is not. This means that Education Departments grant a small proportion of parents or communities permission to carry out 'home schooling' or 'community schooling'.

In each State and Territory formal links between government schools and parents and the wider community have existed for many years, through Parents' and Citizens' Associations or their equivalent who mainly raise funds and carry out volunteer maintenance work with the schools rather than becoming involved in more formal school activities. Parents' Associations have been able to contribute to the wider educational debate about such formal activities through their elected representatives on various education committees.

Since the publication of a Schools' Commission Report in the early 1970s which emphasised the need for closer co-operation and collaboration to occur between schools and homes in the running of schools, the perceived and actual roles of parents in school decision-making have changed markedly, particularly in the last ten years. The official rhetoric as well as the formal mechanisms laid down for the administration of government schools now make it mandatory that, through School Councils, parents are to be given a significant formal role in a wide range of each school's activities. This is discussed more fully towards the end of this chapter.

Education systems: policies, curricula and training issues

Educational policy and accountability systems

Since the formation of the Australian federation in 1901, constitutional responsibility for school education has belonged to the separate States and Territories. However, the federal government still plays a significant role in funding the education of the indigenous people and migrants, as well as multicultural education, Asian studies and women's studies. In addition, the federal government promotes national consistency and coherence in the provision of education across Australia.

Each of the eight State/Territory governments is responsible for determining acceptable teacher qualifications, recruiting and appointing teachers in government schools and supplying buildings, equipment, and materials (McKenzie 1994: 419), as well as for establishing and paying teachers' salaries, setting school curricula and so on.

Changes of government at the national level and particularly at the State/Territory level can lead to quite significant changes in policies and in the subsequent work of schools and teachers. The education ideologies of the major political parties differ in some respects in that the Labour party is more likely 'to emphasise equitable access, the need for compensatory programs, and the importance of teacher and parent involvement in decision-making. The Liberal and National parties tend to place more weight on the need to maintain academic standards, parental choice of school, and vocationally relevant curricula' (McKenzie 1994: 416).

In sum, educational policy-making consists of the Australian federal government determining and funding broad policies dealing with 'the national interest' from time to time, but policies relating specifically to schooling are determined by the State/Territory governments and administered through the respective Ministers for Education, who issue guidelines for schools to follow. Within these Ministerial guidelines, the implementation of some policies may require negotiations to take place between schools and their local communities through School Councils. Formal lines of accountability mean that teachers in government schools are responsible, in an administrative sense, to their principal (not to their School Council) and, in a legal sense, to their Minister for Education who, in turn, is responsible to the ruling government.

The nature of curriculum

Australia does not have a national curriculum for its schools, although it came very close to doing so in 1993 following several years of negotiation. Some of the reasons put forward in the literature to explain the rejection by States and Territories of the national curriculum include:

- the States/Territories perceived this federal initiative as being excessively centralist and thereby impinging on 'States' rights' (during the debate fears had been expressed about national government control of educational outcomes and about nationwide testing of primary school children);
- the States/Territories resented the way in which the federal government had seized the agenda of the Australian Education Council from the mid-1980s onwards and had used it to pursue federal political and economic imperatives;
- the political landscape in a number of States changed dramatically in the 1992–1993 period, with more Liberal/National parties coming to power while the Labour party continued to hold power in the federal government.

In 1991 agreement was reached on eight 'national learning areas' as well as on certain other aspects of schooling (see Marsh 1994: 20–21) as follows:

- English;
- science;
- mathematics;
- languages other than English;
- technology;
- studies of society and the environment;
- the arts;
- health and physical education.

Special areas

- English as a second language (ESL) band scales;
- special education.

Cross-curricular areas

- The environment;
- information technology;
- personal and interpersonal skills;
- vareer and work education;
- literacy;
- numeracy.

Groups with special needs

- Girls;
- aboriginal and Torres Strait Islanders;
- the geographically isolated;
- children in poverty;
- those who leave school early.

These 'national statements' provided a framework for curriculum development by specifying a national position for each of the eight areas of learning. Each statement contained a 'profile' indicating 'outcomes' across eight levels of proficiency that students should seek to achieve over their twelve to thirteen years of schooling. Interwoven through the profiles were

> a number of cross-curricula perspectives as well as principles of inclusivity, ensuring that the profiles [used] gender-inclusive language and that the knowledge, skills and understanding identified [were] inclusive of the knowledge, experience and interests of women and of Aboriginal and Torres Strait Islander people.
> (Australian Bureau of Statistics 1996: 274–275)

As far as current curriculum implementation practices are concerned, Kennedy *et al.* (1995) assert that:

- the national curriculum statements and profiles have now become resources which are being used to meet local needs and conditions;
- all eight systems now seem to be committed to outcome-based reporting, which they claim represents 'a significant change in philosophy at the State level';
- there is now widespread use of the eight key learning areas as the basic units of the school curriculum.

Within the primary school curriculum, Science and Technology tend to be combined to form one curriculum area and, as yet, not many primary schools are teaching the area of 'languages other than English'.

Marsh (1994: 14–15) argues that a focus in the new curriculum documents on pupil outcomes and pupil behaviours rather than on teacher inputs means 'there is less emphasis on what methods a teacher might use, so long as certain, well-defined outcomes are achieved'. The danger here is the one drawn by Galton (1995) in relation to the UK post-NC scene, in that an overemphasis on student outcomes may result in classroom pedagogy not being given the full attention and consideration which it deserves in the consciousness of teachers and principals, education bureaucrats, politicians and the wider community.

The purpose of primary education

National curriculum negotiations did bring about certain achievements, for example, ten 'national goals' for schooling which include the following turns:

- to provide an excellent education for all young people, one which develops their talents and capacities to full potential and is relevant to the social, cultural and economic needs of the nation;
- to enable all students to achieve high standards of learning and to develop self-confidence, optimism, high self-esteem, respect for others, and achievement of personal excellence;
- to respond to the current and emerging economic and social needs of the nation, and to provide those skills which will allow students maximum flexibility and adaptability in their future employment and other aspects of life;
- to provide a foundation for further education and training, in terms of knowledge and skills, respect for learning and positive attitudes for life-long education;
- to provide students with an understanding and respect for our cultural heritage including the particular cultural background of Aboriginal and ethnic groups.

The federal government subsequently sponsored a number of initiatives involving business, unions and government closely examining and advising on vocational training in post-compulsory studies in schools and colleges. These have resulted in a policy drift which has occurred not only from non-compulsory education down to compulsory secondary education but also from compulsory secondary education down to primary education, thereby representing, in a sense, a double 'top-downness' influence on the development of the current primary curriculum.

However, the competences developed were surprisingly generic and applicable to all levels of schooling and education. For example, the seven broad Key Competencies for effective participation in work identified in the Mayer Committee's Report (Mayer 1992) specified each individual's ability to:

1   collect, analyse and organise information;
2   communicate ideas and information;
3   plan and organise one's own activities;
4   work effectively with others and in teams;
5   use mathematical ideas and techniques;
6   solve problems;
7   use technology.

These broad competences were likely to secure hearty endorsement from primary and secondary teachers alike. Sedunary (1996: 371) argues strongly that the 'new vocationalism', as expressed through the Key Competences and associated documents, is actually in sympathy with, rather than antipathetic towards, many of the principles usually associated with 'progressive' or 'radical' education (for example, an emphasis on 'enquiry and performance rather than passive acquisition and regurgitation of knowledge'). Such an interpretation of the new curriculum differs markedly from alternative constructions which have tended to equate the emerging vocationalism in education with narrow-minded instrumentalism.

Evaluating the effectiveness of primary education

Up until the mid-1970s the effectiveness of government schools and teachers was measured by State/Territory Department of Education inspectors. However, since then there has been considerable devolution of responsibility to regional education offices and schools. Most government schools are now required to undergo review and evaluation every few years, with the focus of such evaluation tending to be on school improvement and accountability to the local community (see Townsend 1996).

Young teachers in government schools are usually required to serve a probationary period of one or two years before they may become eligible for permanent employment. Experienced teachers are required to undergo formal appraisal on a regular basis although there are variations across jurisdictions in the level of involvement of Departmental officers, principals and peers (McKenzie 1994). Merit, rather than seniority, is now a major criterion in promotion decisions.

Since the late 1980s there has also been an increasing focus on pupil assessment and the development of education indicators, with governments tending to shift their attention away from monitoring resource inputs to monitoring pupil outcomes. For example, a number of States use standardised pencil-and-paper tests to assess the achievement of pupils in the areas of basic literacy and numeracy. However, while some (such as the current Federal Minister for Schools) have argued that such tests should be employed as key measures of an 'effective' school and that test results for all schools should be publicly available, the tests have not achieved the prominence that their proponents would desire (Townsend 1996: 118). So far, test results for individual schools have remained the confidential property of the separate Departments of Education and the schools themselves.

In recent years, aspects of school effectiveness have been investigated in a considerable number of federally-funded and State-funded studies (Townsend 1996: 119). One of these, the Effective Schools Project (McGaw *et al.* 1992: 174), representing almost 30 per cent of the total population of schools, investigated two particular perceptions held by these school communities about: (1) that which is regarded as important in schooling and (2) how accountability should be measured, and found that:

- school effectiveness is about more than maximising academic achievement. Learning, and the love of learning; personal development and self-esteem; life skills, problem-solving and learning how to learn and the development of independent thinkers and well-rounded, confident individuals all rank highly as measures of success in the outcomes of effective schooling;
- accountability is a local issue, a matter of direct negotiation between schools and their communities. There is remarkably little interest in large-scale testing programmes, national profiles and other mechanisms designed to externalise the accountability of schools.

Teacher education

Teacher education courses at primary level prepare students for the teaching of children aged 5/6 years to 12/13 years of age, with a number also preparing those who will teach 3- to 8-year olds. Initial early childhood/primary teacher education consists of a three-year or four-year undergraduate university degree. Most of the thirty-eight universities provide pre-service primary teacher education courses. In 1995, there were 4,881 ITE courses for early childhood teachers and 13,452 training for primary.

The curriculum for preparing primary teachers typically consists of four clusters of subjects, as follows:

1. some background subjects in liberal arts, scientific studies and creative arts, in order to develop further the students' general education;
2. subjects dealing with content and specific pedagogy associated with each curriculum area taught in the primary school;
3. subjects dealing with the theory and practice of education (such as

educational psychology, sociology of education, comparative education, history of education, philosophy of education, special education);

4   subjects dealing with general classroom pedagogy linked in with students' practice teaching in schools.

Students usually complete school practice sessions once or twice a year. Lecturers in teacher education are commonly involved in the supervision of teaching practice, working in partnership with supervising teachers in the schools.

Development of teachers through inservice training and professional development programmes has now been largely devolved to the schools, and funding levels are generally low. The provision within all of the State of Victoria's primary and secondary schools with access to an educational satellite learning network enabled Allard *et al.* (1995) to use innovative technology to deliver a range of interactive professional development programmes to widely dispersed teachers.

Both pre-service and inservice teacher education seem to be lacking in preparing teachers for an increasingly multicultural society, especially one which will include an increasing proportion of people with Asian backgrounds. This is of some concern because:

> Current Federal and State government policy is seeking to locate Australia economically, politically and socially within Asia, with some of the strategic initiatives being centred on education including the teaching and learning of Asian languages, cross-curricular Studies of Asia, and related resource development.
>
> (Halse and Baumgart 1995: 1)

Fox and Iredale (1994) found that few pre-service teacher education courses at universities offer more than an elective in English as a second language, let alone offering courses specifically dealing with multicultural strategies, anti-racism, intercultural communication or ethnic studies.

Australian schools and classrooms: practices/processes

The influence of school management on classroom practices

The management of government schools has undergone profound change over the last ten years. Principals now have greater power over staffing, recruitment, promotion and job allocation as well as budgets. However, principals and schools are still subjected to strong accountability mechanisms which provide feedback from the periphery to the centre (Blackmore

1995; Sachs *et al.* 1994). Many changes have occurred recently in the operation of government schools which include:

- moves to school-based curriculum and professional development;
- implementation of social justice and curriculum inclusivity initiatives;
- reduction of centrally provided services;
- revision of promotional procedures;
- introduction of requirements for quality assurance.

Perhaps the greatest impact of change on the management of Australian government schools is the recent introduction of School Development Planning (SDP). Sachs *et al.* (1994: 2) write that the initial step in the process requires the school community's involvement in 'reviewing its present thinking and practices about curriculum, pedagogy, assessment evaluation, organisation, structures, administration, budget, staff and parent development, and relations with its community and employing authority'.

Needless to say, the nature, extent and sheer number of these changes has brought about a 'diversification' of the teacher's roles and responsibilities, with many teachers feeling 'de-skilled and devalued' as a result (Blackmore 1995). However, the extent to which all of these changes have exerted any influence on the actual classroom practices of teachers remains unknown at present. This area has been inadequately researched to date.

One indication that teachers' classroom behaviour might not have undergone much change is implied within the findings of several studies (e.g. Scott 1994; Brady 1995; Aspland *et al.* 1995) all of which indicate that the classroom practice of Australian teachers seems to be largely unobserved and unmonitored by supervisors. Perhaps then, in reality, teachers' actual classroom teaching behaviour may not have been be required to change much at all in response to new curriculum initiatives.

Curriculum perceptions of educationalists

The new curriculum in schools has not escaped criticism by some academics. One recent debate among educationalists has centred on the educational desirability of locating an outcome-based approach (inherent in the competencies in the curriculum documents) within an Australian education *milieu* which favours constructivist approaches to learning and teaching. In his summary of the strengths and weaknesses of the outcome-based approach, Brady (1996: 10) asserts that 'In Australia the traditional positivist behaviourist approach is not strong in general schooling, though it has always had its adherents in special education' and that 'the constructivist view by which learners are perceived as independent makers of knowledge arguably has a stronger hold'.

It is interesting that a number of the competences for beginning teachers compiled recently as part of the National Project on the Quality of Teaching and Learning (summarised in Preston and Kennedy 1994: 23) are constructivist in their orientation (e.g. 'recognising and responding to individual differences amongst students'; 'fostering independent and co-operative learning'; and 'engaging students actively in developing knowledge'). Constructivist orientations also feature in the NSW Department of School Education document *Desirable Attributes of Beginning Teachers* (Boston 1993) where one competence related to 'The practice of teaching' specifies:

> All beginning teachers should be able to demonstrate that they . . . [3.6] Are able to improve learning outcomes for all students by implementing an increasingly wide range of teaching approaches and strategies that provide alternatives to transmission teaching, and reflect contemporary mainstream theory and practice. The following are examples of practice and do not constitute a definitive list . . .
>
> - varying patterns of classroom interaction
> - collaborative and co-operative learning
> - differentiated curriculum materials
> - drama method (enactments, role plays, simulation gaming)
> - negotiated learning and peer assessment
> - teaching practices that cater for different learning styles
> - techniques of integration to bring areas of the curriculum together
> - activity based methods, including play.
>
> (Boston 1993)

The outcome-based approach is not, however, without its adherents. For example, in late 1995 the New South Wales Board of Studies held a forum in which two of the three presentations were from academics with backgrounds in special education programmes in universities. Both of these extolled the virtues of outcome-based approaches to learning and warned of certain dangers associated with constructivist approaches to teaching/learning (Hotchkis 1995; Westwood 1995).

It is likely that discussion of this particular issue will figure prominently over the next few years, as has been the case in the UK. Sedunary (1996: 389) proposes that the various competences and the 'progressive' elements in the academic curriculum should not be viewed as antithetical but rather should be seen as complementary because together they help cultivate an 'instrumental intellect' which, she argues, is eminently suitable for survival and growth in the current economic and social climate.

Curriculum implementation in primary schools

Within certain guidelines, government primary schools are individually responsible for determining the ways in which they implement the curriculum. Usually 'curriculum committees' interpret departmental guidelines and then individual teachers translate the schools' interpretations into classroom practice. This relative autonomy seems not to have produced a wide diversity of approaches – as McKenzie (1994: 421) has observed, 'the curriculum differences between schools in any system . . . would be relatively minor'. This observation is probably also true of differences in primary schools across State/Territory systems.

A detailed case study carried out by Scott (1994) of the extent to which sixteen teachers in one NSW primary school were implementing the mandatory *Mathematics K-6* key learning area document revealed a wide variety of curriculum implementation levels and associated classroom practices within that school. For example, 'well-above-average implementers' had classrooms with a completely language-based, problem-solving focus where children investigate mathematical questions with real-life applications, often generated by themselves, in small groups. Learning is largely negotiated and children have free access to any resources. Mathematics lessons are not independent of other key learning areas and the dominance of mathematics within any one lesson will vary from group to group and day to day. Assessment is done on an ongoing basis and children frequently assess themselves and their peers.

In contrast 'below-average implementers' were found to show spasmodic evidence of some of the more complex teaching practices. They worked from largely whole-class instruction and the semi-irregular use of concrete materials. Investigation was almost non-existent although some attempts to integrate mathematics with other key learning areas were evident. Number dominated. These teachers largely teach from texts or workbooks with the use of very few concrete materials. What is also clear is that these teachers seemed to have been free to choose what and how they taught in their classrooms.

Through detailed case studies, Brady (1995) researched the ways in which the new State Profiles in English were being used by eight teachers in four NSW primary schools and reported that outcomes were:

- generally well understood by these teachers;
- helping teachers to focus their assessment and reporting of pupils' progress;
- perceived as facilitating planning and programming;
- perceived as empowering the pupils by allowing them to set their own targets.

Brady's description of the approaches to assessment and reporting adopted by these teachers contains frequent references to the collection and analysis of samples of pupils' work which were supplemented by the use of check-lists based on the new State Profiles. However, teacher support for the new approach was not entirely unequivocal. During interviews, one teacher expressed the reservation that 'an approach that is purely driven by out-comes is so structured that it may constrain creativity in teaching/learning activities' and another teacher cautioned that 'outcome-based education could be mechanistic in its insistence on the demonstration of behaviour'.

The adoption of 'local' versions of national curriculum frameworks might also be regarded as a kind of 'hybridisation' occurring at the macro-level (Galton 1995: 19–21). When these various elements are combined with other factors, such as (a) the apparent freedom of teachers to choose to be 'non-implementers' (Scott 1994); (b) principals seeming to give teachers a large degree of freedom in their day-to-day teaching (Cresswell and Fisher 1995); and (c) the current absence of national or regional testing of the specific curriculum competences contained in the Profile Statements, a strong impression is gained that the implementation of the primary curriculum will continue to be characterised by 'hybridisa-tion'. Of course whether or not this is desirable is an entirely different issue.

Models of teaching and learning in the 'typical' classroom

In a 'typical' Australian primary class the teacher would probably teach all six curriculum areas. Except in handwriting lessons, whole-class instruc-tion would be relatively rare. Direct instruction would be more likely to occur in some mathematics and some English lessons but this would probably take place with the class formed into three or four groups, based on the teacher's estimates of the children's ability. Teacher-prepared work-sheets would tend to be employed in these lessons, particularly with the more academically able children, thus enabling the teacher to work directly with the less able pupils. Textbooks or other commercial resources would tend not to be used in the classroom (Watt 1994; Reynolds and Lewis 1995).

In science and in human society lessons, and in some English and mathematics lessons, mixed-ability groups would be likely to be used where the teaching strategies would emphasise group work, cooperative learning, problem-solving and pupil research (Killen 1996). Worksheets would tend to be used here to record pupils' work. There would probably be at least one computer in the classroom and this would be used most often for individual or small group work. Lessons in discrete curriculum areas would be supplemented by lessons which adopted an 'integrated' approach in which knowledge and skills from within a number of curriculum areas would be called upon during class activities.

Children with 'special needs' might be withdrawn from this 'typical' class from time to time to attend special classes. This would particularly be the case if the school had large numbers of non-English speaking background (NESB) children where English as a second language (ESL) programmes would be taken by specialist teachers. If this 'typical' classroom did include a number of NESB children, the teacher's approach might exhibit certain deficiencies. For example, Vialle (1994) found that NESB children were being positioned as non-achievers through the following teacher attitudes and behaviour:

- teachers equated usage of standard English with level of intelligence;
- ESL sessions typically provided children with an impoverished linguistic environment rather than an enriched one;
- children from particular ethnic groups were treated homogeneously rather than as individuals;
- compliance was highly regarded in NESB children.

Some special withdrawal classes might also be held in a school for children with learning difficulties but it is unlikely that there would be special classes or programmes for talented and gifted children. There might be an intellectually and/or physically disabled child with a teacher's aide and this child would be included in as many different classroom activities as possible. (Since the early 1980s there has been an increasing emphasis on integrating disabled pupils into mainstream schools and classes.)

If such a 'typical' class was situated in a school located in a difficult-to-staff area, its teacher would be likely to be young and inexperienced. Watson and Hatton (1995) report that difficult-to-staff areas are likely to be found where there are distinct sub-populations such as recent immigrants, indigenous people, the poor, or isolated rural dwellers. Watson and Hatton argue that children in these less favoured areas tend to be taught by the least experienced teachers who stay for the minimum time. High teacher turnover in such areas also means that a disproportionate number of beginning teachers are being asked to teach some of the most demanding pupils (Watson and Hatton 1995).

Curriculum evaluation and assessment

Assessment of pupils' learning consists of a combination of formative and summative procedures. Teachers maintain ongoing records of children's progress in academic and social components and summative reports are usually issued to parents on at least two occasions during the year. The formal report cards for primary children normally contain two sections –

one section reports on academic performance (with each area usually being scored in relation to one of three or four 'bands' rather than in terms of a percentage or a numerical mark) and the other section describes the pupil's 'application' or 'effort' in each area (also usually scored in 'bands').

Within these reports, curriculum areas such as mathematics and English are usually broken down into a certain number of components (some of which are now starting to reflect the terminology used in the new curriculum frameworks, such as 'Space', 'Measurement' and 'Number' and 'Talking and listening', 'Reading' and 'Writing'). Other curriculum areas tend not to use separate components for formal-reporting purposes. The report cards are also likely to contain a section which describes the development of the child's social skills, such as 'co-operation with other children', 'willingness to participate in class and school activities', 'initiative' and so on, described in terms of 'bands' and/or by open-ended comments. There is a growing trend for primary teachers (particularly those in lower year groups) to prefer parents/carers to visit the school and discuss the child's progress in relation to specific 'outcomes' and to see samples of the child's work, rather than relying on report cards to communicate more general information.

Some States/Territories use basic skills tests which are relatively generic in focus and are not tests of the extent to which specific competences contained in profile statements are met. The results are usually sent to parents, as well as to the school and the individual Departments of Education and consist of a summary in terms of broad performance 'bands' which indicate where the student is located within the State-wide group serving comparative purposes. Some test results also provide an item-by-item analysis of correct and incorrect responses by individual pupils and the State results on each item.

At the school level, evaluation of the curriculum and learning is usually undertaken by a quality review procedure which gathers its information through structured interviews with a cross-section of pupils, teaching and non-teaching school staff, and the parent community. The team also observes throughout the school and analyses documents, such as school plans, budgets and reports. The Quality Review process is not simply a matter of the school doing its own evaluation of its key areas and preparing its own documentation. For example, in a fifty-two–page document containing 'School review guidelines', principals are given a four-page checklist of tasks to complete prior to, during and after the review (Hatton 1994).

Following the review, a written report for public consumption is sent to the school by the QA team summarising the school's perceived strengths and weaknesses and suggesting strategies for improvement and development. Hatton (1994) is quite critical of some aspects of this review process because, she argues, many of the features are much easier to realise in middle-class urban contexts than in predominantly working-class areas or in some rural locations.

The roles of support staff and community members

Teachers in government schools are commonly required to interrelate with parents and community members within the formal workings of School Councils and teacher–parent Committees. It must be said that if the findings from some recent research studies of these emerging formalised and intricate teacher–parent relationships (Sachs et al. 1994: 1) are representative of the wider scene, then the collaborative ideals espoused in departmental documents and pursued by advocates of participatory decision-making in schools remain some way from being successfully realised in practice.

Although School Councils were established to facilitate democratic decision-making, it seems that in many schools the Councils are not always fully representative of the parent body. For example, parents who are migrants (especially from non-English-speaking backgrounds) or are low income earners, or are unskilled, or are unemployed tend not to be on School Councils (Pettit 1984).

Some schools have experienced difficulty in getting parents from any sector of the parent population to participate in Council or parent committees, even after extraordinary efforts have been made to involve them (McKibbin 1995). In some schools the opposite occurs – Roe (1994) reports that not one member of the teaching staff in the school he studied considered that a School Council would improve the educational work of the school, while parents were much more optimistic.

McKibbin and Cooper (1995) similarly report that the differing roles and statuses of the parent, the teacher and the principal are significant factors in hindering parents' success in participation in schools. Howard (1994) describes the parents' involvement which she observed as 'tokenistic pseudo-participation' because no opportunities were provided by the school for parents to exercise initiative and yet teachers seemed to be quite happy with the level of parental input. McKibbin's (1995) research found that parents reported a lack of confidence to speak in formal school settings; that there appeared to be greater recognition in the school for the more 'traditional' parent role; and that decision-making was made difficult for parents because of their lack of prior knowledge of school procedures.

Soliman (1994) notes that some teachers tend to exhibit 'boundary-maintenance' in their dealings with parents, an attitude which is well illustrated in the following statement:

> I would be very concerned if they [parents] became involved in selection of specific aspects of the curriculum . . . . I think it

would be most unfortunate if people came to tell me, for example, how after twenty years of teaching that I should use a particular technique in my classroom.

(Soliman 1994: 13)

However, teachers' 'boundary-maintenance' attitudes and behaviours are sometimes supported by parents who also see no need for parents to be advising teachers on what to do, as Soliman (1994: 13) goes on to illustrate: 'What are teachers doing long difficult courses to become teachers for if they're not professionally really capable of knowing what to teach and how to teach it?'

Hatton (1994) asks 'What is the school community?' and proceeds to argue that the concept of 'community' on which many of the recent school reforms rest implies a 'commonality of interests' and a 'unity of purpose' as well as an absence of inequalities based on class, gender and ethnicity which simply do not square with the realities of Australia's social structure. The assumption of power being equally distributed and of all school communities being able to come together to articulate uniform and coherent views is, in Hatton's view, a flawed utopian view of community which is not sustained by the data.

In predicting 'Major problems for the year 2000' in relation to Australia's education system, McKenzie (1994: 422) writes: 'Finding an appropriate balance between central political responsibility for education and the encouragement of local school initiatives is still likely to be problematic'.

Conclusion

As these contextual factors illustrate, the provision of schooling for an increasingly multicultural population located largely within cities and for a somewhat less culturally diverse rural population located at considerable distances from city centres and from each other, all under the umbrella of eight separate State/Territory jurisdictions and a federal government, is a complex operation and one which continues to present Australia with a number of challenges.

References

Allard, A., Dick, B., McKernan and H. Ryan, J. (1995) 'Lessons on the satellite: what teachers say about professional development via the interactive satellite learning network'. Paper presented at the Annual Conference of the Australian Association for Research in Education. Hobart, 26–30 November.**

Aspland, T., Elliott, B. and Macpherson, I. (1995) 'Using an NPDP experience to propose a changing conception of professional development'. Paper presented at the Annual Conference of the Australian Association for Research in Education. Hobart, 26–30 November.**

Australian Bureau of Statistics *Year Book Australia 1996.* (1996) Canberra: Australian Government Publishing Service.

Australian Education Council. (1989) *Common and Agreed National Goals (Hobart Declaration).* Canberra: Australian Government Publishing Service.

Beckett, L., Bode, M. and Crewe, K. (1995) 'Sex and gender: what parents want'. Paper presented at the Annual Conference of the Australian Association for Research in Education. Hobart, 26–30 November.**

Blackmore, J. (1995) 'Where's the level playing field? A feminist perspective on educational restructuring'. Paper presented at the Annual Conference of the Australian Association for Research in Education. Hobart, 26–30 November.**

Blackmore, J., Kenway, J., Willis, S. and Rennie, L. (1996) 'Feminist dilemmas: an Australian case study of a whole-school policy to gender reform'. *Journal of Curriculum Studies* 28(3), 253–279.

Bordieu, P. (1977) *Reproduction in Education, Society and Culture.* London: Sage.

Boss, P., Edwards, S. and Pitman, S. (1995) *Profile of Young Australians: Facts, Figures and Issues.* Melbourne: Churchill Livingstone.

Boston, K. (1993) (Chair) *Desirable Attributes of Beginning Teachers.* Report of the Ministerial Advisory Council on Teacher Education and Quality of Teaching. Sydney: NSW Department of School Education.

Brady, L. (1995) 'A case study of implementing curriculum outcomes'. Paper presented at the Annual Conference of the Australian Association for Research in Education. Hobart, 26–30 November.**

Brady, L. (1996) 'Outcome-based education: a critique'. *The Curriculum Journal* 7(1), 5–16.

Connell, R.W., Ashenden, D., Kessler, S. and Dowsett, G. (1982) *Making the Difference.* Sydney: Allen & Unwin.

Connell, R.W., White, V.M. and Johnson, K.M. (1991) *The Disadvantaged Schools Program in Australia: 'Running Twice as Hard'.* Deakin: Deakin University Press.

Cresswell, J. and Fisher, D. (1995) 'Assessing principals' interpersonal behaviour'. Paper presented at the Annual Conference of the Australian Association for Research in Education. Hobart, 26–30 November.**

Ellerton, N.F. and Clements, M.A. (1994) *The National Curriculum Debacle.* Perth: Meridian Press.

Foster, L. and Harman, K. (1992) *Australian Education: A Sociological Perspective* (3rd edn). Sydney: Prentice-Hall.

Fox, C. and Iredale, R. (1994) 'Immigration and education: issues of equity'. Paper presented at the Annual Conference of the Australian Association for Research in Education. Newcastle, 27 November–1 December.*

Galton, M. (1995) *Crisis in the Primary Classroom.* London: David Fulton.

Halse, C. and Baumgart, N. (1995) 'Do teachers regard Australia as part of Asia? An educational and political dilemma'. Paper presented at the Annual Conference of the Australian Association for Research in Education. Hobart, 26–30 November.**

Hatton, E. (1994) 'Corporate managerialism in a rural setting: a contextualised case study'. Paper presented at the Annual Conference of the Australian Association for Research in Education. Newcastle, 27 November–1 December.*

Hatton, E., Munns, G. and Dent, J.N. (1994) 'Dealing with diversity: three Australian primary school responses'. Paper presented at the Annual Conference of the Australian Association for Research in Education. Newcastle, 27 November – 1 December.*

Hotchkis, G.D. (1995) 'The nature of the learner versus the nature of instruction'. Paper presented at a forum conducted by the NSW Board of Studies. Sydney, 26 October.***

Howard, S. (1994) 'Parent involvement in the introduction of human relationships education in Queensland state primary schools'. Paper presented at the Annual Conference of the Australian Association for Research in Education. Newcastle, 27 November–1 December.*

Kennedy, K.J., Marland, P. and Sturman, A. (1995) 'Implementing national curriculum statements and profiles: corporate federalism in retreat'. Paper presented at the Annual Conference of the Australian Association for Research in Education. Hobart, 26–30 November.**

Killen, R. (1996) *Effective Teaching Strategies: Lessons from Research and Practice*. Wentworth Falls: Social Science Press.

Long, P. (1995) 'The education of intellectually gifted students in Australia: past, present and future'. Paper presented at the Annual Conference of the Australian Association for Research in Education. Hobart, 26–30 November.**

McGaw, B., Banks, D., Piper, K. and Evans, B. (1992) *Making Schools More Effective*. Hawthorn: Australian Council for Educational Research.

McKenzie, P. (1994) 'Australia: system of education'. In T. Husen and T.N. Postlethwaite (eds) *The International Encyclopedia of Education*. London: Pergamon.

McKibbin, C. (1995) 'Can everyone have their say?'. Paper presented at the Annual Conference of the Australian Association for Research in Education, Hobart, Nov. 26–30.**

McKibbin, C. and Cooper, T.J. (1995). 'Decentralisation, change reactions and community commitment'. Paper presented at the Annual Conference of the Australian Association for Research in Education. Hobart, 26–30 November.**

Marsh, C. (1994) *Producing a National Curriculum: Plans and Paranoia*. Sydney: Allen & Unwin.

Mayer, E. (1992) (Chair) *Employment-related Key Competencies*. Report commissioned by the Australian Education Council. Canberra: Australian Government Publishing Service.

Pettit, D. (1984) 'Governing in equal partnership'. *Education News* 18(8), 38–41.

Preston, B. and Kennedy, K. (1994) 'Models of professional standards for beginning practitioners and their applicability to initial professional education'. Paper presented at the Annual Conference of the Australian Association for Research in Education. Newcastle, 27 November–1 December.*

Regan, L.J. (1992) *An Evaluation of the 'Getting Girls into Technology' Project*. Lismore: NSW Department of School Education (North Coast Region) and NSW Department of Health (North Coast Region).

Reynolds, R. and Lewis, R. (1995) 'The teaching of human society and its environment in primary schools in the Hunter Region of NSW'. Paper presented at the Annual Conference of the Australian Association for Research in Education. Hobart, 26–30 November.**

Roe, J.W. (1994) 'Pragmatic policy development in the establishment of the

School Council at Fairvale Primary School'. Paper presented at the Annual Conference of the Australian Association for Research in Education. Newcastle, 27 November–1 December.*

Sachs, J., Logan, L., and Dempster, N. (1994) 'Changing times, changing conditions: the work of primary teachers'. Paper presented at the Annual Conference of the Australian Association for Research in Education. Newcastle, 27 November–1 December.*

Scott, D. (1994) '"Fidelity" mentality is no reality: a message for curriculum developers'. Paper presented at the Annual Conference of the Australian Association for Research in Education. Newcastle, 27 November–1 December.*

Sedunary, E. (1996) '"Neither new nor alien to progressive thinking": interpreting the convergence of radical education and the new vocationalism in Australia'. *Journal of Curriculum Studies* 28(4), 369–396.

Soliman, I. (1994) 'Whither school councils?' Paper presented at the Annual Conference of the Australian Association for Research in Education. University of Newcastle, 27 November–1 December.*

Townsend, T. (1996) 'School effectiveness and improvement initiatives and the restructuring of education in Australia'. *School Effectiveness and School Improvement* 7(2), 114–132.

Vialle, W. (1994) 'Racism in the classroom'. Paper presented at the Annual Conference of the Australian Association for Research in Education. Newcastle, 27 November–1 December.*

Watson, A.J. and Hatton, N.G. (1995) 'Staffing of schools: quality and equality'. Paper presented at the Annual Conference of the Australian Association for Research in Education. Hobart, 26–30 November.**

Watt, M.G. (1994) 'A study of practices used to select curriculum materials in Australia's schools'. Paper presented at the Annual Conference of the Australian Association for Research in Education. Newcastle, 27 November–1 December.*

Weppler, M. (1995). 'Teachers, supervisors, principals: gender interplays'. Paper presented at the Annual Conference of the Australian Association for Research in Education. Hobart, 26–30 November.**

Weppler, M. and Bourke, J. (1994) 'Advanced skills teachers: dilemmas and demands'. Paper presented at the Annual Conference of the Australian Association for Research in Education. Newcastle, 27 November–1 December.*

Westwood, P. (1995) 'Current issues in effective teaching and learning'. Paper presented at a forum conducted by the NSW Board of Studies, Sydney, 26 October.****

Key to Symbols

    *   This paper is available on the Internet at http://www.swin.edu.au/aare/conf94.html.

    **   This paper is available on the Internet at http://www.swin.edu.au/aare/conf95.html.

    ***   This paper is available on the Internet at http://www.opennet.net.au/partners/bos/learner4.html.

    ****   This paper is available on the Internet at http://www.opennet.net.au/partners/bos/learner5.html.

10

PRIMARY SCHOOLING IN HONG KONG

Bob Adamson and Paul Morris

Introduction

The turn of the millennium is seen as a period of major transition for Hong Kong as it adjusts to the return of Chinese sovereignty after a century-and-a-half as a British colony, but, for educational planners and providers in the territory, transition merely represents the status quo. Transience has epitomised life in Hong Kong, especially since the Second World War and the Chinese Civil War, as successive influxes of political and economic migrants from East and West have sought refuge on this once barren rock, many using it as a stepping-stone to greener pastures. More than one Director of Education has compared the task of providing education in the territory to attempting such an undertaking in a mainline railway station (Sweeting 1990, 1993).

Under such circumstances, educational planning and provision have proved difficult and have tended to be reactive, taking the form of crisis management, often in response to local manifestations of economic and political shifts in China. This scenario was reinforced by the very tenuous legitimacy of the colonial government and by the pursuit of a minimalist or *laissez faire* approach to the provision of public services (Sweeting and Morris 1993).

This chapter first provides a description of the education system through a historical sketch of the development of primary schooling in Hong Kong, and of the main features of the present system. Secondly, it analyses the key prevailing issues that are evident in schools and classrooms and the reforms that are designed to address them. Finally, it attempts to locate both the nature of the system and the issues which affect it in a broader social, economic and political context.

The educational system: antecedents, policies and curricula

Historical development

The public provision of primary education for the Chinese sector of the population (i.e. more than 98 per cent) did not appear on the government's agenda until after Britain reclaimed the territory following the Japanese occupation during the Second World War. Government provision of education for the local populace had previously been limited to producing an academic élite who could act as go-betweens in trade and administration (Sweeting 1992). Other demands for schooling had been met by private schools offering a traditional Chinese education. Even when the government did turn its attention to public provision, its actions appeared half-hearted: the post-war expansion of primary, and subsequently secondary, school places was initially a result of private provision by a combination of benevolent and profit-making organisations, who responded rapidly to public demand, and, for the minority sectors of the population, by international schools.

The decline of Britain's imperial strength in the post-war period was a serious blow to Hong Kong, whose livelihood hitherto had been based on its role as a far-flung entrepôt of the Empire and whose only significant natural resource was Victoria Harbour. Meanwhile, a tide of humanity was flooding over the border from China to escape from the ravages of the civil war in the late 1940s; however, instead of proving to be a burden, these refugees provided the life blood for an economic miracle, founded initially upon the production of textiles and plastic goods, which resulted in 'Made in Hong Kong' becoming household words to describe cheap mass-produced goods. Once China's economy started to develop, the port of Hong Kong again provided an entrepôt service, this time for the Communist régime to trade with capitalist counterparts without mutual loss of face.

The government eventually reacted to the public demand for schooling and the concomitant educational needs of the burgeoning workforce, which increasingly comprised young females and child labour in particular, by embarking, in 1954, upon a seven-year expansion programme in primary education. The programme included – supposedly as a temporary measure – the establishment of bi-sessional schools, in which school buildings were used in the morning by one set of staff and pupils, and in the afternoon by another, with class sizes fixed at an average of forty-five (Sweeting 1993). Given the nearly threefold increase in population in the late 1940s and 1950s, the attainment of universal and compulsory primary education by 1971 was a considerable achievement for a government better known for its *laissez faire* policies.

Issues related to quality rather than quantity of educational provision then became the centre of debate. Further social and economic changes occurred in the territory as the People's Republic of China emerged from the anarchy of the Cultural Revolution and pursued a programme of economic modernisation from 1977. Hong Kong weathered the shift of its manufacturing base to mainland China, because the growth of the service and financial sectors filled the vacuum, especially as a result of China trade. The shift fundamentally altered the nature of the workforce required by employers, because a basic education that prepared workers for employment in factories was insufficient for the demands of the sophisticated high technology that now characterises the industrial profile of Hong Kong. At the same time, an affluent middle class emerged, with greater expectations for their children and seeing education as the main conduit to achieve these. There was an increasing awareness, particularly among citizens who had studied and worked overseas, of global educational trends, and of political issues in the wake of the Sino-British Joint Declaration on the future of Hong Kong, signed in 1984, and the crushing of the student movement in Beijing on 4 June 1989. Dissatisfaction at current provision expressed by parents and various pressure groups, along with the desire to be seen to be keeping up with international trends, spurred the Education Department to initiate innovations, such as the introduction of the Activity Approach in 1975. The culmination was a major reform of the primary school curriculum in 1989, in the form of the Target Oriented Curriculum (TOC), an uncharacteristically comprehensive and well-resourced attempt to align the curriculum with the needs of a post-industrial society. These initiatives are analysed later in this chapter.

The emergence of highly politicised pressure groups towards the end of colonial rule increased the profile of educational issues. The government's response included the addition of cross-curricular themes which were designed to promote personal and social values in the school curriculum. Civic education was introduced in 1985 as a response to the demands for increased political awareness, and revised in 1996 to incorporate a greater sensitivity towards Hong Kong's status as a Special Administrative Region after the return to Chinese sovereignty in 1997. Moral education was introduced in 1981, and environmental education appeared in 1992. Essentially, these initiatives were perceived as rhetorical and largely ignored by schools (Fung and Lee 1993) and served, through the use of a discourse which stressed school-based approaches to curriculum development and teacher empowerment, to locate responsibility for their implementation in schools (Morris and Chan 1996).

Contemporary primary education

In this section we describe the key features of primary schooling in Hong Kong, with reference to the following dimensions: provision, curriculum, schools and a typical school day.

Provision

Hong Kong has 900 primary schools, with a student population of 467,000 and a teaching force numbering 18,000. The Education Department (ED) relies heavily on charitable private organisations to run independent or aided schools as a complement to its own schools (which represent less than 10 per cent of the total). Curriculum policies are formulated by a variety of advisory bodies which includes: the Education Commission, a panel of educationalists, politicians and government officials concerned with macro policies; the Board of Education, which advises the government at the school level; and subject specialists within the Curriculum Development Council (CDC). All these bodies incorporate a large representation of non-government members, but their freedom of independent action is somewhat curtailed, as the government maintains control of the agenda and membership selection (Morris 1996a). The government, through the ED, also sets the Hong Kong Attainment Tests (HKATs) at Primary 6 Level, which help to determine the secondary school each child will enter. Likewise, school syllabuses are developed by the Curriculum Development Institute (CDI), which is part of the ED, in accordance with the aims and objectives set out by the CDC; the CDI also vets textbooks produced by commercial publishers, and the ED's Advisory Inspectorate monitors the work of schools.

Curriculum

As with other aspects of educational policy-making, curriculum development is centralised and bureaucratic, with some traces of independent input (Morris 1996b), especially when crises arise or when there is intra-government conflict. The influence of various interest groups upon curriculum decisions at different levels is shown in Table 10.1

Although the West has been perceived as the source of solutions to particular problems, Hong Kong's curriculum has also been heavily influenced by its proximity and relationship with China, upon whom the territory relies heavily for its economic survival, not to mention cheap water, electricity and foodstuffs. During periods of hyper-politicisation in the mainland, the ED sought to bar any form of Communist (or Nationalist) propaganda from schools, as this was seen as potentially subversive. In contrast, during periods of close co-operation, efforts have been made to

Table 10.1 Curriculum decisions and sources of influence

	ED, CDC and CDI	Textbook publishers	Schools	Teachers	Parents
Aims and objectives	Strong influence. Decided by CDC	No influence	Weak influence, but schools can decide on adoption	No influence except as members of CDC	No influence
Content	Strong influence. CDC specifies content; developed by CDI	Some influence: determine depth of coverage	Weak influence, but schools can decide on adoption	Weak influence, but select content to emphasise and can overteach	No influence
Teaching method	Weak influence: just advise and recommend	Some influence: strong if teachers follow textbooks closely	Some influence, especially if supportive of staff development	Strong influence	No influence or weak influence
Assessment	HKAT controlled by ED; strong influence on schools' internal assessments	Some influence: internal assessments are often based on textbook content	Some influence on internal assessments but tend to mirror HKAT	Some influence on internal assessment	No influence except on the language of assessment
Language of instruction	Limited influence. Use of Chinese encouraged but not required	Some influence. Most primary textbooks are in Chinese	Strong influence. Schools decide official language policy	Strong influence: choose language to use in classroom	Strong influence: can choose school on basis of language policy

Source: Adapted from Morris 1996b.

depoliticise the curriculum, for fear of offending China. The latter tendency became more pronounced with the advent of the change of sovereignty. Since the signing of the Joint Declaration in 1984, which settled the return of Hong Kong to China, the content of school subjects has become less remote and Anglo-centric, and more relevant to the local context.

Parents have little influence upon the primary curriculum, other than as a group whose offspring schools seek to attract – although this factor has become more critical as a result of the decline in the school-age population and the related problem of under-enrolments and school closures. The importance of English for future tertiary study and emigration entices some parents to place their children in private English-medium primary schools to allow immersion from an early age, a practice which is not officially encouraged by the ED, whose one such school is specifically for ethnic minority groups. Schools which succeed in helping pupils to enter higher-band secondary schools (i.e. for the academically more able) also attract more attention from ambitious parents. One result of this striving for success is the importance that schools and parents attach to indicators of academic achievement, such as report cards, test scores and homework, as these serve to define and distinguish school quality for parents.

Pupils begin primary school, which is of six years' duration, at age 6 but the large majority will have already received three years of kindergarten education, which is provided by a variety of private businesses, charities and community organisations. At the end of primary schooling, examinations are conducted to stream children into five bands for placement in secondary schools. As a result, primary schooling is often perceived as a transition stage between kindergarten and secondary education, a perception reflected in official statement of aims for primary schooling issued by the ED:

> The general aims of the primary curriculum share, to some extent, the enabling and preparatory nature of the aims of the kindergarten curriculum. The primary curriculum mediates between kindergarten and secondary curricula. On the one hand, it encompasses and reinforces the same areas of development as in the kindergarten curriculum – intellectual, communicative, social and moral, personal and physical, and aesthetic. On the other hand, it enlarges the achievements of kindergarten tasks and furnishes children with the knowledge, skills and attitudes, in rudimentary form, required for approaching the tasks of the secondary curriculum satisfactorily. In particular, the primary curriculum should aim at enabling children to achieve their optimum levels of attainment against the targets to be set from time to time in specified curriculum areas.
>
> (CDC 1993: 8–9)

Parents similarly tend to see this stage as merely a forerunner to secondary and, hopefully, tertiary education. As Bond (1991) points out, this view may be related to the fact that, in imperial China, education and success in the civil service examinations represented the means to social advancement, and, as a result, 'parents exert massive pressure on their children to do well in school. Homework is supervised and extends for long periods, extracurricular activities are kept to a minimum, effort is rewarded, tutors are hired, and socialising is largely confined to family outings' (Bond 1991: 18).

The primary curriculum is subject-based, with a common core of seven constituent subjects: Chinese language, English language, mathematics, general studies, music, art and craft and physical education. The first three subjects form the basis of the Secondary School Placement Allocation Exercise and, as a result, tend to exert curricular hegemony over other subjects. The CDC recommends the integration of various subjects to ease pressure on the timetable. Consequently, social studies, health education and primary science can now be taught as a single subject, general studies (CDC 1993: 56). To break down further the barriers between individual subjects, the CDC suggests that all subjects should, where possible, contribute to general aspects of learning and experience, such as values education. This interrelationship is expressed in Figure 10.1

The CDC advises that most attention should be paid to Chinese language, which is particularly complex for a number of reasons. Cantonese, the local dialect of Chinese, is the medium for the majority of primary schools. The written form of the language is classical Chinese, and removed from standard spoken Chinese in terms of structures and vocabulary. The links between Cantonese and classical written Chinese are even more remote. The change of sovereignty has brought a move towards including *putonghua*, the standard Chinese of the mainland, in the curriculum, with the added complication that the mainland uses simplified characters whereas Hong Kong uses full-form traditional characters. In effect, therefore, pupils are expected to learn spoken Cantonese, written Chinese and English, as well as, possibly, *putonghua*, although simplified characters are not currently taught in Hong Kong. Not surprisingly, therefore, the CDC advocates according a large proportion of class periods every week to Chinese language (Table 10.2). Pupils are also expected, in principle, to have mastered a minimum of 2500 characters by the end of primary school, and, as an ideogrammatic language, the written characters contain few, if any, phonetic links to their oral forms. This requires the children to spend hours practising and memorising how to write the characters. Accordingly, the pedagogic emphasis is on repetitive learning and diligence, which then tends to pervade other areas of the curriculum.

Primary schools have freedom to determine their own curriculum, with reference to the CDC guidelines. The greater emphasis that schools tend to place on Chinese language, English language and mathematics is reflected in the distribution of lessons in the curriculum map in Table 10.3, which comes from a typical primary school run by a Christian organisation. In

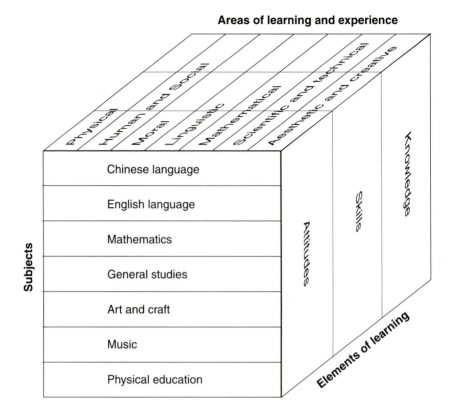

Figure 10.1 Diagrammatic representation of the primary curriculum (CDC 1993: 56)
Note: The emphasis of learning and experience may vary in different subjects

this school, English Language is actually accorded up to double the minimum allocation of class periods recommended by the CDC, thus reducing the time allocation of subjects such as art and craft to below the recommended figure.

Usually, each class has a variety of subject teachers, although one member of staff serves as class teacher in charge of pastoral and administrative matters. Most teachers teach three or more subjects within the school, as illustrated in the teacher's timetable in Table 10.4.

Schools and classrooms: practices and issues

A typical school

A typical school comprises a multistorey building, with a total site area of approximately 4000m^2. Most schools do not have their own sportsground,

Table 10.2 Suggested minimum weekly allocation of periods for subjects in the core curriculum

Subject	Level					
	P1	*P2*	*P3*	*P4*	*P5*	*P6*
Chinese language	11	10	9	8 (9)*	8 (9)*	8 (9)*
English language	5	6	7	8	8	8
Mathematics	5	5	5	5	5	5
General studies	5	5	5	5	5	5
Art and craft	3	3	3	3	3	3
Music	2	2	2	2	2	2
Physical education	2	2	2	2	2	2
Total	33	33	33	33 (34)*	33 (34)*	33 (34)*

Source: CDC 1993: 47.
* If *putonghua* is offered at P4–P6 levels.

Table 10.3 A curriculum map for a primary school

Subject	Level					
	P1	*P2*	*P3*	*P4*	*P5*	*P6*
Chinese language	10 (*11*)†	10 (*10*)	10 (*9*)	19 (*8*)‡	9 (*8*)‡	9 (*8*)‡
English language	10 (*5*)	10 (*6*)	10 (*7*)	10 (*8*)	10 (*8*)	10 (*8*)
Mathematics	7 (*5*)	7 (*5*)	7 (*5*)	7 (*5*)	7 (*5*)	7 (*5*)
General studies*	5 (*5*)	5 (*5*)	5 (*5*)	5 (*5*)	5 (*5*)	5 (*5*)
Art and craft	2 (*3*)	2 (*3*)	2 (*3*)	2 (*3*)	3 (*3*)	3 (*3*)
Music	2 (*2*)	2 (*2*)	2 (*2*)	2 (*2*)	2 (*2*)	2 (*2*)
Physical education	2 (*2*)	2 (*2*)	2 (*2*)	2 (*2*)	2 (*2*)	2 (*2*)
Library	1	1	1	1	1	1
Biblical knowledge	1	1	1	1	1	1

† Figures in brackets are CDC suggested minimum allocation of periods.
‡ The school does not offer *putonghua at P4–P6 levels.*
* Social studies, science and health education.

possessing just a small playground, part of which is often covered and incorporates a tuckshop. The classrooms, each accommodating around forty children, are usually located according to age group, with Primary 1 children situated on the first floor and the Primary 6 children on the top floor. Lower primary classes have clusters of tables, particularly if the school has adopted the Activity Approach, while the upper primary classes are more likely to have rows of desks. There is limited storage space, and the children have to carry textbooks, exercise books and stationery to and

Table 10.4 A teacher's timetable in a bi-sessional (afternoon section)

School time	Monday	Tuesday	Wednesday	Thursday	Friday
1.00–1.35	Class period	Class period	Class period	Class period	Class period
1.35–2.10	English P1C		English P5C	English P1C	
2.10–2.45	English P1C	English P1C	English P1C	English P5C	Health education P1D
2.45–2.55	Recess	Recess	Recess	Recess	Recess
2.55–3.30		English (TV) P5C	English P1C	Science P1B	English P1C
3.30–4.05		Science (TV) P3B	Art and craft P1A	English P1C	English P1C
4.05–4.40	Art and craft P1A	Science P1B	Art and Craft P1A	English P5C	Science P3B
4.40–4.50	Recess	Recess	Recess	Recess	Recess
4.50–5.25	English P5C		English P5C		English P5C
5.25–6.00	English P5C	Science P1C		Science P1C	English P5C

from school, which has led to concern in medical quarters about spinal damage caused by heavy school bags.

A typical day

Apart from those attending afternoon sections of bi-sessional schools, a child's day starts early. This eases the pressure on the transport system, and also, in the case of bi-sessional schools, allows for two eight-period time-tables to operate. One girl, in an upper primary class of a Christian bi-sessional (morning section) school, describes a typical day as follows:

It is six o'clock, so I have to wake up to brush my teeth, wash my face and wear my uniform. After that, I go down to wait for the school bus.

When I arrive school, I hand in my homework. Usually we are quiet except Wednesday. There is a lot of noise. Some of us talk, some of us study and some spell words with each other. Why? Because we will have our English Dictation in the fifth lesson.

After two lessons we have a small recess. It lasts for five minutes. We are not allowed to eat, but drink. After the recess, we have an assembly. Sometime the theme is about Jesus, and sometimes it is about morals.

One hour later we have a recess again. During this recess we are allowed to eat, drink and buy food at the canteen . . . . But one thing we are not allowed, is run. So our teacher have chosen some prefects to write down the names of the pupils who run and give them to the teacher. Then the teacher will punish them.

Now let's talk about some happy things. We have PE lesson twice a week, we do our exercises and play ball games in winter. In summer, we'll have our swimming lesson.

School finish at about twelve forty. I carry my heavy bag and go home by school bus happily.

The day does not end there, for the heavy bag will be burdened with homework. Every day, pupils are usually required to do homework in at least three subjects – Chinese language, English language and mathematics – in accordance with parental expectations.

In the late 1980s, a movement towards a major overhaul of primary schooling resulted in a series of reforms designed to address several features that had emerged from the historical processes described earlier, and which were considered problematic. Before examining the reforms in detail, it is helpful to identify first the particular areas for concern.

Issues in primary education

The reforms that were outlined in a series of reports by the Education Commission, especially ECR 4, 5 and 6, addressed a range of problematic features, several of which are interrelated, including the provision of primary education, curriculum issues, teacher quality, school environments and bi-sessional schools.

Provision

Since the mid-1980s there has been an increasing awareness and criticism of the level of expenditure on education and its relative distribution between the sectors of education. This has resulted in frequent calls, especially by the elected members of the Legislative Council, for both an increase in the level of spending and a redistribution towards the primary sector. The statistics do suggest that in comparative terms the level and distribution of spending are respectively low and heavily geared in per capita terms towards the tertiary sector. In 1995, 2.7 per cent of GDP was spent on education compared to an average in Asia of 4 per cent and of 5 per cent in Europe. This represents about 17.0 per cent of total government spending. In per capita terms the government spent on average in 1995 $200,000.00 per annum on each tertiary student, $29,000.00 on each secondary student and $18,000.00 on each primary pupil. This ratio of 11:1 between spending on tertiary and primary pupils contrasts with ratios in 1990 of 2.8:1 in the UK and 6:1 in Singapore (UNESCO 1993). In concrete terms, this low level of resourcing is manifested in a number of features of primary schools, some of which, such as bi-sessionalism and the paucity of facilities, have already been noted. Other features include: the absence in most schools of any forms of modern technology, especially computers; the lack, in most schools, of a gymnasium or specialist rooms, and crowded staffrooms. In terms of teacher salaries, which comprise the largest single item of expenditure, only recently were graduate posts created in primary schools, which remain predominantly staffed by non-graduate (or Certificated) teachers commanding a significantly lower salary.

Curriculum issues

Despite the transitional nature of society, and the regular adjustments to the educational system as a result of socio-economic and political influences, the orientation of schooling in the territory has been notably resistant to change. For instance, a visiting British School Inspector commented in 1950 on:

> the traditional Chinese enthusiasm for education, a tradition in which education is the necessary means to social status and material success. Traditional Chinese education is literary and mathematical in content, didactic in method and dominated by examinations. Its teaching is secular, its scope largely confined to the classroom, its curriculum emphasizing the theoretical rather than the practical, and learning by heart rather than the application of learning.
>
> (Fisher 1950: 10)

More than forty years later, the Advisory Inspectorate portrayed primary classrooms in very similar terms:

> Most pupils were found to be obedient, attentive and hardworking in the lesson. However, their learning attitude was considered to be a bit passive and lacking of independence.

Most lessons tended to be teacher-centred. While due emphasis was placed on the teaching of grammar and pronunciation, the training of the four language skills was in general inadequate. Students were not given enough opportunity to put the language into meaningful use.

Teachers in general adopted the teacher-demonstration approach in classroom teaching. Teaching aids were often used by teachers. Classwork sessions were arranged in most of the lessons observed but not used to the best effect. Some teachers still assigned class-work at the very end of lessons after they had delivered their expository teaching. Some teachers were too textbound. They were unable (or unwilling) to make due adjustments to the depth of treatment of individual topics to cope with different abilities of pupils.

(Education Commission 1994: paras 1(2), 2(6), 3(8))

The HKATs and internal assessments, both of which contribute to the selective Secondary School Places Allocation Exercise, exert a strong back-wash influence upon primary schools, with special attention being devoted to the three key assessed subjects: 'like internal assessments, the HKATs do not always have a positive effect on classroom teaching and learning since, in the main, they test discrete items of knowledge rather than problem-solving' (ECR 4 1990: 69).

A resistance to change, or more accurately the prevalence of tried and tested patterns of teacher–pupil interaction, was also evident in the impact of several curriculum innovations, including the 'activity approach' and the 'cross-curricular guidelines', which attempted to promote curricula that were, respectively, more child centred and activity based, and socially relevant. Actual classroom implementation of the approach was problematic and characterised by the adoption of the form rather than the substance or deep structure of the innovation. In some schools, the activity approach consisted merely of a replacement of the rows of desks by groups of tables, but group work and self-initiated learning were rarely in evidence. The reasons for this were various: the incompatibility of the innovations with prevailing conceptions of knowledge, learning and assessment; the shortage of space for movement around the classroom or for the display corners advocated by the ED; the lack of a school library for independent learning, particularly in bi-sessional schools, where they are seen as an administrative minefield, for instance in determining responsibility for the purchase of new books; the lack of teacher involvement in the planning of reform and the brevity of training courses for teachers; and the inflexibility of timetabling and schemes of work. Further, the transient nature of classrooms in the bi-sessional schools did not encourage their decoration as home-base rooms for individual classes, thus reducing any sense of belonging for the pupils.

Whilst there are outstanding examples of innovative practices in some schools, the importance attached to testing and selection has generally contributed to resistance to attempts at curriculum reform. Schools feel constrained by parental pressure to concentrate upon academic achievement and HKAT success, which militates against innovations in pedagogy and paying greater attention to non-examination subjects. Sadly, in extreme circumstances, primary school children have responded by committing suicide, often by jumping from a window of a high-rise apartment block. In one such tragic case, a 10-year-old boy left a note laying bare the cause of his despair:

> Everyday, there are many homeworks. They are not only in large quantity, but also difficult to do. Each recess is engaging for 10 minutes. If getting one day more holiday, [I] will be given 10 odd homeworks. Especially in long vacation, the homeworks will be more. [I] can get no rest in any day. Dictations, quizs [sic] and examinations will be more. Though after 12 o'clock in every night I still have to revise my homeworks. I can't go to bed until 1 o'clock odd. At 6.50 hours in the morning, I have got to get up. [I] am so hard. I do wish no studying.
>
> (Reported in *South China Morning Post*, 11 May 1991)

Teacher quality

The quality of the teaching force was a further cause for concern. Until 1993, there were no pre-service teacher education programmes designed specifically for primary teaching. Those entering the profession possessed either a general Teacher's Certificate acquired after two or three years' study at one of the four Colleges of Education, or no professional qualifications, and there was little incentive for teachers to further their studies, in terms of promotion or increased salary. ECR 5 (1992: 43–44) recognised the problem:

> Because of the additional demands being placed on primary schools by new policies and higher community expectations, there is a growing mismatch between the quality of the service expected and the level of expertise available to deliver that quality. If teachers are to keep up to date and provide effective service all through a career, sustained professional development is needed. A considerable proportion of secondary school teachers acquire higher qualifications during their career; but the current primary

school staffing structure offers little motivation for teachers to acquire the level of skills that the schools now need.

The establishment of the Hong Kong Institute of Education, which amalgamated the four Colleges of Education and the Institute of Language in Education as an autonomous entity in 1994, was the most significant move towards upgrading the quality of the pre-service and inservice training of primary teachers. As well as running Teacher Certificate courses, the institute was to offer a range of degree programmes, with a view to enabling 35 per cent of primary school teachers to possess first degrees by 2007. Other initiatives included a streamlining of qualifications and the career structure for teachers, and the recommendation that, by 2007, all school principals should possess a degree.

School environments

The physical environment of schools, most notably the shortage of space, has constrained developments in curriculum and other aspects of school work:

> New areas of study such as sex education, moral education and civic education need storage space for teaching kits and materials. New approaches to teaching generally need more space than the traditional 'chalk and talk' approach. New teaching posts require staff room space. The greater emphasis on guidance and counselling has shown the need for small rooms where teachers, students and parents can talk privately. Space must be found to process large numbers of documents, including application forms for various financial assistance schemes, and to store examination papers.
>
> (ECR 5 1992: 19)

ECR 5 goes to on propose the phased expansion of existing schools suffering from a severe lack of space, and an enlargement of 15 per cent in the standard site area for new primary schools.

Other problems include noise pollution, as many schools are situated close to major roads and building sites. The government has introduced measures to provide double-glazing and air conditioning in schools in especially noisy locations.

Bi-sessional schools

Bi-sessional schooling, introduced as a temporary measure in 1954, was still prevalent more than forty years later, as governmental spending priorities had shifted first to the secondary and later to the tertiary sectors. In 1989, only 20 per cent of primary schools were uni-sessional (ECR 4 1990). The long-standing pledge by the government to shift to whole-day primary schooling was restated by the Education Commission in 1990, who linked the issue to, *inter alia*, concern over a rise in juvenile delinquency, even though official police figures for 1989, the year before ECR 4 was published, showed that the total number of crimes committed by primary school children was 1050, the lowest total for five years.

Nevertheless, bi-sessionalism places a number of constraints on schooling. It requires pupils to transport all their books to and from home each day; it restricts the extent to which a classroom can be personalised; and the time for extra-curricular activities is limited, as is the willingness of schools to provide common facilities, especially school libraries. Despite the social and educational disadvantages of bi-sessional schools, many teachers prefer half-day schooling, as it means shorter hours at work for the same salary as received by whole-day school counterparts, and many school principals express concern as to which of the two sessional head-teachers would become the principal of the combined whole-day school.

ECR 4 proposed phasing in a mixed-mode of schooling by the year 2000, with Primary 1 to Primary 4 operating a half-day system, and Primary 5 and Primary 6 operating on a whole-day basis. This proposal was deferred as a result, mainly, of the negative response from bi-sessional principals. The government, which had not been enthusiastic to the original proposal, was quick to use the response of the principals as a reason to defer the decision and the associated cost implications.

Target Oriented Curriculum (TOC)

The TOC is a fundamental reform in that it addresses, at the same time, three principal curricular components: the orientation of the curriculum, pedagogy and assessment. The existing curriculum was perceived, as noted above, as being concerned with established factual knowledge; being taught through teacher-centred and textbook-driven pedagogy, and assessing children's learning through norm-referenced procedures. In terms of Bernstein's (1971) framework, the curriculum had all the features of a 'collection code' orientation in so far as there was a strong degree of separation between the subjects, a low degree of teacher and pupil control of the curriculum, and a focus on established knowledge. The TOC, on the other hand, promotes: generic competencies which are seen to transcend the goals of individual subjects; child-centred and task-based learning with criterion-referenced assessment; and a focus on constructed knowledge (see Figure 10.2).

The TOC framework envisages a hierarchy of learning targets for each subject and five cross-curricular principles of learning: communicating,

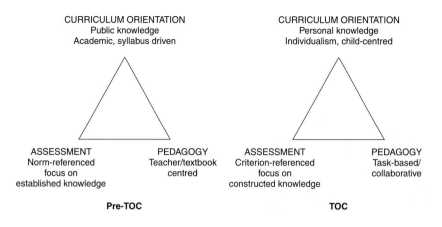

Figure 10.2 Elements of TOC reform

enquiring, conceptualising, reasoning and problem-solving, as well as criterion-based assessments. Progression is divided into three Key Stages (Primary 1 to 3; Primary 4 to 6; and Secondary 1 to 3). The learning targets comprise subject targets, subject dimension targets, and within dimension targets, which are to be achieved through learning tasks. The learning targets are designed to encourage: the development of higher thinking abilities and of ever-improving capabilities; the integrative use of knowledge; a learner-centred approach to all aspects of the curriculum; a stress on the processes and construction of learning rather than its products; and an emphasis on the five cross-curricular principles of learning, namely problem-solving, reasoning, enquiring, communicating and conceptualising.

Although conceived as an integrated curriculum with common strands across subjects, the TOC was initially introduced only in the three core subjects, English, Chinese and mathematics, at Key Stage 1 in 1996. Examples of the hierarchy of targets for these subjects are shown in Table 10.5.

The discourse used to promote the TOC resembles that which accompanied the introduction of the national curriculum in the UK, especially with regard to the need for greater public accountability and the identification of clear targets for learning. However, in a number of important respects, the TOC embodies features which distinguish it from the goals of the national curriculum. The two most critical features are, firstly, the pedagogies promoted by the TOC stress the importance of group work, catering for individual pupil differences, subject integration and the need to promote generic skills. This is in marked contrast to the promotion in

197

Table 10.5 Examples of TOC learning targets

Subject	TOC *learning target*
English	
Subject target	To develop an ever-improving capability to use English to think and communicate; to acquire, develop and apply knowledge; to respond and give expression to experience; and within these contexts, to develop and apply an ever-increasing understanding of how language is organised, used and learned
Dimensions	Interpersonal Dimension Knowledge Dimension Experience Dimension
Within dimension targets (example)	Interpersonal Dimension Target 1 (Key Stage 1) to establish and maintain relationships and routines in carrying out classroom activities
Mathematics	
Subject target	To develop an ever-improving capability to inquire, communicate and reason mathematically; formulate and solve mathematical problems; appreciate the beauty of mathematics; and apply mathematics to different contexts through the learning of the knowledge, concepts and skills/procedures in number, measures, algebra, shape and space and data handling
Dimensions	Number Dimension Measures Dimension Algebra Dimension Shape and space Dimension Data handling Dimension
Within dimension objectives (example)	Number Dimension Learning Objective 1 (Key Stage 1) Learners read, write and order numbers up to 5 digits, and understand the meaning of place value
Chinese	
Subject target	To develop an ever-improving capability to read, write, listen, speak and think in Chinese. To develop knowledge of the Chinese language and culture. To develop interest in learning Chinese, thinking skills, personal character, and a sense of social responsibility
Dimensions	Listening Dimension Speaking Dimension Reading Dimension Writing Dimension
Within dimension targets (example)	Listening Dimension Learning Objective 1 (Key Stage 1) Listening to children's stories: fairy tales, stories about everyday life, nature stories and fables

the UK of whole-class teaching and subject-based curricula. Secondly, the Reform Act in the UK was perceived as an attempt to create a centralised national curriculum which would effectively reduce the degree of teacher autonomy and professionalism, in that key curriculum decisions would no longer be taken by teachers. In contrast, the TOC was introduced into an educational environment which was characterised by a high degree of centralised control by the state, and low levels of teacher autonomy. A central feature of its rationale involves the goal of promoting greater teacher involvement in curriculum decision-making.

The reform has not enjoyed a happy history to date, principally because of its complexity and problems in resolving the nature of assessment. An early document setting out the TTRA was couched in arcane theoretical language, which was rendered even more obscure in its Chinese translation. The bewildered and subsequently hostile response of many members of the teaching profession was picked up by the press and general public. In some quarters, there was a perception that the TTRA was designed to enhance the status of English in primary schools, and an attempt to impose 'Western' values on schools and to select pupils for English medium secondary schools. Forced on to the defensive, the ED then reviewed the TTRA and renamed it as the Target Oriented Curriculum (TOC), partly to allay parents' and teachers' concerns that the initiative was focusing solely upon assessments. It also signalled a shift towards more concern for improving the quality of learning and the curriculum generally.

Early indications are that the TOC is being interpreted in a wide variety of ways within schools and across subjects. In some schools, it is associated with the activity approach; in others, with 'mastery learning'. In English, there is a movement towards holistic language use, whereas Chinese remains more focused on individual skills areas. Mathematics has seen an increase in contextualisation: topics are made more relevant to children's real-life experiences. The ED, meanwhile, has invested in school-based teacher education programmes and resource centres to support the initiative.

Social, economic and political considerations

The social context

The above portrayal of primary schooling invites comparison with the patterns which prevail elsewhere. Such comparisons have the potential to provide powerful insights into the educational systems of other countries and to allow us to understand better our own systems and problems. By stepping outside our limited experiences and assumptions we can reflect on our own situation. The potential pitfall of such comparisons is the belief that we can easily identify and transplant policies from one context to another. When education becomes a key item for reform on the political agenda, as in the UK and USA, so educational policies are frequently derived from or justified by reference to educational practices elsewhere. For example, Reynolds and Farrell (1996: 3) comment with regard to the UK that 'references to the superior achievements of "Pacific Rim" economies or the "Tiger" Economies now pepper the speeches of Government and Opposition spokespersons, as does acknowledgement of the educational reasons for their success'. To do this without a recognition that schooling is inevitably a reflection of deeply rooted social, political, economic and cultural factors is highly problematic. Below we identify a range of features of the social context of Hong Kong which influence the nature of schooling and thus provide a basis for a more substantive understanding of the patterns identified.

Demographic and economic factors

Since the end of the Second World War the population of Hong Kong has grown tenfold, largely as a result of waves of immigration from mainland China. There has also been over that period a rapid decline in the birth-rate and a rise in the average age of marriage. Two consequences arise from this: first in a society where the majority of people are the offspring of refugees, social status is an achieved rather than an ascribed phenomenon and primarily reflected in economic terms. This ensures that access to education is the primary determinant of social mobility and the private rates of return to each level of schooling are high. Basically, therefore, access to schooling is the key determinant of life chances in a society with a very uneven distribution of wealth and a very limited welfare system. Not doing well at school, enrolling in a poor school or leaving school early all have clearly understood economic consequences.

Secondly, the decline in the birth-rate and rise in the average age of marriage have meant that Hong Kong is close to averaging – albeit without the support of legislation – one child per family. The implications of this for schooling relate to parental expectations of their children and of schools which are now focused on far fewer offspring. Given that the majority of parents will depend on their children in old age, this only serves to reinforce the perceived value of schooling and pressure on pupils to succeed.

Political factors

Since the early 1980s, politics has been dominated by the impact of the transfer of sovereignty in 1997, which generated a climate of uncertainty exacerbated by the events in Tian'anmen Square in 1989. With a large proportion of Hong Kong's population being descendants of people who fled the political and economic turmoil of mainland China, the prospects of returning to Chinese rule were not viewed with optimism. The response has been for some to obtain foreign passports or to emigrate. The preferred destinations (Canada, Australia and the USA) of potential emigrants give priority to those who are better educated, speak English and have some prior connection with the country. This has served to reinforce the perceived importance and value of schooling and qualifications generally, and of studying in English specifically.

A political factor of a more long-term nature derives from the colonial status of the government. This has meant that it has had a very tenuous legitimacy and only used its full powers when the survival of the state was threatened. The preferred style of governance was described as 'positive non-intervention' and the government tended to avoid pursuing policies which were strongly opposed by any sector of the community. The consequences for education of this was an approach to educational reform which relied on exhortation and rhetoric and avoided matters of implementation. Thus, parental expectations and market forces exert a powerful influence on patterns of schooling. An example of this is the prevalence of mixed-code teaching in secondary schools whereby the oral language of the classroom, with the exception of key terminology, is mainly in Chinese and the written components (textbook, homework, examinations) are undertaken in English. This pattern prevails despite long-standing policies to encourage the use of Chinese as a single medium of instruction.

Socio-cultural factors

The concept of culture is elusive but important. Chinese societies in East Asia have been primarily portrayed in terms of embodying a Confucian cultural heritage, although Taoism and Buddhism are also important influences (Lau and Yeung 1996). The precise nature of this concept has been subject to a variety of emphases which have variously stressed its classical roots, its core values or its manifestations in a modern industrial context. The key elements which are common across these definitions include an emphasis on the role of the family, respect for authority and established knowledge, an emphasis on diligence and perseverance, concern for morality, and the promotion of social harmony through a collectivist ethos. The educational consequences of this amalgam of values are far reaching. Pupils generally accept the authority of the teacher, expect to learn in school and see performance as a function of effort rather than ability. Similarly, parents generally expect schools to stretch their pupils and to give them homework. Teachers expect pupils to be attentive, to work hard and to learn. Knowledge is viewed as a fixed commodity which is embodied in books and it is the task of the teacher to impart this to pupils. This is not to suggest that schools do not experience discipline

201

problems – it is not unknown for primary pupils to have links with Triad gangs – or that all pupils are motivated learners. With increasing affluence, mass education and the pervasive influence of the mass media, social values are changing. However, they continue to exert a sufficiently powerful influence on schooling to ensure that Hong Kong classrooms are dissimilar to those in the West, especially in terms of classroom climate and expectations of pupils and teachers.

These same values are manifested in the society's views of children and childhood. For the first few years of life, children are mollycoddled by their families. However, with the transition to primary school, attitudes harden, as this transition is associated with *tung chi*, the Chinese age of reason (Ho 1986; Bond 1991). The pressure on children to achieve academically often changes the parental role, from patient indulger to strict overseer. This must come as a shock to many children. Even kindergartens offer an academic curriculum centred around Chinese characters, basic English and arithmetic, with homework for good measure.

An awareness of socio-cultural differences is necessary if we are to avoid the tendency for educators steeped in Western models of education to interpret schooling elsewhere through their own cultural understandings. A key example of this is the tendency to portray the prevailing teaching and learning strategies used in Hong Kong as meaningless, superficial 'rote learning' (Murphy 1987; Ginsburg 1992). Biggs (1996) argues that, in reality, what occurs is better described as 'repetitive' learning, which is meaningful and focused on accurate recall; together with a complex 'ecosystem' of cultural factors, including diligence and a climate of positive interpersonal motivation, this approach contributes to promoting deep learning. Consequently, 'innovative' pedagogical practices, often derived from Western models, might be viewed as unnecessary.

Conclusion

This chapter has described primary schooling in Hong Kong with reference to its historical, political and socio-economic contexts. The picture that emerges has the following features:

- the government has relied heavily upon the private sector in the provision of schooling;
- the curriculum is academic and targeted at matriculation;
- bureaucratic inertia and lack of resources have hampered many attempts at curriculum reform.

According to McClelland (1991), these features are not unique to Hong Kong: indeed they are typical of schooling developed in territories under British administration, which, in all areas of public provision, was reluctant to do more than what was minimally necessary to maintain the colonial system. However, other features of primary schooling are shaped by particular characteristics of Hong Kong, such as the rapid and large-scale demographic changes, the shift from manufacturing to service industries, the transfer of sovereignty, and the kaleidoscopic complexity of interaction between Chinese and Western values. The result has been a number of tensions that have prompted the government to undertake a fundamental reform of the primary and, eventually, secondary curriculum. The tensions include questions relating to quality versus quantity of education provision, academic versus whole-person curricula, and general contents versus Hong Kong-specific subject-matter.

There are two particularly surprising features of primary schooling in Hong Kong. The first is that, given the wealth of the territory, primary schooling has remained almost primitive and under-resourced. The second is the extent of achievements made despite the lack of funding. Hong Kong pupils are widely admired around the world for their academic success in certain fields, but it appears that this stems not from government investment in education, but rather from intrinsic motivational values, such as diligence and the extrinsic motivation of keen competition.

The turn of the millennium sees primary schooling in a typical transient state, as the TOC initiative, grafted from the West, takes root. Unusually, however, this initiative has been nurtured with relatively rich resources. How, or, indeed, whether TOC will flourish in the complex ecosystem of Hong Kong schools, and an uncertain socio-political climate, remains to be seen.

Acknowledgements

We are very grateful to Ms Ada Au Mei-Yee and her pupils, Ms Karen Chui Wai Mun and Professor Lau Sing for their help in the preparation of this chapter.

References

Bernstein, B. (1971) *Class, Codes and Control*. London: Routledge & Kegan Paul.

Biggs, J.B. (1996) 'Western misperceptions of the Confucian-heritage learning culture'. In D.A. Watkins and J.B. Biggs (eds.) *The Chinese Learner: Cultural, Psychological and Contextual Influences*. Hong Kong: CERC and ACER.

Bond, M.H. (1991) *Beyond the Chinese Face: Insights from Psychology*. Hong Kong: Oxford University Press.

Curriculum Development Council (CDC) (1993) *Guide to the Primary School Curriculum*. Hong Kong: Government Printer.

Education Commission Report Number 4 (ECR 4) (1990) *The Curriculum and Behaviour Problems in Schools*. Hong Kong: Government Printer.

Education Commission Report Number 5 (ECR 5) (1992) *The Teaching Profession*. Hong Kong: Government Printer.

Education Commission (1994) *Quality in School Education: Report of the Working Group on Educational Standards: Technical Annex 4F* Hong Kong: Government Printer.

Fisher, N.G. (1950) *Report on Government Expenditure on Education in Hong Kong 1950*. Hong Kong: Noronha & Company.

Fung, Y.W. and Lee, J.C.K. (1993) 'Environmental education in Hong Kong secondary schools'. Paper presented at the UNESCO Conference: 'Overcoming the barriers to environmental education through teacher education'. Australia: Griffith University.

Ginsburg, E. (1992) 'Not just a matter of English', *HERDSA News*, 14(1), 6–8.

Ho, D.Y.F. (1986) 'Chinese patterns of socialization'. In M.H. Bond (ed.) *The Psychology of the Chinese People*. Hong Kong: Oxford University Press.

Lau, S. and Yeung, P.P.W. (1996) 'Understanding Chinese child development: the role of culture in socialization'. In S. Lau (ed.) *Growing Up the Chinese Way: Chinese Child and Adolescent Development*. Hong Kong: The Chinese University Press.

McClelland, J.A.G. (1991) 'Curriculum development in Hong Kong'. In C. Marsh and P. Morris (eds) *Curriculum Development in East Asia*. Lewes: Falmer Press.

Morris, P. (1995) *Curriculum Development in Hong Kong* (2nd edn). Faculty of Education Papers No. 7. Hong Kong: The University of Hong Kong.

Morris, P. (1996a) 'The management of participation in the policymaking process: the case of the Education Commission in Hong Kong'. *Journal of Education Policy* 11(3), 319–336.

Morris, P. (1996b) *The Hong Kong School Curriculum: Development, Issues and Policies*. Hong Kong: Hong Kong University Press.

Morris, P. and Chan, K.K. (1996) 'Cross-curricular themes and curriculum reform in Hong Kong: policy as discourse'. Paper presented at AERA Conference. Boston, USA.

Murphy, D. (1987) 'Offshore education: a Hong Kong perspective'. *Australian Universities Review* 30(2), 43–44.

Reynolds, D. and Farrell, S. (1996) *Worlds Apart? A Review of International Surveys of Educational Achievement Involving England*. London: HMSO.

Sweeting, A. (1990) *Education in Hong Kong, Pre-1841 to 1941: Fact and Opinion*. Hong Kong: Hong Kong University Press.

Sweeting, A. (1992) 'Hong Kong education within historical processes'. In G.A. Postiglione, (ed.), *Education and Society in Hong Kong: Toward One Country and Two Systems*. Hong Kong: Hong Kong University Press.

Sweeting, A. (1993) *A Phoenix Transformed: The Reconstruction of Education in Post-war Hong Kong*. Hong Kong: Oxford University Press.

Sweeting, A. and Morris, P. (1993) 'Educational reform in post-war Hong Kong: planning and crisis intervention'. *International Journal of Educational Development* 13(3), 201–206.

UNESCO (1993) *World Education Report 1993*. Paris: UNESCO.

CURRICULA ACROSS CULTURES

Contexts and connections

Martin Cortazzi

Introduction

As a finale to the whole book on international primary curricula, this chapter presents a framework for reviewing curriculum perspectives across cultures. It suggests that in order to learn from international perspectives the significance of cultural continuity and cultures of learning must be taken into account. The framework is applied in discussing primary teaching in China.

No one can doubt that broadening our professional vision with international perspectives is worthwhile. The acceleration of global processes that increasingly bind diverse peoples together is hard to ignore; it is shown in increasingly multicultural classrooms. More than ever, a greater number of children, and some teachers, go to school in cultures that are additional to the one in which they were born. London is the cutting edge: children in London primary schools between them speak 200 or more languages and represent a fantastic diversity of cultures and communities. In places where this is not the case, teachers still need to prepare children for futures in which it will be so; citizenship has a global future of multicultural living.

Most of the official primary school curricula around the world not only contain the same subjects, but give them the same relative importance (Benavot and Kamens 1989; Lockheed and Verspoor 1991). How such curricula are implemented and what they mean to the participants, however, varies greatly according to a wide range of situational factors. How the curriculum of another country is perceived also varies enormously, depending on the context the commentator brings to such interpretations and the sets of presuppositions that frame someone's current perspective. All teachers develop ideas out of their experience (a current British approach to teacher reflection encourages this). It is more difficult to develop experience out of ideas, and even more difficult to develop experience from the ideas of another culture (yet many children of ethnic minorities have to do so daily). To widen our perspectives on a curriculum, we need awareness of what we see, but also of who sees and how, and how others, including children and parents from different backgrounds, might see that curriculum. Such a broadening of vision includes a raised awareness of our own curriculum and of ourselves as viewers.

To substantiate the relevance of any comparison it may be helpful to think of applications on different levels: we might find greater knowledge of new concepts and other systems (a source of professional enhancement), and some of this may give insights towards a new understanding of our own teaching situation (a cause for reflection), or suggest implications for policy or practice (an impetus for change), or be of direct application (an agenda for action). In the end, we may feel that our current endeavours and practices are confirmed as being appropriate; more likely, we will want to extend them, to question them, and perhaps to transform them.

A framework for learning from international perspectives

A culturally oriented framework for learning from international perspectives can be suggested. It consists of seven Cs:

- change;
- challenge;
- continuity;
- collaboration;
- communication;
- context;
- cultures of learning.

This minimal framework will be elaborated in relation to the following cameo of activities seen in a kindergarten in China, for children aged 2–6.

A class of 25 children is sitting on the floor learning to read the Chinese characters for different animals. On the wall there is a poem about a little fat pig. The teacher reads the poem several times in a very clear voice, then the class reads it in chorus. The teacher holds up cards with written questions. The class reads the questions aloud and individual children find the answers in the poem. At each answer, the teacher does not give individual feedback but first asks the class if the answer is correct or not. If it is, everybody claps in a collective evaluation of the answer. Next, groups of children sequence cards with individual words to make one of the sentences of the poem. The teacher is using the task for a collective assessment of reading rather than for practice. All

206

children are expected to maintain the same level of achievement. With the whole class the teacher now uses other cards, which are familiar to the children. Each card has a question about animals, e.g. 'What are the tail, eyes and ears of a dog like?' Children in chorus – later individually – read the questions aloud and answer rapidly. This happens at a smart pace; everyone works with the same material at the same speed; older children read textbooks in the same way. The teacher orchestrates everything, strictly but in a kind manner. She conducts rapid changes of class activity on the same topic: a song, an action rhyme, a dance movement, picking characters and words from boxes, matching characters with others on the wall. Later, children paint a bird: the teacher demonstrates each stroke, the wing, the head, the beak; children trace each one in the air before painting it. Now there are 25 birds, each like the teacher's model. Children are consistently attentive: listening, speaking, moving together in a disciplined chorus. No one, except the teacher, asks a question, but all children listen to the answers. They can all read the characters involved in the lesson. They clearly have a sense of achievement: they are learning to read around 100 characters each term. Most will learn the poem by heart, older children will probably memorize their reading texts.

(Cortazzi and Jin 1996: 175)

Some 'Western' observers of such kindergarten and primary classes are impressed by the discipline, concentration, hard work and achievement. Many are concerned about the emphasis on the whole class, by an apparent lack of giving individual attention and meeting individual needs, and by the absence of creativity. The classroom processes look worrying: too much transmission, imitation and reproduction of a defined product by rote learning. There seems to be little active participation by children, except as a whole class or as individuals performing in front of the class. The whole lesson looks like a performance; visitors may even conclude that it has been rehearsed in order to impress them.

Before coming to such conclusions, the cameo can be re-examined in terms of the seven features of the framework.

Change

Which aspects of primary education are changing, how and why?

The Chinese interpretation of this aspect will probably first draw attention to the scale of the enterprise, then to the role of education in modernisation. The numbers are staggering: in 1995 there were some 132 million children attending primary schools in China (compared to 61 million in

1967). This can be seen in the context of variable enrolment changes in 'developing' countries: by 1990, 76 per cent of 6- to 11-year olds in developing countries were in school, but while primary education is now almost universal in East Asia and Latin America, and steady progress is being made in the Middle East and slower progress in South Asia, the gross enrolment ratio actually fell to 50 per cent in Africa (Burnett 1996: 217). Thus the Chinese enrolment rate of 98.4 per cent in 1995 (86.6 per cent complete primary school) represents remarkable progress. The country with the largest number of children can move from implementing primary education for all towards considering quality of learning and school effectiveness (Levin and Lockheed 1993; Little *et al.* 1994). Some urban primary schools are large: perhaps 3,000 pupils and 200 teachers. In these teachers teach one subject only. Other schools, particularly those in rural areas are smaller, perhaps with only one teacher.

Education is seen as crucial in China's modernisation. It has been increasingly linked to China's remarkable economic growth. Outsiders will perhaps point to ways in which schools respond to political changes, most obviously in the Cultural Revolution (1966–1976) when most primary schools were closed for long periods so that children, and teachers, could receive political education elsewhere.

Challenge

What do participants consider as challenges for development and how do they intend to meet these challenges?

One set of challenges is to respond to social and economic factors. Teachers of young children are highly conscious of socialisation. Since the one-child policy of the 1970s, whereby to alleviate population pressures only one child is permitted in urban families, it is rare for a child to have brothers or sisters. Teachers report that many children are initially spoilt or wilful ('little emperors'); they are not used to playing or working with others. Teachers therefore stress obedience, self-control, conformity to the group and awareness of others. In fact, these have been significant aspects of Chinese tradition since Confucius.

Class sizes (forty to fifty children in a primary class is usual, sometimes seventy) might be seen as a challenge. In fact, primary pupil to teacher ratios are about 23:1, which is much less than the mean for developing countries of 39 (Colclough and Lewin 1993: 93). A normal primary teaching load in China is fifteen to twenty periods of forty-five minutes per week. The challenge for Chinese teachers is how best to use this time. This is usually interpreted as how to organise a good presentation with appropriate explanations, interesting examples, intensive practice and revision, as in the cameo. Many teachers make very detailed notes on the use of the textbook, planning and timing each section. Teachers' free periods are spent in preparation. Teachers are also involved in extra-curricular activities, home visiting or staff meetings. Some meetings introduce new methods; teachers are keen to try these out, if they believe they are effective.

China's economic success has left some schools behind. There are significant disparities in primary schools between coastal and inland areas, and between urban and rural settings. Many schools are short of qualified teachers: in the 1980s about half the primary teachers were unqualified (World Bank 1984). This has improved greatly recently, but the relatively low salaries of teachers leads to attrition. School facilities often need upgrading: some primary schools obtain funds to solve this problem by entrepreneurial involvement in the new market economy. This gives pupils experience of productive work. Some schools have their own factories, sometimes several – occasionally, less effective teachers are quietly transferred into them.

Continuity

Which elements of the curriculum and curriculum
management show continuity and stability and why?
Are these elements desirable?

In times of change, with high awareness of the challenge to improve, continuity of the curriculum is important, both in the sequence of topics and in the sense of general stability. Too much change of too many aspects can become unsettling, demoralising or deprofessionalising.

The curriculum in China is highly centralised, a 'confined' system (Rudduck and Kelly 1976) in which the role of curriculum development is a matter for the central authorities, seen particularly in standardised national textbooks for all subjects. In a huge country with many developments, disparities and local variations, this standardisation is considered important for stability and continuity. In schools known, until 1995, as 'key' schools, there is more innovation. Originally these schools (around 5 per cent of all schools) were allocated better resources and teachers, with a selective intake, in order to focus limited resources and prepare primary pupils for (key) middle schools and (key) universities. Recently the emphasis has changed so that they have a modelling role in relation to other schools and an experimental role in using new materials and textbooks. These are often localised. This allows more economically developed areas to teach an advanced curriculum, while the standardised textbooks provide a minimum level to be achieved in rural areas.

Two notable features of cultural continuity in China, which underlie ways in which current changes and challenges are met, are a moral collective orientation and the centrality of models. The first is a central theme of the two thousand years of Confucian tradition, whereby elements included in the curriculum must be conducive to learning or implementing moral conduct and social goals. In this 'social utility criterion' (Munro 1977) the moral, social and political elements of the curriculum determine the legitimacy of other elements. These three are often indistinguishable in Chinese thinking, whereas elsewhere they are generally separated. In the Chinese tradition, continuing in current socialism, the social or collective always comes first. The individual is expected to develop strong awareness of, and conformity to, the group. In Chinese, 'individual' has the negative connotations of being self-centred or selfish. The cultural trend is that the Chinese are oriented towards collectivism, while the British or North Americans tend towards individualism (Triandis 1995). Where British primary schools might teach the topic 'People who help us', in China the topic would be 'People who help others', or rather 'How we can learn from people who help others'. Where British teachers are highly conscious of individual child development, meeting individual needs, and individualising work, Chinese teachers are more aware of the collective goals, meeting social and moral responsibilities, and classwork, as seen in the cameo. The collective standard is formed by individual achievement and all children are believed to have the right, and potential, to achieve a high standard.

In modern China, this moral collective orientation is seen in the fusion of 'Red and Expert' aspects for teachers, learners and curriculum content. 'Red' (the political, moral, social element) frames 'Expert' (knowledge, skills, facts), and the unity between them is what matters. This guides curriculum selection, emphasis and presentation. The result is not necessarily a political or moral text; the crucial point is how the text is treated in class – whether it is studied with the proper attitude and commitment to 'serve the people'. This moral collective orientation is exemplified in the ordering of the oft-quoted five aspects to be cultivated in children: *de zhe ti mei lao* – moral, intellectual, physical health, artistic, physical labour. These are linked: when all children are involved in cleaning the school for ten minutes every day this is moral education through physical work. The syllabus for moral education for 5-year-olds shows similar links: love (for parents, family, friends, teachers), friendship, courtesy and politeness, cleanliness, festivals, visiting shops, factories and other workplaces.

The centrality of models underlies the Chinese emphasis on the teacher as a source of knowledge, a model of learning and of morality. It underlies the demonstration–mimesis–practice–performance approach characteristic of so much classroom work, and seen earlier. Teachers have a strong sense of their responsibility, 'As teachers we must be moral models and engineers of the soul'. They often quote the classic formula, *shen jiao sheng yu yan jiao*, 'A physical model (deeds) is more effective than an oral model (words)'. Children learn best by being exposed to examples of good practice, and the teacher is an embodiment of practice. As long as the teacher presents a good model, careful observation, imitation, and personal practice with effort will be considered good ways to learn calligraphy, art, dance or mathematics. Personal creativity or originality will come later, after mastery of skill, technique or knowledge and prolonged practice. This Chinese notion of careful apprenticeship is somewhat the opposite of a British or American approach, in which knowledge or skills develop through exploration, discovery, learning through play, trying things out and being creative (Gardner 1989).

The centrality of models also underlies the text-centred approach that is practically universal in China from primary schools to university. Texts are taught and learned in exhaustive detail. A common Chinese expression for 'teach' is *jiao shu* or 'teach the book' (balanced by *yu ren* or 'cultivate people'). The text is a model, of form and content. Therefore, intensive reading, much questioning, deep study, reflection, reciting and memorising will help with understanding and eventually internalising the model. This process will be incomplete unless it leads to action or some practical outcome to fulfil the moral collective demand. This long-term view is therefore not simply rote learning.

The centrality of models has another aspect in China: model teachers and pupils. Model teachers are outstanding teachers, 'red' and 'expert', who are recognised by titles such as 'excellent teacher', and given rewards and bonuses. Other teachers are encouraged to acquire knowledge and techniques from the model teachers. Teachers may also encourage pupils to become models by observing, identifying and publicly recognising outstanding pupils with honorific titles, thus developing confidence, encouraging group respect and support, and providing incentives. Among Chinese pupils each one commonly knows who is better at different areas of the curriculum and each is encouraged by parents and teachers to reach the standard of the best.

Collaboration

How are learners involved in active participation in learning and what other kinds of collaboration are there?

The moral collective orientation implies strong collaboration from all participants in schools. This collaboration is evident when even experienced Chinese teachers commonly plan lessons together. Student teachers also do this; they practise with each other before entering the classroom, watch each other teaching, and later the group share comments and observations. Similarly, as inservice training, primary teachers systematically observe others teach for ten hours per term (fourteen hours for new teachers). Teachers from other schools are invited to give demonstration lessons. Through such collaboration, changes and innovations are disseminated face-to-face.

While class teaching characterises the common Chinese approach, some teachers have developed pair and group work, notably in Chinese and English language lessons. This is an innovation in Chinese contexts. For example, in a Taiwanese primary school the teacher sets a problem and gives children time to think about it; in groups huddled round tables (not the usual desks in rows) children discuss approaches and solutions; each group has a chairperson, who notes or remembers main points and results; in turn, each chairperson reports to the class from the front, while the teacher (unusually) stands completely aside; the chairperson then tackles comments and questions from the whole class. Through collaboration between teachers (demonstration, observation, discussion, group planning) such group work has spread to every year group throughout the school. Children are disciplined, observant, fluent and confident.

Communication

What kinds of language and communication patterns are used for learning?

Not only is language a major subject in the curriculum, it is the medium through which the rest of the curriculum is encountered. This medium changes for large numbers of children around the world, who learn in a second or third language. In China, apart from the Han majority, there are indigenous ethnic minorities speaking over sixty languages and using twenty-one scripts. The Chinese language itself has a single script but many mutually incomprehensible spoken forms. Teacher training therefore stresses good speech in *putonghua*, Mandarin, since this is the standard form that is used in classrooms. It is effectively a second language for millions of children and many teachers.

Second language considerations are critical when cultural values about communication differ. There are many schools in Britain which value talk for learning and see the implemented curriculum as being created on the tip of the tongue, in interaction (Wells 1986; Mercer 1995). From the cultural perspective of learning by talking through meanings, the Chinese children in the cameo seem to participate only in chorus, and many seem passive. Yet their cultural value of 'being active' and 'interacting' is different (Cortazzi and Jin 1996). In China, this is cognitively oriented; children are taught to learn through listening, observing carefully and thinking. Only when this input has been absorbed and mastered will many feel ready to produce creative output. Classroom discourse is teacher centred but organised for high quality whole-class interaction. Children's speaking is fluent and confident, but usually after preparation, following a model, and when one has something worth saying. In China, there are moral dimensions to this. This difference of perception of the value of talk is important in multicultural situations, as shown in the following dialogue, noted in Britain (author's data). A Chinese parent is talking to her child:

Mother   You children, talking all the time at home. We parents try to listen, but your talk is empty. Don't talk so much. Think before you speak. Don't just speak out. You must listen to other people, see what they have to say.

Child   But my [British] teacher says we have to speak out, just give our own ideas and opinions, just talk, don't think hard, just say what's on your mind.

Mother   I see you children in the playground, notice everyone talking. No one listening. Children may have opinions, but they are no good unless they listen to others. Those British children are very conscious of themselves, but not of others.

Context

What is the context of the central value system underlying the critical features that influence the curriculum?

Beyond the immediate political, economic, or social contexts influencing the curriculum there is the context of the central value system that underlies both the content and style of the curriculum. In East Asia, despite obvious surface differences between countries, there is a clear long-standing Confucian heritage that has been highly influential on their central value systems. Arguably, this is a crucial factor behind East Asian top performances in international studies of school mathematics and science, and for their countries' economic success (Rozman 1991; Wingert and Greenberg 1996). Arguably, too, this is a key reason for the widely perceived educational success of the children of East Asians in America, even their 'achievement beyond IQ' (Flynn 1991).

This two thousand-year-old Confucian heritage stresses diligence, dedication and self-discipline; an extraordinary aspiration for learning; the conviction that attainment depends on effort rather than ability; that persistence, practice and memorisation will result in mastery of skills and concepts; that teachers and learners have reciprocal relations of care and respect, and mutual responsibilities and duties towards each other; that virtuous leadership can produce moral and diligent behaviour in others (Chen 1990; Rozman 1991; Tu *et al.* 1992). Such ideas, with brief exceptions as in the mid-1970s, have continued as a major element in the central value system in modern China. They form the basis of current early socialisation in the Chinese family. They are a key element in the cameo context. Children come to believe 'If others can learn to do it, I can learn to do it'.

This context is changing with modernisation. A familiar dilemma is how to reconcile Chinese tradition and identity with new Western knowledge and technology: in one famous formula, 'Chinese learning for the substance, Western learning for the function' (Smith 1983: 247). Many would go further, seeking to develop Western individualisation, creativity and the acquisition of problem-solving skills, but there is little evidence of this in the present primary curriculum.

Cultures of learning

What are the crucial norms, beliefs, values and expectations of teaching and learning which make up a culture of learning and are participants aware of these?

Much of the enactment of the curriculum is set within presuppositions and expectations about what constitutes good teaching and learning, about what books are for, or about talking. These are aspects of a culture of learning, a cultural tool-kit that defines how tools of learning and classroom interaction are used. Cultures of learning are often taken for granted and are rarely made explicit to learners.

A Chinese culture of learning includes key notions that the teacher and textbook are sources of knowledge and models; learning means moral development and the teacher is a moral model; teaching and learning are performances with good presentation, pace, variety and virtuosity; teachers and learners have responsibilities to each other, the teacher is an authority, an expert, but caring as a parent and friend; learning means preparation, imitation, reflection, practice; memorisation, even by rote, is part of progress; with effort, everyone can learn.

These values contrast with a British culture of learning. That children do perceive such differences is illustrated by a Chinese Year 2 child (author's data) who compared the British school with his Chinese Sunday class: 'I go to school to do work but I go to the Chinese class to learn'.

Since cultures of learning are part of cultural identity they may be resistant to change, especially in older children, who are likely to believe their way is 'correct'. For teachers to change their culture of learning seems to challenge their professional and personal identity.

Connections and crossings

There are many countries where, in a colonial era, the curriculum was transferred from one culture to another, with relatively little regard to local context or people. Legacies of this still remain in some places, if not exactly in curriculum subjects then in curriculum style: primary textbooks reflect anglophone or francophone academic cultures in parts of Africa and there are recent ministry proposals to 'Indianise' the perspectives and examples in textbooks in India (Suroor 1997).

In reverse, more recent population movements have led to representatives of different cultures coming to a single curriculum, resulting in multi-cultural classes in America and Western Europe. It is important to learn from the cultures brought by different populations, including their cultures of learning. Discussions of assimilation, pluralism, multiculturalism or anti-racism often revolve around tensions between a national curriculum, stan-dards, equity, perceptions of others, representation and important religious, ethnic and linguistic rights. The challenge of future world citizenship demands reconciliation between such tensions; between globalisation and localisation, between important rights and responsibilities, without imped-ing cultural identities. In the connections and cultural crossings of curri-cula that strive to meet this challenge, it is necessary to consider cultural continuities (whose culture?) and cultures of learning (whose culture of learning?) Since each cultural group has valuable contributions to make to larger social units – ultimately global units – some kind of mutual learning, not a one-sided affair, is required. While children need to learn about – and learn through – the culture of learning of their teacher, teachers need to learn about – and develop professionally through – the cultures of learning of their pupils (Jin and Cortazzi 1993, 1995). In this cultural synergy everybody needs to learn about how others learn, without losing their own sense of personal, cultural or professional identity.

Acknowledgement

This chapter has benefited greatly from discussion and collaboration with Lixian Jin, to whom many thanks are due.

References

Benavot, A. and Kamens, D. (1989) *The Curriculum Content of Primary Education in Developing Countries* (PPR Working Paper No. 237). Washington, DC: World Bank.

Burnett, N. (1996) 'Priorities and strategies for education – a World Bank review: the process and the key messages'. *International Journal of Educational Development* 16(3), 215–220.

Chen, J. (1990) *Confucius as a Teacher: Philosophy of Confucius with Special Reference to its Educational Implications*. Beijing: Foreign Languages Press.

Colclough, C. with Lewin, K.M. (1993) *Educating all the Children, Strategies for Primary Schooling in the South*. Oxford: Clarendon Press.

215

Cortazzi, M. and Jin, L. (1996) 'Cultures of learning: language classrooms in China'. In H. Coleman (ed.) *Society and the Language Classroom*. Cambridge: Cambridge University Press (pp. 169–206).

Flynn, J.R. (1991) *Asian Americans, Achievement Beyond IQ*. Hillsdale, NJ: Lawrence Erlbaum.

Gardner, H. (1989) *To Open Minds: Chinese Clues to the Dilemma of American Education*. New York: Basic Books.

Jin, L. and Cortazzi, M. (1993) 'Cultural orientation and academic language use'. In D. Graddol, L. Thompson and M. Byram (eds.) *Language and Culture*. Clevedon: Multilingual Matters (pp. 84–97).

Jin, L. and Cortazzi, M. (1995) 'A cultural synergy model for academic language use'. In P. Bruthiaux, T. Boswood and B. Du-Babcock (eds.) *Explorations in English for Professional Communication*. Hong Kong: City University of Hong Kong (pp. 41–56).

Levin, H.M. and Lockheed, M.E. (eds.) (1993) *Effective Schools in Developing Countries*. London: Falmer Press.

Little, A., Hoppers, W. and Gardner, R. (1994) *Beyond Jomtien, Implementing Primary Education for All*. London: Macmillan.

Lockheed, M.E. and Verspoor, A.M. (1991) *Improving Primary Education in Developing Countries*. Oxford: Oxford University Press for the World Bank.

Mercer, N. (1995) *The Guided Construction of Knowledge, Talk amongst Teachers and Learners*. Clevedon: Multilingual Matters.

Munro, D.J. (1977) *The Concept of Man in Contemporary China*. Ann Arbor: University of Michigan Press.

Rozman, G. (ed.) (1991) *The East Asian Region, Confucian Heritage and its Modern Adaptation*. Princeton, NJ: Princeton University Press.

Rudduck, J. and Kelly, P. (1976) *The Dissemination of Curriculum Development*. Slough: NFER.

Smith, R.J. (1983) *China's Cultural Heritage, the Ch'ing dynasty, 1644–1912*. Boulder, Colorado: The Westview Press.

Suroor, H. (1997) 'Indian bookworms turn'. *Times Higher Education Supplement* 7–2–9, p. 48.

Triandis, H. C. (1995) *Individualism and Collectivism*. Boulder: Westview Press.

Tu, W., Hejtmannek, M. and Wachman, A. (1992) *The Confucian World Observed, A Contemporary Discussion of Confucian Humanism in East Asia*. Honolulu: Institute of Culture and Communication, East–West Center.

Wells, G. (1986) *The Meaning Makers, Children Learning Language and Using Language to Learn*. London: Hodder & Stoughton.

Wingert, P. and Greenberg, S.H. (1996) 'At the top of the class' (Report of the Third International Mathematics and Science Study). *Newsweek* 2 December, 54–55.

World Bank (1984) *Report on Chinese Education*. Washington, DC: World Bank.

ENDPIECE

Linda Hargreaves and Janet Moyles

The contributors to this book have examined the origins and nature of primary curricula from a range of theoretical viewpoints and have provided an international set of detailed practical examples of primary curricula in a variety of geographical, social and political contexts. Readers, we hope, will have sought out the messages most relevant to their own local and national educational concerns. To try to conclude with a synthesis of all that is represented here would be an extensive project. It would also be a flawed undertaking since every author in Part II expressed anxiety about the representativeness of the particular perspective they were presenting. Each one was concerned to point out the huge range of curricula within their particular world region. It is important, therefore, to be cautious in generalising from each single example to neighbouring states or countries. In this concluding section we will draw out some very general implications for future directions in the primary curriculum.

The book addresses in Part I the *deep*, generative forces which predispose societies to express certain long-term aims of education and, in Part II, the *surface* economic and political configurations which precipitate curricula fashioned to meet relatively short-term objectives. It could be argued, with Cortazzi in Chapter 11, that although perceptions of primary curricula differ enormously, those presented here are similar in many ways. In content, for example, the lists of curriculum areas to be covered overlap considerably, with similar emphasis placed on basic numeracy and literacy at the expense of artistic expression or creativity. The medium of instruction is essentially verbal, varying chiefly in the extent to which children must depend on skills of listening (but not necessarily speaking), reading and writing. Children's tasks are highly decontextualised, in spite of the evidence of children's learning capacity and capability in solving real-life problems (Donaldson 1978; Lave and Wenger 1991). Where there is a determination to ensure active learning, as for example in parts of the Japanese curriculum, the typical class format of one teacher to a large number of children generally necessitates the *manufacture* of learning opportunities as opposed to engagement with real problems. Methods of assessment continue to represent a further abstraction from reality and a commitment to the narrow confines of what can be tested. There are attempts to increase the use of portfolios, records of achievement and teacher-based assessment, for instance, and to introduce more task-based assessment, but such approaches have had difficulties in being accepted; reliability remains a problem and, although such methods may be more valid in their representation of school work, they remain disembedded from real life, and offer limited scope for recognising children's individual styles and extra-curricular talents (Gipps *et al.* 1995; Sternberg 1997). The majority of children receive neither support nor recognition of their skills which exemplify practical intelligence (Sternberg and Wagner 1986) or musical, spatial, bodily-kinaesthetic intelligences (Gardner 1983). Much less is there any formal recognition of inter- or intra-personal intelligence, or teaching children to co-operate, to develop their social skills or to indulge in reflective or metacognitive activity.

Since most learners experience primary education only once and usually within one education system, the vast majority will know nothing of any alternative system. This limited but common experience across generations of children instils a popular belief in the 'rightness' of formal education whatever type, and an expectation that it will be provided, allowing successive administrations to legitimise and perpetuate the original system. Thus, formal education gradually becomes a cultural tradition and joins the ranks of the 'deep' forces, perceived to be a societal need. In consequence, fundamental educational change is made difficult to achieve without some momentous critical event, as in Japan and South Africa, or where impending major socio-political change is known about for a long period in advance, as in Hong Kong's return to Chinese rule. Further, while the nature and function of formal universal educational provision may not be questioned, the wealth, and effects, of the practical intuitive teaching and learning taking place within a community but outside the school may go unrecognised. A curriculum designed to develop the creative, co-operative and problem-solving potential of children to meet their own personal needs, or to help establish or sustain community harmony, and eventually to contribute to their society's adaptation to global change is a luxury for the few who have the confidence to step outside the official curriculum and who can afford to do so.

What then of the primary curriculum in the West, and particularly in England and Wales? High costs of education and modest performance in international comparisons of educational attainment have provoked some reappraisal of purpose. Employment and educational achievement are no longer closely related (Berliner 1997) and there is loss of faith in education and lack of respect for teachers. Despite the priority afforded education in political agendas, the curriculum models advocated are regressive, suited to a previous world order but at a time when world markets and producers are shifting their needs and outputs, and we are at an advanced point in an information and communications revolution (see Chapter 5). Meanwhile, Western policy-makers are selective about the results of educational research and the discourse of national press concerning education is demoralising (Alexander *et al.* 1992; Berliner and Biddle 1995). The application of principles of school improvement have led to increased managerialism, loss of natural collegiality and headteachers who give up their curriculum leadership roles (e.g. Webb and Vulliamy 1996). In other words, these advanced industrialised countries have lost a clear view of any unified educational purpose.

In the midst of these challenges, the chapters here identify two common factors facing education. One is the need to recognise the voice of the child, the learner, the majority group within education, the actual consumer of educational resources, and the group with no formal power to influence the curriculum (Newell, 1991). The second is the rapid advance of the information superhighway. Information and communications technology is crossing basic social boundaries created by differences in gender, race, age and physical ability; physical boundaries between countries and districts; and age and time-linked boundaries between home, school and work (see, for example, the collection of papers in Wood, 1996). When such tangible differences are removed, how much more vulnerable are the artificial boundaries the curriculum places between subjects. The multimedia world of information technology blurs the distinctions between knowledge systems which are largely verbal, spatial, symbolic or musical by making each of these more accessible to people. Information from the Internet is not neatly packaged into school subjects and curriculum designers need urgently to acknowledge this. Critically, communications technology is empowering learners to have their voice heard.

These widely recognised challenges for primary curricula point to a future in which the school with its closed classrooms, predefined curricula and male-dominated hierarchies will be replaced by the gradual emergence of open schools, stronger links between school and community and home-based learning. In so far as the examples from the USA, Australia and the UK reveal a disparate set of educational purposes and decreasingly predictable range of backgrounds, contexts and needs, it can be speculated that information superhighways and electronic communications offer ways forward from their diverse predicaments. It remains for the curriculum to provide for children to learn the skills needed to exploit such systems, and not be exploited by them, and to develop the social skills and understanding required to strengthen, in face-to-face interactions, or group-to-group liaison, the bonds created through electronic networks. Teachers themselves, as Ryan points out in Chapter 3, hold the key. They are uniquely placed, if they were permitted and motivated to do so, genuinely to hear, advocate and respond to the learner's voice. Teachers have unique access to the community and to the parental interest which exists there (Hughes *et al.* 1993). By involving parents, teachers gain access to the wealth of situated learning and intuitive teaching which takes place outside schools (e.g. Tizard and Hughes 1984; Lave and Wenger 1991). Thus, while many teachers may need support in adapting to new learning environments and loss of complete control of learning and teaching sources, as the Australian experience shows (Chapter 9), teachers represent a major investment by national governments. Their special knowledge of children and their links with homes and community could be developed to much greater effect, as shown in the development of the national curriculum in the Netherlands (Chapter 5). What is lacking, apart from the opportunity to use this specialist resource, are the channels of communication between teachers and policy-makers: channels to mediate between schools and policy-makers and ensure two-way communication.

But difficulties exist and, as Fullan (1992: 16) points out, 'There is no point lamenting the fact that the system is unreasonable, and no percentage in waiting around for it to become more reasonable. It won't'. Far from feeling threatened by the moves towards the information society and the need to ensure that children develop the social skills and understanding required for global citizenship, teachers should feel empowered by their special position. Fullan (1993: 145) expresses this thus: 'Macrocosm is the learning society and the learning world. Microcosm is Monday morning. Teachers above all in society must have a foot in both "cosmos" because they cannot be effective in one without being plugged into the other'. He concludes:

> Teachers are privileged and burdened with the responsibility of helping all students become inner and outer learners who will connect to wider and wider circles of society. Teachers cannot do it alone. At this stage, they have to do it despite the system. But this is how breakthroughs occur. And they will find allies.
>
> (Fullan 1993: 147)

In terms of the primary curriculum, teachers internationally face the tensions referred to in the first sentence of the book. They have, also, the practical expertise and personal experience of implementing the curricula in existence. Perhaps the gaps which communication technology needs to bridge are those between schools, communities and governments. Some countries are achieving this, but these are vital bridges to build to empower teachers and the children they teach to contribute to the creation of primary curricula which meet the needs, and develop the talents, of all learners, teachers, parents and communities internationally.

References

Alexander, R., Rose, J. and Woodhead, C. (1992) *Curriculum Organisation and Classroom Practice in Primary Schools: A Discussion Paper*. London: Department of Education and Science.

Berliner, D. (1997) 'Uninvited comments from an uninvited guest'. *Educational Researcher* 25(8), 47–50.

Berliner, D. and Biddle, B. (1995) *The Manufactured Crisis*. Reading, MA: Addison-Wesley.

Donaldson, M. (1978) *Children's Minds*. London: Fontana.

Fullan, M. (1992) *What's Worth Fighting for in Headship?*. Buckingham: Open University Press.

Fullan, M. (1993) *Change Forces: Probing the Depths of Educational Reform*. London: Falmer Press.

Gardner, H. (1983) *Frames of Mind*. New York: Basic Books.

Gipps, C., Brown, M., McCallum, B. and McAlister, S. (1995) *Intuition or Evidence?*. Buckingham: Open University Press.

Hughes, M., Wikely, F. and Nash, T. (1993) *Parents and their Children's Schools*. Oxford: Blackwell.

Lave, J. and Wenger, E. (1991) *Situated Learning: Legitimate Peripheral Participation*. Cambridge, MA: Cambridge University Press.

Newell, P. (1991) *The U.N. Convention and Children's Rights in the UK*. London: National Children's Bureau.

Sternberg, R. (1997) 'Practical Intelligence'. Paper presented at the American Educational Research Association Annual Meeting (Symposium: 'Expanding our concept of intelligence: what's missing and what could we gain?'). Chicago.

Sternberg, R. and Wagner, R. (eds) (1986) *Practical Intelligence: The Nature and Origins of Intelligence in the Everyday World*. Cambridge: Cambridge University Press.

Tizard, B. and Hughes, M. (1984) *Young Children Learning*. London: Fontana.

Webb, R. and Vulliamy, G. (1996) *Roles and Responsibilities in the Primary School*. Buckingham: Open University Press.

Wood, J. (ed.) (1996) *Education Superhighways: The Future of Multimedia, the Internet and Broadband Networks in Schools, Colleges and Universities*. London: Financial Times.

INDEX

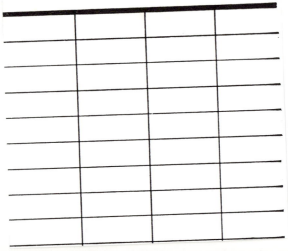